Persons, Sou ls nd

ALSO BY DAVID H. LUND

Death and Consciousness
(McFarland, 1985)

Persons, Souls and Death

A Philosophical Investigation of an Afterlife

DAVID H. LUND

McFarland & Company, Inc., Publishers
Jefferson, North Carolina, and London

LIBRARY OF CONGRESS CATALOGUING-IN-PUBLICATION DATA

Lund, David H.
    Persons, souls and death : a philosophical investigation of an
afterlife / David H. Lund.
       p.   cm.
    Includes bibliographical references and index.

    ISBN 978-0-7864-3487-9
    softcover : 50# alkaline paper ∞

    1. Future life.   2. Mind and body.   3. Parapsychology
and philosophy.   I. Title.
BD421.L86   2009
129—dc22   2008050569

British Library cataloguing data are available

Cover image ©2009 Clipart

Manufactured in the United States of America

McFarland & Company, Inc., Publishers
  Box 611, Jefferson, North Carolina 28640
   www.mcfarlandpub.com

To Gregory, Matthew, and Rebecca

Acknowledgments

I wish to thank my wife, Elaine, for the many hours spent in word-processing the manuscript.

Table of Contents

Preface

The question of whether nonexistence follows biological death is one that we all must raise at some point in our lives, even if we do not carry it much of the time just outside the focus of our consciousness in our day to day activities. For many of us it is a more or less regular companion, often within sight, as we make the journey through our lives. But dealing with the issues that arise in any sustained attempt to address it in a thoughtful and open-minded way brings to light a number of difficulties that must be confronted by those who wish to apply their own critical thought in their attempt to find the truth about what death brings. Some of the general difficulties are rather evident. Since we move closer day by day to our own deaths, it might be difficult to maintain the objectivity and the open-mindedness that would be relatively easy to achieve for a dispassionate spectator who regards our question as holding only an intellectual interest. But we can rise to the occasion and meet the challenge posed by that difficulty. Another difficulty comes into view when we see the full complexity of what must be taken into account in arriving at the most plausible interpretation of the cases on which we will focus in the second part of our study—remarkable if not astonishing cases providing what seems to be evidence that at least some people have survived bodily death and have revealed to us that they continue to exist.

But the difficulty I wish to emphasize at this point is less obvious and appears to be the most formidable of them all—the difficulty we encounter in trying to grasp what it is that, in the ultimate analysis, *persons* should be understood to be. What is it that must survive bodily death if *we* are to survive? What is it that *must* exist for a person to exist and yet is *all that is needed* for the existence of a person? This question about the identity of persons, though often largely if not entirely circumvented in studies of death, is crucially important if our aim is to determine, as best we can, whether the existence of the person ends with bodily death. For if the identity of a person just is the identity of the living body that perishes with death, then, of course, the existence of the person would thereby end as well. But even if a person is distinct from her living body, her existence might, as a matter of fact, depend upon the (causal) support provided by her body.

These questions about what ultimately constitutes a person and about how the person-body relation should be understood reach a depth and a complexity that might strike you as more than a bit daunting. I deal with these questions primarily in the sections entitled "Minds, Souls, and Persons" and "Mental-Physical Relations." If these sections prove to be difficult to understand, at least on a first reading, it might be helpful to point out that some summarization of the reasoning found there, along with the role it plays and the significance it has in the overall study, can be found at various places in the text. You will find such summarization mainly in the sections entitled "Our Investigation So Far" and "Overview of Our Investigation into the Essence of Persons."

Introduction

The Perennial Question

Through the ages countless numbers of people have believed that death does not mark the absolute end to their existence, apparently convinced that an afterlife awaits them. They clung to their afterlife beliefs even though they could observe, as we can, what happens to the bodies of human beings when they die. What should we make of this? Should such beliefs be understood as nothing more than the superstitions of a relatively primitive age when people lacked the extensive knowledge of the natural world that we have today? Can there be any rational grounds for them in view of our science-based knowledge of the enormous size and alien character of the physical universe, of the evolutionary development of life forms on our planet, and of how deeply embedded we are in the world of nature? Though a negative answer to the third question may seem unavoidable, we shall see that this is not the case.

With this book I invite you to undertake the daunting task of thinking through that clusters of concepts, theories, and data that must be taken into account in any intellectually honest search for the truth about what happens to us when we die. Does our existence simply come to an end with the death of the body, as indicated by ordinary observations of bodies no longer alive, or do we continue to exist as individuals with conscious states, however that continued existence is ultimately to be understood? This large question, which inevitably arises with our awareness of our mortality, is one to which few, if any, can remain entirely indifferent. For many, it both engages the mind and stirs the heart. It is mind engaging as it leads us to think deeply about what the broader dimensions of the world would have to be to include an afterworld in which we exist after bodily death, and also about what our deep nature must be if continued existence were in store for us. Clearly, if we continue to exist after our bodies have perished, we must be something distinct from them, despite the fact that we are so deeply embodied that thought about what we could be apart from them may seem quite confused

3

if not simply incoherent. And we might find it quite engaging to focus on precisely what it is that we are imagining when we imagine, or seem to imagine, our continuing existence beyond death. What are we imagining ourselves to be under such conditions, and what kinds of experiences are we imagining ourselves to have?

It is on the level of our passions, however, that the question has its strongest grip upon us. Even those who are unmoved by what many find to be intellectually engaging can hardly remain entirely dispassionate—indifferent on the level of feeling—about their own approaching deaths. After all, we are dying, even though death has not yet arrived. A keen, and sometimes painful, awareness of this fact can hardly fail to be deeply moving.

Still, some have argued that indifference would be better for us, and more rational as well. The ancient Greek philosopher, Epicurus, famously argued that a rational person should become indifferent to death after reflecting on the fact that while we are alive, we are not dead ("death is not with us"), and when we are dead, we do not exist. Thus we should be led to see that death should not be of concern to us in any state we could possibly be in. But would we really be better off, and more rational, if we could become indifferent to death? The answer may become clear when we see what becoming genuinely indifferent to death would require of us.

As we reflect on this matter, let us momentarily assume what Epicurus assumes—that death results in permanent nonexistence. What would we have to become to become indifferent to our own approaching annhilation, our reduction to nothingness. It is true that a few people say that they are indifferent to death, even if it brings nonexistence. But some of these haven't given the matter much thought, preferring to avoid thinking about such "morbid questions." And among those who have confronted such questions in reflective thought are some who are victims of a self-deception motivated by a powerful desire to convince themselves that death will not harm them in any way, and thereby come to terms with death more easily. However, one would suppose that none (or at least very few) of these people would agree that their claim about being indifferent to death would commit them to the position that they would never *prefer* death, even over the alternative of, say, spending the remainder of one's life in terrible agony. Under such circumstances, they would *not* be indifferent to death, but *prefer* it to the alternative. So apparently their indifference is a limited one: they believe that death can sometimes be a good thing and thus sometimes preferable to the alternative, but can never be a bad thing because it cannot bring harm.

Now our focus has shifted to the issue of whether a limited indifference to death is an attitude we would be better off having and thus something we should strive to attain. Such indifference would be beneficial only if death cannot bring harm. But it can and does bring an important kind of harm if we are harmed by the loss of important goods we could have had if we had lived. To judge that such losses are not harmful to us is, in effect, to make a very dim assessment of the worth of those things that death prevented us from having. If the loss of those goods is insignificant, as they must be if we are not harmed by their loss, then the value they would have had if we had enjoyed them must be equally insignificant. But among the goods lost are those that make our lives worth living. We derive enjoyment from activities that keep our lives interesting and from the pursuit of goals whose attainment would be immensely fulfilling. We have life-affirming desires whose satisfaction makes our lives meaningful. All this is lost in a death that deprives us of the opportunity to have any experience.

What is lost are the goods that provide our reasons for living, which are precisely our reasons for not dying, and thus what blocks our becoming indifferent to death. If, as it now appears, our becoming indifferent to dying requires our becoming indifferent to living, then we should not strive to become indifferent to dying. It would be better for us to believe that death can be, and often is, a bad thing than to believe that life cannot be good. So let us proceed with the assurance that we would not be better off if we could become indifferent to the fact that we must die.

As we reflect upon the numerous ways in which our awareness of our approaching death affects our lives and note that in this respect we are no different from countless others throughout the ages struggling with their awareness of their mortality, we might be led to thoughts about how different the human condition would be if we lacked the capacity for such awareness, as seems to be the case with the lower animals. Though the capacity to become conscious of ourselves and of the fact that we must die is one that we cannot choose to leave unexercised, and should not wish to do so even if we could, it also imposes upon us a burden from which the lower animals are free. Our efforts to make our lives meaningful are shaped and sometimes hindered by this burden created by our awareness of our mortality. Its presence may seem at times to cast a long shadow over our lives that may have some effect upon us even when our attention is largely devoted to other matters. Though it reminds us of the brevity of life and the importance of the day, and may even inspire us to become more than we would have been without its motivating force, it also prompts a somber, if not dismal, assessment of our human condition.

Given the near universal awareness of mortality, one might have thought that a great many people would be quite concerned to critically examine the matter of whether anything follows death for the person who dies. But this seems not to be the case. Apparently, some have little interest in critically thinking through any intellectually challenging matter, and others lack the capacity or the determination to do so with much success. Perhaps of more concern are those who believe that investigating such a matter is a waste of time and energy, maintaining that questions about what follows death are unanswerable. For confusion lurks here. An unanswerable question is one to which there is no answer, not one whose answer is unknown. Clearly, the question of what follows death *has* an answer. There is some *fact of the matter* as to what death brings that would answer this question even if we never come to know what that fact is. But our failure to know what it is does not imply that it is unknowable. The claim that something is unknowable is a very strong one, implying that knowledge of it is impossible in principle. It would imply the failure of every actual *and every possible* argument for and against concluding that nonexistence follows death. We would have to wonder what grounds we could possibly have for accepting such an implication.

Others fail to think critically about the question of what death might bring because they believe that they already have the answer, at least one that they deem sufficient for themselves. Many of these appeal to religious beliefs, often claiming to "know," perhaps "by faith alone," that they will survive bodily death. Such claims, however, express mere conviction rather than knowledge and imply that evidence for the truth of these beliefs is irrelevant. But if evidence is irrelevant, then *what one believes* by faith alone becomes entirely arbitrary. One might just as sensibly *reject* "by faith alone" what others believe on that basis. Perhaps recognizing such problems, others may contend that evidence is needed but must be supplemented by faith to yield the religious conviction that the beliefs are true. Indeed, they may acknowledge that faith in the truth of certain religious claims is needed for these claims to be seen as evidence that people have survived bodily death or will survive it. Clearly, such faith-based beliefs do not encourage an open-minded search for the truth or critical thought about what happens when we die.

A Philosophical Approach

A philosophical approach to the issues involved in our central question requires that we put our initial beliefs about the matter at some risk as we begin our study. It would discourage any attempt to look only at considerations that support the beliefs we wish were true, while ignoring those considerations that weigh in on the other side. In other words, the philosophical spirit in us would prompt us to engage in an intellectually honest search for the truth of the matter, remaining as open-minded in our treatment of the relevant issues as we can be, even though we realize that such a search might lead us to conclusions we would not like to accept.

Clearly, an open-minded, truth-seeking approach is beneficial in that it increases the likelihood of success in clarifying the issues and in arriving at an informed view of the various considerations that can be advanced for or against thinking that our existence ends with biological death. Even though any rational certainty that we have arrived at the truth of the matter may be beyond our reach, we will be in a better position to assess the probabilities. We will be able to assess the strength of the case for each of the alternative possibilities, and to determine which is the more rational to believe to be true. But a second benefit of our philosophical approach is a result of the logical rigor that it encourages. In adopting it, we subject our beliefs to the tests of logic and thereby run the risk that they will not measure up, at least as they presently stand. More specifically, we will subject the concepts involved in our beliefs to logical analysis in an effort to clarify our thinking and to see precisely what we believe in holding them to be true. We will try to expose hidden obscurities or ambiguities in them, and may even find that some are logically inconsistent with others. We will identify and examine arguments (understood as instances of reasoning from premises to conclusions) for or against a variety of conclusions (a central one of which is that death ends our existence) and evaluate them in an effort to see if any are sound. We will need to weigh (and thereby determine the significance of) evidence provided by factual claims and by the arguments we consider. We will, for example, weigh the evidence provided by well-documented reports of people having survived bodily death and try to determine their overall significance to the survival question. And throughout our investigation we will try to remain alert to any unexamined assumptions we might have been unaware of making so that we can evaluate them to see if our reliance on them is justified. The rigor involved in such an approach should maximize our chances of finding our way through the maze of considerations to be taken into account in reaching a fully informed answer to our central question.

What is perhaps the greatest value of a philosophical approach comes clearly into view when we see that many of the issues to be considered are philosophical in character, requiring conceptual analysis and an examination of the logical relations among the concepts employed in thought about the issues, rather than simply issues about what the relevant empirical facts are. To illustrate, it seems clear that the reality of one's consciousness must be acknowledged, but there is surely an issue about what one's consciousness should be taken to be or how it should be conceived. And though it is an empirical fact that one's conscious states are intimately connected to certain states of one's brain, the nature of the consciousness-brain connection or relation cannot be decided on empirical grounds alone. Some contend that this relation is one of identity—that conscious states are identical to certain brain states. Others contend that the relation is a causal one, maintaining that two different kinds of entities or events are in a cause-effect relationship. This issue, like so many of those bearing on the question of what death brings, is not about what facts have been observed, but about how they are to be interpreted, explained, or understood.

Not only is it true that philosophical analysis is needed throughout our investigation but some philosophers have tried to show by such analysis alone, independently of what the empirical facts may be, that death must bring nonexistence. Some have argued that the very idea of a person's continuing to exist after bodily death is a logically incoherent notion—that such an "idea" doesn't even make sense. A closely related argument is that a person would have to be an essentially nonphysical being to survive the death of the body, and that the notion of a nonphysical substance is logically incoherent. Another purports to show that conscious states cannot be nonphysical by contending that if they were nonphysical they would lack any mass or energy and so could not be causes or effects of brain activity.

Our critical examination of such arguments will, of course, involve philosophical analysis, which we will use to reveal their flaws. More generally, I will argue that all such arguments fail not only because of their own defects, but by showing that individual survival of bodily death is conceivable. I will present a rather detailed conception of individual survival—of what could constitute one's continuing to exist after bodily death. The logical coherence (i.e., the internal consistency) of such a conception, grounded in what we presently experience ourselves to be, would have the added benefit of showing what is necessary and sufficient for our existence as individual persons, irrespective of whether we survive bodily death.

If successful, these arguments would show that survival is logically possible (i.e., that the concept of it is internally consistent) and that the survival issue depends upon the most plausible interpretation of the relevant facts—the facts that appear to indicate the continued existence of some deceased persons. Our philosophical approach would have led us to see that the issue is primarily a factual one. But it will continue to serve us well in helping us assess the significance of the relevant facts. Among other things, it will be of help to us in determining which facts are the relevant ones, in conceiving of the various possible ways in which they might be interpreted, in arriving at the most plausible interpretation of them, and, finally, in drawing inferences based upon them about the likelihood that we will survive bodily death.

The Influence and Scope of Science

Science has become a dominating force in shaping our conception of ourselves and our place in the natural world. The remarkable advance of natural science, especially in its scientific study of human beings in such areas as brain science and evolutionary biology, has had a profound effect upon us in laying out in such detail the material conditions of our existence. Natural science finds nothing in the world except complex arrangements of physical elements and thereby fosters the view that there *is* nothing else. In this view, persons are seen as entirely material beings whose existence must end with the destruction of the complex material organisms that they are. This materialist view of persons has attained the status of an orthodoxy in the contemporary intellectual culture and is especially well received in contemporary philosophy of mind. One form of this view, for example, is embraced by such eminent philosophers as Armstrong and Smart, who argue that a person is nothing more than a highly complex physico-chemical mechanism.[1]

The success of science undeniably has been of great benefit to us, but it has led many to exaggerate what science is capable of revealing, suggesting that the type of understanding exemplified by science will prove to be sufficient for a full understanding of reality, or at least of the natural world. Clearly, this greatly exaggerates the scope of its power as a truth-finding method. Though science uncovers the laws of nature, as it informs us of the constitution and behavior of matter, its unparalleled effectiveness is within the domain of the publicly observable—of objects and events accessible to the third-person viewpoint. But it has no place for the irreducibly subjective character of our conscious states, for they are directly accessible only to the person having them. It has no language to describe them, nor any way to acknowledge their existence among the items available to its objective, third-person viewpoint. And in having no place for our conscious states, at least as they appear to us to be in having them, it leaves out much more than we might have thought. For, as we shall see, when we are conscious or, in other words, having conscious states, what seems to be present to us is not only our *consciousness* but also what we are being conscious *of*. Since at least some elements *of which* we are conscious (e.g., the "contents" or intentional objects of consciousness) are accessible only to the first-person viewpoint (the viewpoint you have in being directly aware of them), they too will fall between the cracks in any science-inspired view that fails to acknowledge the existence of anything that science cannot find from its third-person view of the world.

The inability of natural science to provide an exhaustive account of the natural world comes into view in a different way when we see that the conception of the world that science investigates is fundamentally a perceptual concept grounded in our perceptual experience. In our sense experience, especially in seeing, hearing, and touching, we encounter a world of independently existing material things that we believe others also perceive. This is the external world—the world that exists externally to our "inner" conscious states—and it is accessible to the third-person viewpoint, i.e., to many observers. Accordingly, it is the world on which natural science focuses.

Natural science tries to reach beyond our perceptual experience of the world around us by theorizing about a micro-world (consisting of atoms, sub-atomic particles, energy waves and packets, etc.) that underlies and explains what happens in the world of larger material things accessible to us in ordinary perception. But whether it is theorizing about the micro-world or the world of extremely large and distant material entities, the confirmation or disconfirmation of its theories must always be carried out in ways involving ordinary sense perception, often by making observations in laboratories and taking note of what highly complicated and sensitive instruments are doing. And all of the theoretical entities studied are conceived in broadly perceptual terms, ultimately grounded in our perceptual experience. They are thought to be in physical space, even if the precise location or extension of some cannot be determined, and to be independently existing entities accessible to the third-person viewpoint. Certainly, the brain and the various activities occurring within it are conceived in this way.

Our concept of consciousness, however, is not a perceptual concept. It is an "introspective" concept, grounded in our direct or unmediated awareness of our own conscious states. This explains why questions about what it would be like to perceive consciousness with our senses (e.g., about what it would be like to see consciousness, or hear it, or taste it) make no sense. We do not become aware of our conscious states by using sense perception. And since our concept of spatiality, of objects located and extended in space, arises out of our sensory experience, we also have an explanation of why questions about where our consciousness is or how much space it occupies seem unintelligible. If such questions were intelligible, then we should expect to have some idea of what it might be to *find* someone's consciousness in the place where it is supposed to be. But we have no such idea. Finding something in the place where it is located is to perceive it there, usually by seeing or touching it; and we cannot even conceive of encountering anyone's consciousness in that way.

Why science fails to find our conscious states in the spatial realm of publicly accessible objects that it investigates now seems clear. What should also be made clear, however, is that such a failure need not diminish our confidence in either its method of inquiry or what, strictly speaking, it finds to be the case. We should not be surprised to find that it cannot reveal every-thing that we can know to be true of us, even if we believe that it is not inher-ently limited in its ability to discover the laws of nature and the constitution of the physical realm.

As we bring to a close our reflections about the influence and scope of natural science, we should note that, though scientific inquiry is a human endeavor of enormous value, its reach is not unlimited; and so we are justified in being skeptical about claims that it has established truths about matters that seem beyond its reach. Examples of such claims are that consciousness does not exist (at least as it appears to us to be in having conscious states), that the mind is nothing but the brain, that consciousness is a brain process, and that persons are nothing more than highly complex physical objects. We shall find that such claims presuppose, often uncritically and unreflectively, that the numerous and complex issues to be considered in evaluating these claims have already been settled, perhaps by science itself. But these issues have *not* been settled, at least to a degree even approaching conclusiveness, and, indeed, are not such that science *can* settle them. Many are conceptual issues, requiring philosophical analysis and a philosophical elucidation of the alternative possibilities. In other words, they are philosophical issues that require an approach different from that of science. So as we consider the rel-evance of scientific investigation to the concerns central to our study, we must make sure that we carefully distinguish what science itself reveals from what we (or others) might be importing by way of unexamined presupposi-tion into our interpretation of the scientific findings.

The Coherence of the Idea of Post-Mortem Existence

To believe that we will continue to exist after bodily death or even to believe that survival of death is possible, however unlikely its actual occur-rence may be, we must have some conception of such existence in mind. To believe is to believe something—to have something in mind rather than noth-ing at all—even though one's conception of this "something" may be quite unclear and incomplete. But arriving at an adequate conception of post-mortem existence will likely prove to be no easy task. Indeed, there are many well-known thinkers who would argue that this couldn't be done, not because what we would be trying to do lies beyond the reach of our conceptual pow-ers, but because the very idea of post-mortem existence is revealed to be incoherent upon careful examination.

The idea of a person continuing to exist as a physical or psychophysi-cal organism after bodily death might strike us as a non-starter, given our awareness that death brings the destruction of that organism. Obviously, it would be incoherent to claim that the organism whose existence is terminated by death nevertheless continues to exist after death. Some have claimed that God re-creates at a later time the person as she was at the moment of death. But because the existence of the organism that the person is would not be continuous, there could be no way of establishing that the re-created person is the original rather than an exactly similar replica. If this cannot be established, then the conceivability of personal existence after death has not been established either. It has been argued that God could keep the person in existence by whisking her away at the moment of death and leaving an exactly similar replica in her place.[2] Though this seems conceivable, it also strikes one as incredible, partly because of how deceptive God would have to be. In any case, such views in which a person is an essentially physical being must be rejected for reasons we shall later consider in some detail.

If (as I shall argue) a person or self is most plausibly viewed as a non-physical conscious being, and thus distinct from the human organism in which it is (deeply) embodied, the conceivability of post-mortem existence of persons is a matter of whether a disembodied person is conceivable. That such a "person" is *not* conceivable is the view of many contemporary philosophers. We have no idea of how such a being could have any location, of how one such being could be distinguished from another, and of what would make a deceased person identical to some such being. Thus McGinn, for example, writes, "How could such a mind be located anywhere without a body to anchor it? How can it have effects in the physical world? How could we manage to pick out and describe one disembodied mind rather than another? We can hardly point to a disembodied mind."[3] Clearly, any attempt to show that the idea of a disembodied self is coherent must include a plausible response to the difficulties suggested by these questions.

Since the issue of the conceivability of a disembodied self or person is inseparable from the issue of what a person essentially is, we shall later examine in some detail the alternative theories of the person. At this juncture, we shall simply note two points. The first is about what is essential to the existence of a self or person—a point that should be made if the suggestion that a person is essentially a nonphysical being strikes us as highly implausible. This suggestion would so strike us if we were thinking of the person as the entire human being. For a human being is a member of a species of animal life and thus is a type of physical organism. But it is legitimate to use the term "person" to possibly include nonhuman beings, provided that they possessed an inner conscious life relevantly similar to our own. It is conceivable that greatly advanced super-computers of the future should come to possess what we judge to be conscious states or an inner personal life, in which case we might well be happy to consider them persons, even though they are not even organic. In any case, it seems easy to conceive of our encountering extra-terrestrial intelligent beings that seem to possess the full array of conscious states that we experience. We would likely find ourselves thinking of them as persons despite the fact that they are not human.

The apparent fact that a person could be a non-human (even if no such beings presently exist) indicates that being human and being a person are different attributes. Though we possess both, they need not have been connected in the way they are in us. Being human is not essential to being a person. What *is* essential comes into view when we ask ourselves why we believe that humans are persons and that certain (possible) non-humans could rightly be considered persons as well—it is because of the inner conscious states we believe they have. Though all of these persons, both actual and possible, are embodied beings, what is embodied (as distinct from the material in which it is embodied) seems to be all that is both essential to and sufficient for the existence of a self or person. But if we have good grounds for thinking that a self or person is something embodied in humans, and in some possible non-humans, then we have such grounds for thinking of a person as something distinct from all of its material embodiments, that is, as unembodied or disembodied, even if it never actually exists in that form.

This conclusion is further supported by thought-experiments in which we try to imagine the full extent to which we could have been different from how we actually are. As we think about our physical characteristics, it seems clear to us that they could have been quite different—we could have had different facial features, different eye, hair and skin color, different size and physical stature, etc. Indeed, it seems easy to imagine experiencing the world through an entirely different body, perhaps a body that is in fact the body of another—some celebrity, for example. Yet, from the first-person view that one has of one's own experience, it seems incontestable that the person experiencing the world—the subject having the experience—is *oneself*. For one cannot even imagine having the experience of another, since one's *having* it is what *constitutes* its being one's own. In other words, though you can imagine having the body of another, you cannot imagine having experience belonging to someone else. To try to imagine the latter is to try to imagine yourself *being* someone else—someone *not* yourself—and thus talk about such an imaginative scenario is clearly incoherent.

This thought-experiment indicates that your identity as a person is in part constituted by the experience you have, but not by the physical organism by which you experience the world. The subject having those experiences could not have been someone other than you, though the body through which you have them could have been a body other than the one you actually have. Thus again, the organism (or other physical system) in which one is embodied appears to be something logically distinct from the person who is embodied, i.e., distinct from the subject having the experience arising from its association with that body.

Though these considerations may seem to justify the conclusion that a person is something non-physical, they do not take us quite that far. A critic could charge that something distinct from all its material embodiments might be understood to denote the manner in which certain material organisms or systems behave or function. To illustrate, though a variety of material things or organized systems of things are considered clocks (e.g., a sundial, an hourglass, a wind-up alarm clock, and a battery powered wrist watch), what makes all of them clocks consists in what they *do*—the way they function enables us to measure the passage of time. Similarly, the critic might argue, talk about the conscious states of humans and possibly other complex material organisms is, when correctly understood, revealed to be nothing more than talk about certain things these organisms do or are disposed to do. But, as we shall later see, this behaviorist/functionalist/dispositionalist interpretation of conscious states is extremely implausible, unable to acknowledge what we find to be true of these states in having them. We shall uncover compelling reasons to conclude that they are not physical themselves nor are they states of a physical thing. They are states of a conscious subject distinct from the human organism to which it is connected, even though its existence may depend upon the existence and proper functioning of that organism. In this view, you are the conscious subject who is now reading these lines and thinking about what they mean. You are visually conscious of your surroundings, perhaps conscious in a tactile way of holding a book in your hands, and conscious in a peripheral way of various sounds in the background and of various bodily sensations. What is both necessary for your existence and also all that is needed (i.e., sufficient) for it is the existence of this conscious subject with its potential for having various states of consciousness. It is what you find yourself to be as you are aware of the world around you and of yourself as the center of your awareness. Thus it is defensibly considered to be what, in the final analysis, constitutes the *person* or self that you are.

The second point is about the number of challenges to be met and the extent of what must be shown if one is to show that an entirely disembodied person is even conceivable. Can we show that thought and talk about such a person is coherent, that is, that it does not fall apart into contradictory claims or a confused muddle when carefully examined? Though this is not the place to try to meet these challenges, it will prove helpful to gain at least a general grasp of what is involved in carrying out such a project. We have already noted, at least implicitly, one challenge to be met. It is to show, or provide good reason to believe, that conscious states are neither physical states nor behavioral/functional/dispositional states of physical systems, more specifically, of human organisms. A closely related, though equally formidable, challenge is to show that what a person or self essentially is is a subject of these conscious states and is itself nonphysical. These are formidable challenges indeed.

What may be the most obvious difficulty comes into view when we wonder how a disembodied self devoid of physical sense organs could have any sensory or perceptual experience. Disembodied existence would be extremely impoverished if any such experience were impossible. Non-sensory conscious states would not be rendered impossible by this difficulty, but they too are exposed to whatever problems arise from the fact that all conscious states are a function of brain activity. However, as we shall later see, functional dependence on the brain or the rest of the body does not by itself imply that conscious states are *essentially* (i.e., necessarily) tied to the body; and such an implication would be required to show that the existence of a disembodied subject of conscious states is inconceivable (and thus could not exist in the actual world or in any other possible one).

Another central challenge to be met consists in two closely related difficulties. On the one hand, there is the problem of understanding what *constitutes* a person's remaining one and the same unique individual over time. In first-person terms, what is it that *makes* the various stages of what I (and others) consider to be stages of my life the stages of the life of one and the same person, namely, myself—the person I find myself to be in having experience? Let us call this the *ontological* or *metaphysical* problem, as it is a problem about what the *reality* is that underlies one's having remained one and the same person over time. Though the matter of how this problem is to be resolved is highly controversial even for persons as they presently exist, it is widely considered to be irresolvable in the case of disembodied persons. Critics of the notion of a disembodied subject or person would charge that we cannot conceive of anything that could make a disembodied person one and the same as some embodied person who has died. If this is inconceivable, then so is the notion of a disembodied person.

The closely related problem is an epistemic one—the problem of *knowing* or being able to find out that a disembodied person is one and the same as (i.e., numerically identical to) some deceased person. This problem would persist even if the ontological problem with respect to disembodied persons could be resolved. For even if it is true that there is something that makes a disembodied person identical to some formerly embodied one, it may be impossible to find out what that is. Moreover, even if what that is can be known generally for persons, it may be impossible to know that it obtains in any specific case, thus rendering impossible the knowledge that a particular disembodied person is in fact some particular person who has died. Though this epistemic difficulty, even if irresolvable, would apparently not prevent our having a conception of a disembodied person, the critic may argue that it would block one's having a conception of one's own disembodied existence after death. More specifically, I would be unable to conceive of my own disembodied existence after death because I would be unable to tell whether the person whose disembodied existence I am conceiving is myself or someone else.[4] I may think that I can conceive of myself in a disembodied state remembering my embodied life, but, so the argument goes, there would be nothing in my conception that would enable me to distinguish someone genuinely remembering my prior embodied life (viz., myself) from someone merely seeming to remember it (i.e., someone else).

Another charge meriting some consideration that will be leveled against the notion of a disembodied self arises out of the work of the twentieth century philosopher, Ludwig Wittgenstein.[5] He argued that a private language (which he understood to be a language only one person *can* understand) is impossible—a conclusion that has been embraced by many contemporary philosophers. Since one committed to the (metaphysical) possibility of a disembodied self is implying that the word "self" refers to an inner private entity that only she can experience, she is thereby implying that this word, along with terms referring to her conscious states, are terms in a private language. Given this charge, along with the other challenges to be met, it is understandable that many philosophers and other thinkers have held that a disembodied self is inconceivable.

The Relevance of the Case for Theism

I shall take theism to be the view (or assortment of similar views) that there is a god who has various attributes of the kind we ascribe to persons. "God" is not a term for some non-personal, unconscious force such as gravity or electromagnetism but for a personal being who is aware of the world, who has the power to act upon it, who values justice and moral goodness, and who cares about us and about how we treat one another. Indeed, many theists have held that God is all knowing (omniscient), all-powerful (omnipotent) and perfect in moral goodness, maintaining that a proper conception of God is the concept of the Greatest Conceivable Being. But God is conceived to be great in virtue of possessing attributes that if possessed to some degree by you and I would make us greater persons than we would have been without them—such attributes as knowledge, wisdom, integrity, compassion, magnanimity, and moral goodness. These are attributes that may be possessed only by persons.

In addition to having such "great-making" attributes, the God of theism is conceived to be an *agent*, that is, a being possessing free will, capable of contemplating alternative courses of action and then choosing among them. An agent considers the reasons for choosing one course of action over another prior to freely choosing one of them, as contrasted with having one's behavior causally determined by prior causes, which, in turn, were causally determined by even earlier members of a causal chain that extends indefinitely far into the past. Clearly, freedom of the will is another attribute properly ascribable to persons and only to persons.

That we do have free will is what we commonly assume. It is the assumption implicit in our deliberations about what course of action to take as well as in our commonsense belief that we are justified in holding ourselves and others responsible for what we do. Though this assumption is taken to be false by many causal determinists, the controversy about whether we actually have free will hardly affects the fact that we commonly (even if only implicitly) think of ourselves and of God as having it. Thus the theistic conception of God is a conception of a conscious agent capable of having a variety of mental states. It is a conception of what a person essentially is, human or otherwise. The philosopher, A. Plantinga, forcefully expresses this point when he writes, "...on the Christian scheme of things, *God* is the premier person, the first and chief exemplar of personhood ... and the properties most important for an understanding of our personhood are properties we share with him."[6]

The next point to establish is that our conception of God is not only a conception of a premier person, but of an *immaterial* person. That God is properly conceived as immaterial seems rather obvious. In Christianity, at least, God is regarded as capable of temporarily manifesting himself to people by way of an appearance that might be interpreted as physical, but his personhood remains immaterial throughout. And Christ has been regarded as the God incarnate, thus implying that embodiment is not the normal condition of the person of Christ. Presumably, Christ is conceived as immaterial both before and after his incarnation period.

If God were conceived as material, there would be formidable difficulties to address. As we shall later see, the case against thinking that any person is essentially material is very strong. But apart from that, a rather obvious problem for the view that God is essentially material—a physical organism, perhaps with physical organs like our own—is that this organism would have to occupy physical space. The problem comes more fully into view when we wonder how there could be a physical space without it bearing some spatial relation to the physical space of the physical universe. But if they were spatially related, as one would think they must be, then God and his realm would be situated in the physical universe, reachable, at least in principle, by a space ship. Clearly, this line of thought is profoundly wrongheaded.

The relevance of the case for theism may be apparent already. If the conception of God as an immaterial person is coherent (i.e., free of internal inconsistencies, and thus meaningful), then so is the conception of an immaterial person who is embodied as a human being. The *conception* is coherent even if as a matter of fact no humans are *immaterial* persons, just as the coherence of the conception of God as an immaterial person is unaffected by the possibility that God does not exist. In other words, both the God of theism and immaterial persons (embodied as human beings) are conceivable and thus possibly exist even if in fact they do not. Roughly speaking, conceivability establishes possibility, but not the factual existence of what is coherently conceived.

We should note that the conceivability of the God of theism is widely acknowledged. Though the issue of whether God exists is highly controversial, the conceivability of God's existence is commonly acknowledged, at least implicitly. The belief that God exists might be rejected as false, but, strictly speaking, its falsity implies its meaningfulness and thereby implies that what is believed is conceivable. A claim or belief must be at least meaningful to be either true or false. If a "claim" or "belief" turns out, under examination, to be incoherent and thus inconceivable, it is not false but meaningless. If I should "claim" that I might have traveled back in time and killed myself when I was eighteen (and thereby bring about my nonexistence and thus my inability to travel back in time), I would be uttering meaningless nonsense rather than making a false claim. In view of this, it is significant that most non-theists seem to be maintaining that belief in the theistic God is false rather than meaningless, and thereby suggesting that the God of theism (i.e., an immaterial personal being) is conceivable.

The case for theism is relevant to our concerns in another respect. If (as I shall argue later in some detail) we are immaterial persons who happen to be (i.e., are *contingently*) embodied as human beings, then we would be such that God (given the power and the desire) could and would keep us in existence, despite the destruction of our physical bodies. If we were identical to our bodies, then it would be metaphysically, i.e., absolutely, impossible[7] (and thus not within the power of even an omnipotent God) to keep us in existence when they do not exist. Perhaps God could resurrect these bodies at a later time, but (because of what makes a *body* one and the same body through time)[8] it would be metaphysically impossible to preserve *us*—the very beings that we are now—in that way.

We see that God's existence would increase the likelihood of our continued existence beyond death when we note how deeply embodied we apparently are. We depend upon our bodies, especially our brains, not only to acquire information about our surroundings and to express what is on our minds but also to *have* anything in mind. All of our conscious states, cognitive as well as perceptual, seem to be functionally dependent upon brain activity. Though this apparent fact is one whose significance we shall explore later, if it is best interpreted as indicative of a natural law that conscious states exist only in association with brain activity, then it is a matter of natural law that we will not survive the destruction of our brains. At this point the relevance of God's existence again comes into view, since an omnipotent and omnibenevolvent (i.e., perfectly good) God could and perhaps would suspend this law of nature to keep us in existence after brain death. For our survival would be only naturally impossible (i.e., contrary to natural law, which might have been different) rather than metaphysically impossible, as would be the case if we were identical to our bodies.

The Nature of Persons and the Laws of Nature

The matter of whether we continue to exist after bodily death depends primarily upon two factors: our own nature and the character of the natural laws that govern our existence. A careful study of these two factors involves two distinguishable though thoroughly integrated parts: (1) a sustained effort to determine what the relevant empirical facts are, and (2) a consideration of a variety of philosophical issues as to how the facts are to be interpreted or understood. This distinction does not presuppose that the question of what the empirical facts are can be ascertained in some interpretation-free manner. Perhaps they cannot be. But we need not try to settle the issue of whether they can. Rather, our awareness of the issue should alert us to the possibility that we are unwittingly imposing some interpretation on what we naively regard as interpretation-free facts, and also to realize the need to consider, as best we can, the variety of interpretations to be taken into account.

We have already reflected, to some extent, upon the issue of how our own nature—of what we are essentially—is to be understood, and on how that understanding is crucial to our present concern. We noted how the possibility that we are identical to our bodies, in conjunction with the fact that death destroys our bodies (and thus destroys bodily continuity)[9] would render our survival not only naturally impossible but metaphysically impossible as well. Our being distinct from our bodies renders our survival metaphysically possible, but fails to establish the natural possibility of survival. Of course, these issues are so central to our present concerns that we must consider them much more carefully in a subsequent chapter.

Perhaps somewhat more precise distinctions would be helpful at this point to further elucidate the issues before us. We shall say that I am metaphysically distinct from my body if my identity is not the identity of my body. It would be a metaphysical truth that I am one entity and it is another. I would be such that I could not *just happen* to be (i.e., be *contingently*) identical to my body. I would be such that *necessarily* I would be one entity and it would be another, however intimately connected these different entities might be. Thus the metaphysical truth that I would not be my body would be a necessary one as well: I could not have been some entity other than the one I am, and thus could not have been identical to my body or to any other entity. For any other entity would have been something else. Consequently, any attempt to show that I am contingently (i.e., in fact, but not necessarily) identical to my body is doomed to fail.

But how can I find out that I am metaphysically distinct from my body (if indeed I am)? In general, the most plausible interpretation of the apparent facts of the matter must be our guide. In this case a first-person approach to the matter must be accorded centrality in our investigation, as we are trying to understand the nature of what the word "I" refers to when one uses it to refer to oneself. In first-person terms, I must search for the most plausible interpretation or understanding of what I seem to find myself to be in having experience, not only at this moment but also as I experience what seems to be my lasting or enduring through time.

As I carry out this introspective investigation, I might find that I am led to think of myself as something other than my body, i.e., my concept of myself is not my concept of my body. I might find that I can conceive of myself having experience extending through time, but entirely in isolation from my body. I might find that in thought I can exclude all my physical states and properties—my entire body. This would justify my claim that I am *conceptually* distinct from my body.

Though conceptual distinctness does not amount to metaphysical distinctness, it is a guide to the latter. Put somewhat differently, conceivability is a guide to metaphysical possibility. To illustrate, my ability to conceive of myself existing in isolation from my (and every other) body is a (fallible) guide to or indicator of the metaphysical possibility of my existing in isolation from it. This possibility would be actualized if I were to continue existing after biological death.

The relevance of natural law to the survival issue may be more precisely elucidated at this point. Even if I am metaphysically distinct from my body and thus such that my continuing to exist without it is a metaphysical possibility, the natural law governing my existence in this world may be such as to prevent that possibility from ever becoming actualized. Though my existence in isolation from my body might be metaphysically possible (and thus a possibility an omnipotent God could actualize), the fact that I actually exist might depend upon the existence of my body (or, at least, upon *some* physical body) in such a way that I could have no actual existence in isolation from it.

If (as I shall later argue) I am metaphysically distinct from my body, my being in a deep and intimate relationship to it in my present embodied existence would be undeniable. This would be a relationship expressible in terms of natural laws—the lawful connections between my conscious states and various physical/functional states of my body, primarily my brain. Some of these connections are known in a general way. When I am in a conscious state of some kind, there is then some kind (or some instance of some variety of kinds) of state or process occurring in my brain. Conversely, when an instance of a certain kind (or a certain variety of kinds) of state or process is occurring in my brain, then I am in a certain kind of conscious state. Such connections can be described in the amount of detail to which they have been determined, and they are ordinarily interpreted as causal connections. These cause-effect relations appear to have one of two directions: from mind to brain and from brain to mind. The appearances are that some brain states cause mental or conscious states, and some conscious states or events cause brain states or events. Though the issue of whether conscious states cause brain states is controversial, what is not controversial is that I must be causally related to my body if I am metaphysically distinct from it. In other words, if I am not distinct from my body (including all its states, properties, and functions), then I would not bear any causal relation to it, as no item is causally related to itself.

How these mind-brain causal connections are to be understood is an issue meriting close attention. The view that the nonphysical cannot bear any causal relation to the physical is widely held among contemporary philosophers of mind. But, as we shall see, this view depends on the plausibility of a certain interpretation of the causal relation; and there are other plausible accounts of how causation is to be understood. In the end, the account of causation that we find to be most plausible is the one that makes most sense of the full range of factual and theoretical/interpretive considerations that must be taken into account in our effort to arrive at an overall understanding of our own nature and our relation to the physical world.

The Case Against
Post-Mortem Existence

Antecedent Probability of Extinction

As we reflect upon the reasons for believing that our existence will end at death, they may strike us as numerous and weighty, if not compelling. We note that physical science finds nothing in us or about us that could survive biological death. The entire physical body dies and decomposes into more elementary material, eventually leaving no trace of that highly organized and immensely complex material organism that was once a living, functioning human being. The human being follows the natural course of all complex living things in the natural world, its life eventually terminating and its body broken down into simpler materials available for the production or sustenance of other living things. We are creatures of the natural world, deeply embedded in nature, however much we may differ even from those of our fellow creatures most like us; and we assume without question that death terminates their existence in an absolutely final way. With death, they are and will be no more. Why should we suppose, or even conjecture, that what death brings in our case is any different from what it brings in theirs? The corpses of at least the higher animals appear in all the relevant respects just like the human corpse, and all are recycled back into nature in accordance with the same natural laws. In view of such considerations, the antecedent probability (i.e., the likelihood suggested by how a phenomenon initially appears to be) that death brings our extinction might seem very high, if not amounting to a certainty.

Empirically-Grounded Support of Extinction

Although the foregoing considerations seem to show conclusively that the *human being* does not survive, one might maintain that the prospects for the survival of the *person* do not look so grim. We have already taken note of some reasons for believing that the person is distinct from the human being in which she is embodied; and, if she is, then the death of the human being does not entail the termination of the *person's* existence. But to defend this view, one would have to face formidable challenges grounded in our ordinary observations of the deep functional dependence of our consciousness upon our bodily states, especially those of the brain. Let us call these challenges "empirically-grounded indicators of extinction."

Even if a person is distinct from her body, our observational evidence of her relationship to it renders undeniable that she is very deeply embodied in it. This relationship may well be such that any conscious states we might imagine her having independently of it are contrary to the relevant laws of nature, i.e., are naturally impossible in the actual world. Perhaps the most obvious evidence of the dependence of consciousness upon brain activity consists in our observations of what happens when brain activity ceases with biological death or when there is major trauma to the portions of the brain associated with consciousness. With biological death, all signs of consciousness cease, as they do after a massive stroke or severe head injury. Apparently, consciousness itself has been extinguished, either permanently or temporarily.

Another line of evidence of functional dependence is of a kind available not only to the third-person viewpoint but also to the person whose consciousness is being affected, allowing that person to witness directly the effect on consciousness. Many drugs affect consciousness by altering brain activity. The affects of alcohol are widely known. More profound effects are brought about by such powerful psychotropic drugs as cocaine, opium, lysergic acid, psilocybin, and mescaline. Of course, there are numerous other bodily states, conditions or activities that, apparently by altering brain activity, bring about changes in consciousness available to the inner, first-person viewpoint. The effects of fatigue and illness are known to everyone, and serious, if not fatal, disease (such as Parkinson's, Huntington's chorea and Alzheimer's) that ravages the brain is directly experienced by their victims, at least in the incipient stages. Other items in this class include yoga postures, meditation, lengthy fasting, and sensory deprivation.

Another line of evidence is contributed by brain science. By machine-generated images of brain activity, often in conjunction with testimony from patients about their conscious states, much has been learned about the correlations between locations, intensities, and kinds of brain activities, on the one hand, and states of consciousness, on the other. By studying the electro-chemistry of the brain, much has been learned about the function of such neurotransmitters as dopamine, serotonin, and norepinepherin, and about how abnormalities in their production or functioning may often be corrected or mitigated by the use of some one or other of the mood-altering medications. Artificial electro-stimulation of the brain provides a striking example of how conscious states can be caused to arise simply by generating tiny electric currents in certain regions of the brain, thus leaving no doubt that certain brain disturbances are (causally) sufficient for bringing about at least some conscious states.

One of the most somber and poignant reminders of the dependency of our conscious lives upon the condition of our brains occurs in the aging process when, as often happens, brain decline and deterioration have been sufficiently advanced to be noticed by their victims in memory loss, difficulty in concentrating, and general cognitive decline. As the mind, including its introspective capacity to note and reflect upon its own states, is what is declining along with the brain, these declines in cognitive function are often first noticed by others. In many cases, the cognitive decline becomes all too conspicuous to others, a grim testament to what is happening to the inner conscious life we cannot directly observe. The appearances are that the mind (and, of course, the person) always goes where the brain goes, and thus eventually to complete destruction and nonexistence.

The phenomenon of aging is one of the most forceful indicators of our deep embodiment. It (though not it alone) provides compelling if not conclusive evidence that the brain is not merely an instrument used by the mind to acquire information about the external world and to express itself in language and bodily action. Such an "instrument view" of the brain is inconsistent with the deep embodiment implied by the apparent effect of diminished brain function not only on perceptual acuity and alertness but also on such higher-order intellectual activities as critical thinking, reasoning, reflective decision-making, evaluation, and judgment. If proper brain function were a causally necessary condition (i.e., necessary in the sense of physical or natural necessity) for having any conscious state, then our being deeply embodied would imply that our being conscious after death would be contrary to the laws of nature (i.e., would be naturally impossible). Of course, we must not overlook the counterevidence that we have free will, in which case we would have, by way of our conscious decision-making events, the power to affect our brain activity and thereby bring about bodily action. Still, we must take these empirically-grounded considerations fully into account and appreciate their centrality in the overall case for believing that persons are in fact destroyed by death, even if they are such that they might have continued to exist had the relevant natural laws been different.

Theory-Based Arguments for Extinction

Though our beliefs about what the observable facts are may always bear some influence of an interpretive element we unwittingly supply, the views we shall take note of now are heavily dependent upon interpretation in that they are attempts to understand and explain why these facts are as we find them to be and not otherwise. These views are attempts to understand the broader setting in which the observable facts fall neatly into place. Much of the fabric of this broader setting is theoretical, consisting of items not observed, but postulated or inferred to exist as part of an overall account purportedly having the merit of providing the most plausible explanation of the observable mind-brain (or mind-body) relations.

We should note at the outset that the observable mind-body relations leave open the possibility that persons are merely embodied as human beings, not identical to them. For whatever else may be essential to what a person is, she is certainly someone who has various experiences or conscious states— states that certainly do not appear to be states of the brain or body. Thus they leave open the possibility that persons survive death in disembodied form, or as embodied differently (perhaps, as we shall see, in a nonphysical "phenomenal" body), either as the regular outcome of natural law or (if God exists) as the result of God's action. What the empirically-grounded indicators appear to show is that the likelihood that this possibility is the one actualized is not very high. Though persons appear to be such that they might have survived bodily death, the likelihood that they will in fact survive appears very low in the light of the mind-brain relations we are able to observe.

The theory-based arguments would push the case against survival even further, since, if successful, they would show that personal survival of death is absolutely (or metaphysically) impossible, at least without miraculous divine intervention. Many are attempts to show, in one way or another, that a person is nothing over and above a human being—that complex physical organism eventually destroyed completely by bodily death. Some maintain that consciousness is a *nonphysical property,* but a property of brain events or processes that are, of course, physical things (i.e., particulars) possessing physical properties. So in these views, persons have the nonphysical property or characteristic of being conscious, but they are nevertheless physical particulars, which, unlike most physical things, have the additional property of being conscious.

We can make these distinctions more precise by introducing at this point a bit more terminology. The former views are forms of *monism* in maintaining that the concrete natural world (i.e., the entire physical universe) is physical in its entirety. All the physical particulars constituting it are physical, and all their properties are either physical or physical-neutral. In other words, none of their properties are nonphysical. By contrast, the latter views maintain that though some properties are nonphysical, all are properties of physical particulars. Thus these views are monistic with respect to particulars (i.e., particulars are all of *one* fundamental kind) and dualistic with respect to properties. For further clarification, we note that a property (or characteristic or attribute) can have an instance in many particulars, such as the property of being blue, which is possessed by all blue particulars. A particular, on the other hand, cannot have instances (for that would be to have an instance in some particular), but is what has or possesses properties. Indeed, it seems that any particular *must* have properties; for when we speak of *what* it is (e.g., a table), we are speaking of the *properties* it shares with certain other particular things, namely tables. A particular is something there can be only *one* of, unlike a property, which can have many instances in different particulars. Its particularity is what accounts for its "thisness"—its being the unique individual that it is and its being (numerically) different from every other individual, even one exactly like it. To illustrate, I am *this particular* person and such that there can be only *one* of *me*, though the property (or set of properties) of being a person has an instance in every other person. My qualitatively identical twin (if I had one) would be exactly like me, both mentally and physically, yet clearly would be *someone else.*

We are now in a position to see that a view in which a person is a single individual or particular distinct from the human body in which she is embodied would express a dualism of *particulars*. And since it would be (metaphysically) possible for one particular to exist in the absence of the other, the post-mortem existence of the person would be metaphysically possible, even if the person-body relation is so intimate that in fact persons perish with their bodies. There seems to be no such possibility in either of the other two groups of views. We have already noted that the views in which persons are entirely material beings effectively exclude this possibility. What we should note now is that this possibility is similarly excluded in those views acknowledging a dualism of properties. For in these views, even though persons have the nonphysical property of being conscious, this is a property of the physical particular that a person is—a human being—and the human being is destroyed in death.

Though some views of the person that effectively rule out the possibility of survival (e.g., materialist functionalism) do not fit neatly into either of the two groups we have been considering, we shall examine them along with the others in some detail as we turn to the next chapter. Our concern will be to determine precisely what they assert about the nature of persons, what grounds they provide for making these assertions, and how well they fare under critical examination. Our overall effort in that chapter and the following one will be to determine what view of persons proves to be the most adequate one, all things considered. Given that view, we will be able to establish (to the degree of certainty that this view expresses the truth about what we are) whether post-mortem existence is metaphysically possible for us. If it is, we would have no rational basis for joining those who routinely dismiss as false without any further consideration those numerous reports, some very well documented and carefully examined, of paranormal occurrences appearing to show that some deceased persons have in fact survived bodily death and have managed to communicate that fact to the living.

Minds, Souls and Persons

The views of the mental and, accordingly, of the person that have received the most attention and the most widespread acceptance among contemporary thinkers engaged in professional study of the mind are forms of a thoroughgoing materialism. According to materialist theory,[1] the (concrete) natural world is constituted entirely of matter in its various forms, one of which is energy. Persons are seen as entirely material (i.e., physical) beings. There are, of course, importance differences that distinguish one view from another within the broader category of more or less extreme materialist theory.

The most extreme is eliminative materialism, according to which there are no minds or mental (i.e., conscious)[2] states at all. Though this extremely provocative view acknowledges that there are mental terms and other mental expressions, it maintains that there are no mental things (i.e., particulars) or mental properties to which any of these expressions refer. Rather, when they refer, their referents are physical exclusively. However, we will not pay close attention to this view here. Not only does it strike one as highly implausible, but it is at least as vulnerable to all of the formidable difficulties that (as we shall see) the less extreme forms of materialism are exposed. The difficulties that seem to render them acceptable have at least as great an impact on it.

Materialist-Reductionist Accounts of the Mental

The various forms of reductive materialism acknowledge the existence of the mental, but find it reducible to (and thus nothing over and above) the physical. One of the earliest of these views on the broadly contemporary scene is analytical or metaphysical behaviorism. In this view, the mentalistic language is correctly understood as analyzable into expressions referring to outwardly observable behavior and dispositions to such behavior. Many of these behaviors and dispositions to behavior are linguistic in character. It may seem that what one believes or knows without giving any expression of

29

it does not succumb to such behaviorist/dispositionalist analysis. But the behaviorist has a ready reply. Your knowledge that the Pacific Ocean is larger than the Atlantic consists in your being disposed to say "the Pacific Ocean" prior to your actually uttering these words when asked which is the larger of these two oceans, much as a pane of glass is disposed to break prior to its actual breaking when struck with a hammer. Thus in this view the mental is nothing over and above the physical—(physical) behavior and dispositions to such behavior. It is a form of reductive materialism since it claims that the mental exists but is reducible to the physical.

In addition to the very great difficulties that (as we will see) stand in the way of accepting any form of reductive materialism, analytical behaviorism must face a difficulty apparently fatal to it. For it must deny what strikes us as an incontestable truth, namely, that we have inner conscious states that cannot be identified with any observable behavior or any disposition to such behavior. The first person access each of us has to his own conscious states (an access whose existence the analytical behaviorist must deny) reveals them to be inner, privately experienced events that simply cannot be what the analytical behaviorist claims they are, though, of course, they are causally connected to external behavior. In effect, the analytical behaviorist denies the existence of consciousness—that we have an inner conscious life—and thereby renders her view simply incredible.

A more widespread form of reductive materialism that avoids this difficulty fatal to analytical behaviorism is the mind-brain identity theory. In this view, mental expressions may refer to mental states or events, but these mental particulars turn out to be identical to brain states, events, or processes. There are mental particulars (that are not outwardly observable behaviors or behavioral dispositions), but each is identical to some physical particular or other. Though there are different forms of the theory, some making stronger claims than others, all subscribe to the (weaker) thesis that mental particulars exist, but each is identical to some physical particular.

Largely because of difficulties in specifying what it is about some brain states that makes them (but not others) mental states, many contemporary thinkers have advocated a *functionalist* view of mental states rather than a form of the mind-brain identity theory. The functionalist *does* specify what it is about a state that makes it a mental state in defining a mental state as a functional state, that is, a state defined by its functional or causal role in the overall activity of the organism as it receives sensory information from the environment, processes that information by way of its central nervous system, and then responds, often in outwardly observable activity. So a pain, for example, is that which fills the causal role of mediating between the stimuli received as a result of bodily injury and the pain behavior that is outwardly displayed. Though, in the view of at least some functionalists, what fills this role need not be physical, it is in fact physical in the case of every human being and ever other natural creature in which there are such roles to be filled. Thus the functionalist understanding of human mentality is materialist. The resulting *materialist functionalism* is currently a dominant view among philosophers and other thinkers specializing in the study of the mind.

Given the current appeal of materialist functionalism and its relevance to the survival issue, a clear understanding of it will serve us well. Two of its features will be central to our subsequent evaluation of it. First, mental states or events are conceived abstractly, as whatever fills certain functional or causal roles. They are defined by reference to the causal relations they bear to other items in a certain kind of causal chain of items. In other words, they are defined by their *relational* properties, not by their intrinsic ones—the properties they have in themselves, independently of their relations to other things. So what makes some state a mental state is not what it is in itself, the properties it has intrinsically, but its causal-relational properties. For example, what is essential to someone's being in a state of pain is not that one is *hurting* (an intrinsic property of pain), but that one is in a state that bears certain relations to other states or events in some appropriate causal chain of such items.

Second, materialist functionalism implies that even though mental states are conceived and defined as whatever (physical or nonphysical item that) fills some one or other of a certain group of causal roles, in fact every such state at least in humans is a physical state. Thus the functionalist who is a materialist is committed to the view that every one of *our* mental states is in fact a physical state and so is, in this respect, entirely in agreement with the mind-brain identity theorist. Consequently, the grounds we have for concluding that at least some of our mental states are not and cannot be physical states are grounds for rejecting all these forms of reductive materialism.

We should note that there are views whose proponents claim are forms of non-reductive materialism. Some of these seem to acknowledge the existence of nonphysical properties, but nevertheless claim to be forms of materialism on the grounds that all particulars are held to be physical. As we have seen, the prospects for survival of death are at least very dim in such views. Functionalism is sometimes claimed to be non-reductive either because its definition of the mental does not exclude the (metaphysical) possibility of mental states that are nonphysical or because of its admission that a mental state of a certain kind might have been "realized" in a variety of kinds of physical states (much as a clock can be realized in a variety of physical structures). But these distinctions are not relevant to our primary concern since, as we have seen, materialist functionalism—the form widely embraced by contemporary thinkers—maintains that all of our mental states are physical and that the concrete natural world is in fact entirely material.

Materialist Theories of Personal Identity

If the mental is reducible to (and thus nothing over and above) the physical, then a person would be entirely physical, identical to the human organism. This would be true even if the mental is more broadly conceived in the functionalist way as functions rather than physical items, since the functionalist who is a materialist must acknowledge that all actual mental events taking place in us and throughout the natural world are in fact physical events. What we shall examine now are the implications such views have with respect to our personal identity in our pre-mortem existence, as well as how any possibility of post-mortem existence should be conceived.

There are two major issues that must be addressed in any adequate account of personal identity. Both have to do with one's existence in time. First, there is the issue of what constitutes a person's identity at some given time, e.g., at this moment. What makes a person at that time the person that she is? Second, what constitutes a person's continuing existence over time? In virtue of *what* has a person remained the selfsame person over time, ultimately throughout one's lifetime, and even beyond death if post-mortem existence is a metaphysical (even if not a natural) possibility.

Though both issues have fundamental importance in thought about what persons are, the second has received far more attention, with the first apparently considered much less problematic. Indeed, the problem of accounting for one's continuing identity through time is frequently called *the problem* of personal identity, as if it were the only one. And there are views in which it *is* the only one, as in them, nothing can be said about which person (or persons) is (are) present in a human organism at some given time, apart from a determination that can be made only when the entire lifetime of the organism can be taken into account.[3] Such (materialist) views collapse the issue of personal identity at a time into the issue of identity over time, but they are highly revisionist and strike one as wildly implausible. Still, both issues (and there *are* two) ultimately must be answered in the same way.

In most materialist views, personal identity at a time is relatively easy to determine. This identity is the identity of the human organism along with the mental and physical states it is in at the time. At a particular time, the human being, like every other particular, is identical with itself. But over time, this being (that is the person in these views) undergoes a great deal of change. Yet despite this change, it is assumed to remain one and the same (i.e., the *numerically* same) being. How is its numerical identity over time to be understood?

The first point to note is that since there are two different concepts of identity over time, there is a question as to which is more properly applicable to persons. The fundamental concept is variously termed the "strict," or "absolute," or "perfect" sense of identity over time. If some particular did not change at all over some period of time, it clearly would have remained one and the same in the strict or absolute sense throughout that period. It could have remained one and the same in this strict sense even if for example it had moved or changed many of its relations to other things. For such changes are not changes in that which makes it what it is. They are not changes that would have affected its identity at a given time.

But not all changes are identity-neutral. Many particulars such as ships, automobiles, and living organisms are complex objects constituted at a given time by many distinguishable parts, many or all of which get replaced over the course of time by others sufficiently similar to preserve the basic structure and function of the complex object. In the case of the human body, the fact seems to be that the material constituting it is gradually but continuously being replaced by similar material at a rate such that after a period of seven to ten years there is no material in one's body that was there ten years ago. All has been replaced, much as the water in an aquarium through which there is a continuous flow of fresh water would all be recycled eventually. Of course, much of the gradual but continuous flow of material through our bodies takes place at a micro-level, consisting of micro-elements small enough to replace cell material, and thus is very difficult to detect. But since all of this material apparently does get replaced and since the identity of the body at a given time consists in the organized material constituting it at that time, it does not retain its identity in the strict or absolute sense. Rather, it retains its identity in only the "loose," or "relative," or "imperfect" sense.

Though the body does not retain a strict identity over time, (not only because of the material-replacement process but because its shape, size, appearance, and other features also change), the changes it undergoes occur in a gradual and continuous way. Its existence as a living organism is continuous from birth to death, despite the numerous and profound changes it undergoes. There is a continuous track, so to speak, in space and time that we can say is made by a single body. Thus the identity of the person over time can consist only in the imperfect identity provided by the continuity of the body.

One might try to resist this conclusion by maintaining that one's genetic or DNA structure fixes one's physical identity and that this structure is retained throughout one's lifetime. Though the genetic material entering into this structure apparently does get replaced gradually by similar material, the new material enters into and forms the structure vacated by the replaced material. Thus if one and the same structure is preserved, it is available to ground personal identity in the strict sense: personal identity over time is genetic identity.

But this view is highly implausible. Even if it were plausible to maintain that personal identity resides in genetic structure and that this structure remains entirely unchanged through time, a structure is something abstract, capable of having many instances (as in, for example, many houses having the same structure), and thus fails to capture the concrete *particularity* of a person. Identical twins possess the same genetic structure, yet each is a particular person as distinct from her twin as from any other person. Whatever else is true of a person, she is a concrete particular, not an abstract entity capable of having many instances.

If, as it seems, the materialist view of the person implies that personal identity over time consists in the physical continuity of the body, the implications for survival are clear: the existence of the person ends when the continuous existence of the living body ends in biological death. Given the break in continuity, there could be no good reason to believe that a body resurrected at some later time would be (identical to) the person who died. Even if the material constituting the resurrected body were one and the same as (i.e., numerically identical to) the material that once constituted the earthly body and were organized in exactly the way it was organized in the earthly body at the time, there could be no assurance that the resurrected person was anything more than a replica, exactly similar to but not one and the same as the original person. There seems to be only one metaphysical possibility consistent with a person's surviving death: God whisks the person away at death, thereby preserving bodily continuity and thus personal identity as well, while leaving only a replica or simulacrum in its place to be buried or cremated.[4]

Though the prospects for survival could hardly be dimmer if the bodily continuity theory were true, there are compelling reasons for believing that it is *not* true. If personal identity (over time) did consist in the continuity of the body, then bodily continuity would be both necessary and sufficient for personal identity. Our concept of personal identity would be our concept of bodily continuity. But these concepts are easily seen to be distinct, indicating that bodily continuity is not only not necessary for personal identity but also not sufficient for it either.

It seems easy to conceive of two persons switching bodies. One can conceive or imagine this from a third-person viewpoint, observing the apparent body-switch from the outside (as in John Locke's famous example of the prince and the cobbler switching bodies). All the indicators of personal identity such as memories, character traits, and beliefs about identity held by the persons involved point to the conclusion that the persons have switched bodies. But any remaining doubt disappears upon taking the first-person viewpoint and imagining finding oneself in a different body, or viewing one's own body from a distance as in an out-of-the-body experience. It is easy to imagine, for example, awakening from sleep to discover that the body in which one has awakened is obviously not the body had when falling asleep.

In these conceivable (and apparently metaphysically possible) situations, the person does not go where the body goes, thereby indicating that personal identity over time does not consist in the continuity of the body. In the switch cases in which the body continues to exist, though now as the body of another, its continuity is clearly not necessary for the identity of the person who once had it. Equally clearly, its continuity is not sufficient for personal identity either, as it may continue to exist as the body of another after the person who once had it has perished or has some other body. That its continuity is not sufficient for personal identity becomes evident again in those actual cases when, due to massive stroke or other great trauma to the brain, one becomes irreversibly unconsciousness. Though the body continues to exist, it is difficult to avoid concluding that the *person* has gone, never to return.

The Immateriality of the Mental

We have been looking at views in which the mental either does not exist or is reducible to (and thus nothing over and above) the physical, and then at accounts of personal identity consistent with such views of the mental. We will now examine the case for believing that the mental is not reducible to the physical, and that persons are not entirely material, if material at all. It is a case for believing that the mental is an irreducible and immaterial reality.

Perhaps the most conspicuous indication that the mental is a reality of a fundamental kind different from that of anything physical comes into view upon seeing that our thought and talk about the mental is very different from our thought and talk about the physical. We might, for example, speak of some physical object as having a certain weight, shape, and size; but it makes no sense to speak of a thought or feeling as having any such features. Conversely, we might speak of a confused thought or a melancholy feeling, but not of a physical object, such as a bridge or a rock, as confused or melancholy. Reflecting on such facts, we are led to the conclusion that there is a deep conceptual or logical breech between the mental and the physical, however this breech is to be explained. Moreover, the most plausible explanation of this great difference between mental and physical concepts is that there is a great difference between the corresponding realities that we grasp by means of them.

As we probe deeper into the nature of the mental (or, at least, into what we conceive the mental to be), we encounter a variety of good reasons to believe that the mental is not and, indeed, cannot be merely some manifestation of the physical—merely the physical appearing in a way confusing to us—and thus reducible to the physical after all. Though we may at times speak of the unconscious mind and of unconscious mental states, we would do well to follow the lead of Descartes[5] and take consciousness to be the mark of the mental. For a focus on consciousness makes clear the formidable challenges that must be met by any materialist account of the mental. We can still speak of unconscious mental states, but will understand them to be certain causes of, or dispositions to have, *conscious* mental states.

One salient feature of a conscious state or event is its directedness—its being *of* or *about* or *directed upon* something. This feature is called "intentionality." Perhaps it is a feature of every conscious state. On the other hand, perhaps *non-intentional* consciousness exists, but we need not address this issue now. The central point to note here is that nothing physical has this feature. Clearly, no physical thing, such as a table or a river, is *about* anything. A photograph of a table resembles the table it pictures, but is not *about* that table. Even though we may say that it is *of* that table, this is a non-intentional "of," which means only that it was (partly) caused by the table and resembles the table as well. It is clearly not of the table in the way that one's consciousness of the table is of (or directed upon) the table. Nor is a brain event or process directed upon, or about, the conscious state to which it is causally connected. It simply occurs, though, of course, as an item in an encompassing causal network. There is no intentionality in either the causal or the resemblance relation.

Since there is no genuine intentionality in the physical realm, what the reductive materialist must do is show how intentionality can be reduced to (and thus understood in terms of) the non-intentional properties and relations that do have instances in the realm of the physical. But there can be no hope for success in this endeavor if, as seems clear, intentionality is an *intrinsic,* and thus a constitutive, feature of consciousness (or, at least, of the ordinary consciousness that concerns us here). The intentionality of consciousness would be basic, not reducible to anything else.

Another feature of consciousness setting it apart from the physical consists in the way it is known. There are two quite different features of the way we know of it, each of which distinguishes it from anything physical. First, it is unlike the physical in that it is not known through sense perception but by way of introspective awareness of what is occurring in one's own consciousness. One's attention is directed inward, rather than outward unto external things. Second, our states of consciousness are directly or immediately known to us: nothing mediates our knowledge of them. What we might be thinking, remembering, feeling or choosing at the time is directly accessible to us, whether or not we can state with precision what that is or remember it later. More generally, we have a direct, epistemic (knowledge-yielding) access to the contents of our own states of consciousness. But as we shall see, it seems that we have no such access to anything physical. Rather, our access to anything physical is mediated by the contents of our conscious states.

We should also note that this direct epistemic access is a *private* access, open only to a single person. More generally, the direct access each person has to her own conscious states is an access open only to her. In first-person terms, no one else can have the direct awareness of (or the direct epistemic access to) my conscious states that I have. It is a privileged access. But there is no private or privileged access to anything physical. Physical things are publicly accessible. They are public things, accessible to more than a single observer, indeed, to any observer suitably equipped and situated.

Closely associated with the privacy of consciousness is its interiority or subjectivity. We might speak of consciousness as necessarily possessing an inner or subjective dimension that eludes description yet is directly known to the conscious person. But nothing physical possesses this feature. A physical object has an inside in the spatial sense, but clearly not in the subjective sense.

The subjectivity of consciousness is one of its *essential* features, one without which it could not exist. But the same is true of its privacy and of the fact that it is directly known by the person whose consciousness it is. These features (if they are more than one) are very closely related in a common source. Expressed in first-person terms, it is in virtue of being in my conscious states that they are directly accessible to me and that my awareness of them is direct. Since only I can be in, or have, them, no one else can have such access to them. Hence my access to them is *necessarily* private. In other words, it is metaphysically impossible for these very states (or, perhaps, this very consciousness) to have been the states (or the consciousness) of someone else. That is, my consciousness *necessarily* belongs to me. It seems intuitively clear that *my* consciousness of, say, the necessary ownership of experience could not have been had by another, though another, of course, could have her own consciousness of this.

But none of this is found in the physical realm. We have already acknowledged the absence of subjectivity and necessarily private access. What we should take note of now is that the necessary ownership of a person's consciousness is radically different from the way in which the constituents of a person's body are owned by it. The material making up the body merely happens to belong to that body: its belonging is not a matter of necessity. Indeed, its being there is only temporary. As we noted earlier, there is a continuous flow of micro-level material through the body at a rate such that no particular material, at this level at least, remains more than seven to ten years. Clearly, this material has an existence independent of the body that it (temporarily) constitutes at a given time and is such that it could have constituted some other human body, or no human body at all, at that time.

Another feature of consciousness that is not found in the physical realm is its peculiar unity—a unity that seems to be absolutely indivisible. This unity of consciousness is present at any given time at which one is conscious, but it also extends through time. Like other features of consciousness, it is directly accessible only from the first-person viewpoint. It comes into view when one focuses on the various experiences one is having at some particular time and notes that, despite their differences, they are bound into an apparently indivisible unity in being all one's own. To illustrate, at this moment I am thinking about this unity, looking at my computer monitor, touching the keyboard, and hearing soft music in the background. Though these experiences differ greatly in qualitative character, they are brought together into a unity expressed (however inadequately) by saying that each is an experience of mine. Though this unity is directly accessible to each of us, it seems to elude adequate description. What is clear, however, is that its divisibility seems inconceivable. If, for example, this case of being visually conscious of the computer could exist even if not brought into the unity, I would not be conscious of it at all. Even though what I would then be conscious of would change, the *unity* would remain intact and unaffected. A necessary condition for my being conscious of something is that my consciousness of it *is* the unified consciousness of whatever I am conscious of at the time.

That this indivisibility also extends over time is strongly indicated, if not conclusively shown, by the deliverances of experience-memory. When I remember an experience, part of what I remember is *myself having it*. It is thereby brought into the unity of my present consciousness. My present consciousness of having had it is the unified consciousness in which my presently occurring experiences are unified. Thus the unity (and apparent indivisibility) of my present consciousness is also the unity that extends through time when in veridical memory I remember myself having an experience.

Though there is much more to be said about the unity of consciousness, especially in the way it extends through time,[6] what is important to note at this juncture is that physical science finds nothing like it in the material world. Every material particular, however small, is extended in space[7] and thus has different parts in the different places of the space that it occupies. This implies divisibility throughout matter. Even if a material thing (e.g., a meson or a quark) is such that it never gets divided in nature, the (meta-physical) possibility of its division is implied by the fact that it has spatially distinct parts that have parts having parts, and so forth without end. Clearly, the unity of a material thing, and certainly of any brain neuron, is not the apparently indivisible, absolute unity exemplified in the unity of conscious-ness.[8] Indeed, the claim that this unity might be the unity of some state, event, or process occurring in one's brain when one is conscious apparently con-tradicts the observable fact that the physical correlate to any conscious state or event is the electrochemical activity of hundreds of thousands of neurons distributed over a sizeable portion of the brain.

Closely related to this unique unity is the apparent nonspatiality of con-sciousness. Though the brain activity that is causally related to conscious states has both location in space and is extended over a spatial region, it seems unintelligible to speak of the conscious states themselves as having either location or extension in space. We might be tempted to claim that consciousness is where the brain activity associated with it is. But such a claim would not be true in a literal sense, but only a figurative way of refer-ring to a relation between consciousness and the brain. This relation is causal and temporal (as certain brain events and the causally connected conscious events occur simultaneously, or approximately so), but apparently not spa-tial. Its nonspatiality is evidenced by the fact that we do not know what could count as finding consciousness in the place where it is alleged to be. Nor is this fact surprising, for locating something in space relies on sense percep-tion at some point. But, as we have noted, consciousness is not accessed by way of sense perception. Yet there can be no doubt that spatiality is one of the essential features of matter. What is not in space cannot be material.

Other truths about consciousness that stand in the way of any attempt to reduce consciousness to something material consist in what conscious-ness either reveals to us or makes possible. In virtue of its intrinsic direct-edness, it enables us to grasp meaning and thereby makes language possible. Language employs signs and symbols directed beyond themselves unto that to which they refer. The world "horse," for example, means or refers to a certain kind of mammal. But whether written or spoken, it does not do this in virtue of its physical properties. Its physical properties such as size, shape, and color are irrelevant to its referring power. In and of itself, it is a mean-ingless mark (or noise, if spoken). Its directedness beyond itself unto that to which it refers is derived from the intrinsic directedness of consciousness. If language essentially involves a grasp of the meaning of signs and symbols[9]—a meaning deriving from the intrinsic directedness of consciousness—then language becomes impossible to understand without acknowledging the irreducible reality of consciousness.

Consciousness enables us to grasp (non-actual) possibility, to envision how the world might have been. We can think about what is not the case and about things that do not exist. What one is being conscious of at a given time (technically, *the intentional object*) may be nonexistent at that time, perhaps no longer in existence, not in existence yet, or such that it never exists. This nonexistent object might be a concrete particular (e.g., a centaur) or a possible fact—what might have been a fact but actually is not. In virtue of our consciousness, we can represent the world (or some aspect of it) to be this or that, and come to hold beliefs about the world in accordance with our representations or conceptions of it. True and false beliefs become part of mental reality. Thus error becomes a reality when our beliefs fail to fit the facts, along with confusion, ambiguity, vagueness, and other such attributes of our conscious states or our conceptions of the way things are. A belief is rational or irrational, justified or unjustified, in the light of the available evidence of its truth. The evidence may be such that a state of indecision or uncertainty rather than belief is the more rational stance to take to avoid error. Along with error and falsehood comes deception. We may deceive others in lying to them, and even deceive ourselves, perhaps in holding a belief for purely personal or psychological reasons (such as a need for security, certainty, or acceptance), without regard for virtually conclusive evidence that it is false.

Propositions or claims become easy to account for with the recognition of the irreducible reality of consciousness. These items expressed in language are those sentences having assertive power. Unlike questions, commands, suggestions and other non-assertive sentences, they make an assertion about what is or is not the case—an assertion that is either true or false. As the bearers of truth and falsity, and constituting *what we believe* when we hold a true or false belief, they fit well into the overall picture of mental reality that features consciousness at its center.

Before proceeding further in our consideration of truth about our conscious states that appear to render them impossible to accommodate within an entirely material reality, let us take note of what is indicated by the truths we have just considered. Possibility apparently has no place in the material realm. Our access to that realm is by way of sense-perception. But our senses reveal only what is actual, never what is merely possible. Possibility arrives on the scene as we reflect upon and interpret the deliverances of perceptual consciousness. We believe, say, that it might rain today. But in the material world, either it rains or it does not rain. Nothing there answers to our notion that "it might rain." If it does rain, it rains because that is what was causally necessitated, and its not raining was causally impossible. Nor are there any nonexistent objects in the material world or anything that is not the case.

Our concept of possibility (at least, as applied to the non-quantum level) expresses our uncertainty. But there is no uncertainty in the material realm.[10] Nor is there any confusion, ambiguity or vagueness. Every material thing or event is exactly what it is at any given time, with each item constituting it being in exactly the place where it is, bearing precise physical relations to every other item. Obviously, it cannot be confused or clear, nor can it be ambiguous or vague in itself.

Similar conclusions must be drawn with respect to error, falsehood, and deception. Material reality cannot be in error, nor can it deceive, though, of course, *we* can err or be deceived in our attempts to understand it. The physical entities comprising it and the events occurring in it are neither true nor false. They simply exist or occur. Truth and falsehood have no application there. Nor do beliefs and propositions or assertions, for they are characterized by their truth or falsity. Only when consciousness enters the picture do they have a place. It is only in virtue of those conscious states in which we take the facts to be as they are, or other than they are, that we are able to hold true or false beliefs about them. And beyond the evaluative judgments that we consciously make, the concept of rationality or rational justification has no application. An unconscious thing or event in nature, say a hurricane, cannot be rational or irrational, justified or unjustified. Only our attitudes toward it and our beliefs about it can have such properties. It seems clear that none of this could be acknowledged to exist in any attempt to reduce the mental to the physical—to try to conceive of it as nothing in addition to the physical realm.

Another dimension of reality to which our consciousness (in particular, our higher-level conscious states) gives us access is generality and abstraction. We can grasp general moral principles (e.g., the Golden Rule), and completely general logical truths such as the principle of identity (which states that every entity is identical to itself) and logical principles of class membership as expressed in the claim, "Every member of a class entirely contained within a larger class is also a member of the larger class." We can grasp generality by abstracting out properties common to a group of particular things and form the concept of a kind, e.g., the kind of tree to which birch trees belong. Finally, we have access to such apparently abstract objects as numbers, classes, and two-dimensional geometrical figures.

But the material realm consists exclusively of concrete particular things and events or states (and, of course, facts pertaining to them). None are general and none are abstract. Though we can, by abstract thought, come to apprehend characteristics some of them share and thereby group them into (general) kinds (e.g., the kind *horse* or *fish*), the material entities themselves are neither general nor abstract. And whatever general moral or logical principles should be understood to be, they are clearly not material entities. The same may be said of such abstract objects as numbers and classes. Finally, there are no two-dimensional figures in the material world.

Though the existence of an abstract reality would block any attempt to see the material realm as the only one, its existence would not constitute the central problem for the reductive materialist. For the materialist could maintain that her thesis is only that the natural world of concrete particulars is entirely material, and that this includes our mental states. The central problem for her is to plausibly explain in materialist terms the mind's power to abstract and grasp generality. It is part of the more general problem of understanding how the mind can reach out and grasp anything in thought if we do not acknowledge intentionality to be an intrinsic and fundamental capacity of the mind. But the problem is put in high relief if, as it seems, the materialist attempts to solve it must be entirely in terms of the activity of material particulars.

As we noted, the mind is able to see generality in things in seeing classes to which we conceive them to belong. Perhaps this generality is actually in them, perhaps it is only a potentiality in them that becomes actualized in thought, or perhaps it is created by the mind and thus not in them at all. We need not enter into that issue. Since the things themselves are particulars, our focus will be on how the mind's grasp of generality is to be understood as the activity of material particulars alone. This grasping (i.e., intentional) relation would have to be understood to be some natural relation between particulars, more specifically between some general word (e.g., the noun "tree," the verb "is running," the preposition "between") and some particular (or particulars) for which it stands. Meaning would have to arise in this way. The meaning of a word cannot consist in an experience of the conscious subject—a grasping of a particular *as* an instance of a kind—for that would be an irreducible mental item. Instead, it must consist in a causal relation between the word and some particular that we say it represents.

The incoherence of such accounts comes into view when we see that the conscious subject, materialistically understood to be nothing distinct from the brain and its functions, could have no access to the nonverbal term of the meaning relation and thus could have no understanding of the content of its own mental states—the states in which it is supposed to apprehend meaning. Since the meaning cannot consist in the mind's irreducible grasp of what its words stand for and since the brain could have no knowledge of what lies upstream in the causal process leading to an effect on the physical items constituting the symbols or words it is supposed to be employing, the mind could have no awareness of what, if anything, the symbols stand for (i.e., no awareness of their meaning or semantic value).[11]

The final difficulty for the reductive materialist that we shall consider at this juncture becomes apparent as we reflect upon our sensory experience. The world as it appears to us in our sensory experience is replete with colors, noises, smells, tastes, and sensations of touching and temperature. But none of these sense qualities show up in the physical world as it is in itself, independently of sensory experience. Contemporary physical science reveals to us a world of matter in motion, a world of physical objects and events that provides the stimulation for our sense organs, but not the sense qualities that appear in, and only in, our sensory experience. The sense qualities are effects in us caused by this stimulation in conjunction with the functioning of our own brains and nervous systems. But they have no place in any part of the physical world that causes them to arise in our sensory experience, neither the portion external to our bodies nor the portion that includes our bodies, brains, and nervous systems. This is, apparently, the conclusion to which we should be led by physical science, not because it focuses upon their not being there, or even mentions them in speaking of physical theory, but because the physical world as conceived and described by it is one in which they do not fit.

What does fit well in that world are the causes of our various sensory experiences. The external cause of (or, more precisely, causal factor involved in) visual and color experience is colorless (indeed, insensible) electromagnetic radiation. The external cause of our experience of hearing something is a vibratory disturbance in some medium, usually the air, that causes our eardrums to vibrate—a disturbance that in itself is silent. In the case of our sensations of hot and cold, the external causal factor is not a hot or cold object or medium, but something whose molecular activity is more rapid (felt as hot) or less rapid (felt as cold) than that in the causally affected portion of the body. But in no case does the sense quality have any place in the external (or internal) cause of the sensory experience in which it appears.

The problem for the materialist that is presented by the qualitative content of our sensory experience seems insuperable. A few materialists have taken an extreme position, in effect maintaining that qualitative content is at best only an appearance that is unreal (perhaps only seeming to exist because of a widespread but false theory of reality) and thus has no existence needing to be acknowledged in an adequate view of the natural world.[12] Reductive materialists have preferred behaviorist/dispositionalist/functionalist accounts of it. But it seems transparently clear, first that sense qualities must be acknowledged to exist, and, secondly, that, say, a color or an experience of one is not a behavior, a disposition to behave in some way, or a function carried out in or by the organism.[13] Neither group is able to acknowledge the reality of the qualitative content of our sensory experiences as it appears to us in our direct experience of it. To illustrate, the blue color that appears to us in our visual experience of, say, looking at the cloudless sky (i.e., "phenomenal color," as it is often called) has no place in either view. Proponents may insist that color exists (e.g., what they call "physical" color or "dispositional" color), but they are not speaking of *phenomenal* color— the color we directly apprehend in our own visual experience. *That* is the color whose reality is denied.

That the reductive materialist cannot acknowledge the existence of phenomenal sense qualities comes into view once more when we see the connection between the mental and the phenomenal. We apparently have no good reason to believe that the phenomenal colors, noises, tastes, etc. that we experience continue to exist when we are not experiencing them.[14] Their existence is experience-dependent, or, in other words, consciousness-dependent. Thus if consciousness were not the irreducible reality directly known to us in being conscious—if consciousness, so understood, did not exist, as the reductive materialist claims—then neither could the phenomenal sense qualities whose existence depends upon it.

It is important to be clear about the significance of such a denial. If we were to imagine a world in which such a denial were true, we would be imagining one without phenomenal color, without phenomenal tone or noise, indeed, without any of the sense qualities that we now encounter in our sensory experience. The world as we know it by way of our senses would have vanished. The world of material substances and events would remain, but if the phenomenal realm provided by our sense experience cannot be acknowledged to exist, it cannot be used to show that we know anything about that world.

We are now in a position to appreciate the enormous force of the case for believing that the mental is real but not reducible to the physical, that, in other words, the mental is an immaterial reality. The fact that our concepts of the mental are so different from our physical concepts should arouse our suspicions that reductive attempts are likely to be unsuccessful. Further examination of the mental-physical relation seemed to show in a most decisive way that such attempts must fail. We focused on consciousness, noting such features as its intentionality, its subjectivity, its essential privacy, and its apparent non-spatiality, none of which are features of matter. Unlike material reality, it is directly accessible to the introspective awareness of the person whose consciousness it is, and not accessible by way of sense perception. Its being necessarily owned or had by the person to whom it belongs stands in stark contrast to the contingent manner in which the material constituting a human body belongs to that body, just as its apparently indivisible unity contrasts sharply with the evident divisibility of the brain processes associated with it.

In addition to such features, apparently having no instances in anything physical, there are truths either revealed to us or made possible by virtue of our being in conscious states which are such that they appear to render our conscious states impossible to accommodate within an entirely material reality. In this context we spoke of our concepts of generality, non-actual possibility, truth and falsity, error and deception, rationality, non-existent objects and facts, and abstract objects—concepts that apparently have no application in a material world devoid of the consciousness we are directly aware of in being conscious. Finally, the entire phenomenal realm disclosed to us in sensory consciousness and dependent for its existence upon that consciousness would have to disappear along with consciousness itself in any account purporting to reduce it to the behavior, behavioral dispositions, and functions of material entities.

It seems that any one of these considerations constitutes a formidable, if not insuperable, problem for any reductive materialist account of consciousness. But taken together they have conclusive force: the mental is an immaterial reality. We will now examine the relevance of this conclusion to our understanding of persons.

Psychological Theories of the Person

We have already noted that though we are persons who are human beings, a person need not be embodied as a human being. There might be, or might have been, non-human persons (e.g., God, alien persons who are non-human). We considered grounds for believing that a self or person is something embodied in humans and in some possible non-humans, and thus is something distinct from these embodiments or perhaps from all of its material embodiments, even if it never actually exists apart from some one or other of them. We found conclusive grounds for rejecting physical theories of the person when we saw that the identity of a person through time cannot consist in the identity of the body through time, that is, in bodily continuity. Rather, it must consist in something other than the body and its continuity over time. We will now explore this view of persons, noting in passing the powerful support it receives from the conclusion that the mental is an immaterial reality. This conclusion is an essential part of the case for believing that persons are essentially immaterial.

There are two types of views that find the identity of persons in the mental or psychological. According to one type, a person or self is a composite being, constituted of numerous elements (more specifically, of experiences strung out over a lifetime) bearing relations to each other and to the body. These relations are what unify the temporally extended bundle of experiences such that it makes up or constitutes a single person, and also makes that person distinct from every other person. One of these is the memory relation: some experiences are experiences of remembering earlier ones. Other relations or connections among them may be expressed by saying that some resemble others or lead to others in a causal way. And all are connected to the one body. The interconnected whole that they form over the course of a lifetime is what constitutes a person in her entirety, and the more or less continuous (temporal) flow of interrelated experiences constitutes the continuing identity of the person through time. Thus personal identity over time consists in psychological continuity—in the continuity of a stream of experiences. Let us call this the "bundle" or "relational" view of persons and personal identity over time.

According to views of the other type, a person is a single subject of experience—experiences that are understood not to be individual things or events that might have belonged to someone else, as in the bundle view, but instead are the various experiential *states* a subject is in over the course of time. What unifies them is not the relations they bear to each other or to the body, but rather the fact that each is a state of one and the same subject. Since in these views the subject is something in addition to the experience it has (whether or not it can exist when not having experience) and since the subject is (or is essentially included in) what the person is, the person is not reducible to her experiences. By contrast, in the bundle view, a person is nothing more than a bundle of related experiences that constitute it and thus is reducible to those constituents. In other words, the bundle view is a *reductionist* view of persons.

There are many other reductionist views of persons. All materialist views of persons are reductionist. For all of them view a person as a complex material organism made up of simpler, more basic material entities to which it is reducible. A person is nothing more than a highly organized system of such entities functioning and being disposed to function in those various complex ways that we identify as a living, functioning human being. The mental (if acknowledged to exist) is reducible to the physical, and the person is nothing beyond the human organism in conjunction with a series of interrelated mental and physical states. Some of these views take the identity of the person through time to consist in the (physical) continuity of the body, others in psychological continuity. The central point is that all these views are reductionist, even those maintaining that the mental or psychological is not reducible to the physical and that personal identity over time consists in psychological continuity. As such, all stand opposed to the non-reductionist view in which a person is, or essentially includes, an irreducible subject of experience. We will now focus on the question of how plausible any of these views are when compared to the non-reductionist view of the self or person.

The Person as Subject of Conscious States

No reductionist view of persons can acknowledge the existence of a subject of consciousness that endures through a lengthy period of time. As we shall see, this failure, by itself, exposes these views to very serious difficulties. The forms of reductionism that are also materialist views of reality must confront the additional difficulties arising from the numerous weighty reasons for concluding that the mental is immaterial, and thus not merely a manifestation of something physical, such as a "higher-level" but yet physical property of the brain.[15] As we noted, the case for believing that the mental is an immaterial reality is compelling if not conclusive. But even those views in which mental events are understood to be immaterial and persons to consist of such immaterial occurrences can offer no more than a "bundle" or "relational" conception of what a person is, since these views too have no place for a continuing subject of consciousness.[16]

One very serious problem for all relational or bundle views of a person (viz., all reductionist views) is the implication that the bundle of interrelated physical and/or psychological states and events that constitutes the person is spread out over time, indeed over the person's lifetime. Even the psychological views maintaining that the (immaterial) mind is what constitutes the person succumb to this problem. For one's mind is a unified set (or bundle) of experiences, along with dispositions to have experiences—experiences that, though strung out over time, are related in such a way as to form the unity of a single mind. The problem comes into view when we see that only a small part of this bundle (and thus only a *small part of the person*) is present at any given time at which the person exists. In other words, a person is a *perdurer*—something that persists through time in a manner such that only a *part* of it is present at each time at which it exists. But this in radical conflict with our commonsense assumption about how we persist through time: *we* are present *in our entirety* at each time at which we exist, though our entire lives, of course, are not. In other words, we assume (though perhaps uncritically) that we are *endurers*. Formidable as this problem may seem to be, it is, as we shall see, only one of many equally serious problems that reductionist views must confront.

Since the concept of a subject of consciousness is at the center of the nonreductionist view of persons, we might begin with a focus on what such a subject is supposed to be and how it is supposed to be known. Suppose that you are now holding this book, reading these words, thinking about what they mean, hearing soft music playing, detecting the aroma of coffee, and paying at least some attention to each. This experience of reading is had by a subject—it is the experience of a subject of experience—as is the experience of thinking, of hearing, etc. Moreover, the subject doing the reading is one and the same as the one doing the thinking and the hearing: *you* are that subject. You are the subject having them and your having them makes them yours. They—these very experiences—could not have belonged to anyone else. In other words, they are *necessarily* yours, even though you might not have had them at all, as you might have been having other experiences, or none at all, at this time.

It is this subject to which you are referring when you use the word "I" to refer to yourself, as in saying "I smell fresh coffee" or "I hear a strange noise." It seems clear that the experience of hearing, for example, is not simply an occurrence, a subjectless event like a rainstorm, as some of the reductionist views imply. The experience is *had* by someone, it is had by a subject, namely, yourself. Perhaps this experience, like any experience, is more accurately expressed as an *experiencing*, in this case the experiencing of a sound. But an experiencing requires a subject to have it or undergo it. Indeed, it makes no more sense to suggest that there could be an experiencing without anything that does the experiencing than to suggest that there could be a branch-bending event without a branch to undergo the bending. Thus the notion of a subjectless experience seems unintelligible.

Still, many reductionists deny that a real subject (as opposed to a mere *concept* of one) exists, typically maintaining that no such entity is found in experience.[17] An introspective search for it, they say, always comes up empty. And they are correct in that the self or subject is not disclosed to us *in the way* that an experience of color, or sound, or pain is disclosed, i.e., as objects upon which our consciousness is directed. But we must question the conclusion that so many have drawn from this fact—the conclusion that there are only subjectless experiences occurring without any subject to have them. For it may be that the presence of a subject undergoing the experience is disclosed in some other way.

Though as we noted, the notion of a subjectless experience or subjectless conscious event seems to make no sense, let us set that problem for the reductionist aside as we try to understand how the presence of a subject of conscious events might be disclosed to us even if it doesn't appear in our introspective search as one more object of introspective observation. Upon reflection we see that if the subject of consciousness did exist, it could not find itself among such objects. For it would be what is doing the finding or observing, and it cannot observe *itself-observing-objects* among the objects upon which it is directing its consciousness. It could form a *conception* of itself, and this object of self-conception could appear among the objects of its consciousness. But that would be only one more object, and thus not identical to the subject for whom it is an object. That this object cannot be the subject for which the subject is searching becomes evident when we see that, though the subject is essentially subjective, it would have to be suitably objectified to be apprehended as an object of its consciousness. But this objectified subject—the object of the subject's thought—would not be the subject thinking the thought. Thus we come to see not only why the subject itself (as distinct from a concept of it) would not appear as an object to its introspective consciousness, but also why a reductionist could acknowledge the existence of a *concept* of a subject while denying that this concept (like the concept of a unicorn) refers to anything.

There is, however, a more profound reason why a subject could never encounter itself as an object of its introspective observation. In first-person terms, even if the subject I was looking for in my introspective search were a possible object of introspective observation and I were able to introspectively observe it, I would be unable to recognize it as myself (i.e., as the subject of *my* experiences) unless I already had an awareness of myself that I possessed independently of any such observation. For I would be unable to identify the introspected self as myself by the fact that it is introspectively observed by me unless I were already aware that it is *I* who am doing the observing; and this is a self-awareness I could not gain by introspective observation.

This fundamentally important truth shows that we have a self-awareness that is entirely nonobservational. In first-person terms, I cannot acquire this awareness by introspectively observing myself because I must already have it to see that the observing is being done by *me* and that *I* am the object of introspective observation. It is an awareness that I must have to be aware of myself at all. Though a self that I could introspectively observe (if this were possible) could be none other than myself, I could have no idea that *I* am that self unless I had an awareness of myself that is independent of any such observation. I might know that a self is introspectively observed and that any self so observed is observed by itself, but I could not know that that self is *myself* if I lacked that primordial, nonobservational self-awareness needed for me to be aware of myself at all.

Our nonobservational self-awareness is fundamental, that is, not based upon or derived from a more fundamental self-awareness. It is direct or immediate—not mediated by any *concept* of oneself, any inference, or any awareness of some truth that proves to be a truth about oneself. It consists in a subject's encountering itself in an immediate experience of being itself, rather than in something distinct from it but nevertheless mediating its self-awareness. As such, it is prereflective, preconceptual, noninferential, not a product of the conceptualizing or interpretive powers of reflective consciousness. Of course, each of us has an I-*concept*, a concept of oneself—a fact that is uncontroversial—but this concept is not just plucked out of the void. There must be some feature or element constitutively involved in our experience that grounds this concept. Once this is recognized, it seems clear that our reflective self-awareness, though originally preconceptual, is what comes to be seen under the I-concept. We could not plausibly explain our possession of an I-concept without acknowledging that we have a nonconceptual consciousness of *I*.

Though the existence of this unmediated, prereflective self-awareness seems undeniable, one might be reluctant to conclude that this self-awareness is the self-awareness of a subject of conscious states. For its existence is compatible with the view that consciousness is (or becomes) aware of itself. But this view implies that consciousness is intrinsically subjectless, an implication that seems patently false, at least when the entire case for believing that consciousness cannot be subjectless is taken into consideration.[18] Among other considerations, the supposition that prereflective consciousness is subjectless implies that such consciousness is intrinsically anonymous or impersonal—an implication that seems to clash head on with its first-personal givenness. In first-person terms, my intuition that the consciousness I am immediately aware of is *my* consciousness seems unassailable. Clearly, it does not occur anonymously prior to my conceiving it as mine.

This important point merits further elaboration. If my higher order, reflective consciousness is intrinsically first-personal—if this experience is by its very nature something *I* have (as it certainly seems to be)—then we must wonder how I could see a first-order or prereflective experience as one of my own unless I were aware of having it and thus tacitly aware of *myself* having it. I must be, or have been, tacitly aware of myself in the prereflective experience to be reflectively aware, in a higher order experience, of having (or having had) it and thus to be reflectively aware of it as one of my own. Otherwise, I would be unable to recognize the prereflective experience as one *I* had. Thus self-awareness, whether in a higher-order or prereflective experience, is also the self-awareness of a subject of conscious states.

What remains to be shown is that this subject endures through a lengthy period of time, indeed the lifetime of the person if it is what the person essentially is (or essentially includes). Many who hold reductionist views of persons would acknowledge that there are no subjectless experiences, that every experience includes a subject, perhaps as a short-lived particular having an experience, perhaps as a mere part of the structure of an experience.[19] In any case, there are successions of different subjects just as there are successions of different experiences. There is no single enduring subject to serve as a plausible candidate for what a person essentially is.

Since our experience does not reveal one subject being replaced by another, these views must accept the implication that any subject-switching process would go on unnoticed. We will now consider whether the view that undetected subject-switching is occurring in our experience is at all plausible. Let us call this view the USS hypothesis.

It seems incontestable that the selfsame subject lasts over at least short, though appreciable, periods of time. At least some experiences (e.g., of hearing) need to have duration to be experienced at all, and so their subject must last long enough to make them possible. The hearing and subsequent understanding of a lengthy sentence is a case in point. The suggestion that different subjects hear different parts of the sentence seems wildly implausible. In first-person terms, I find myself as incapable of doubting that I am the subject who heard the beginning of the sentence as I am of doubting at the time of hearing the ending that I am the one hearing it. It seems undeniable that the same subject continues throughout such mental activity in which one's attention is continuously focused on a task.

Some of the most persuasive grounds for rejecting the USS hypothesis come into view when we focus on the implications of the first-person character of experiential memory—the remembering of experience, as distinct from other facts about the past. Such memory is not just a matter of being exposed to a past experience as it was for some subject having it. When I remember an experience in this way, that is, "from the inside" (rather than simply remembering *that* some experience occurred), what is apparent to me is that the experience is one *I* had. Indeed, it seems clear that part of what I remember is *myself having the experience*, even though the experience may have occurred long ago. That the experience I am remembering (from the inside, of course) was had by me and *not* by some other subject seems no less certain to me than that the present experience of remembering this is one *I* am having. No deliverance of memory seems more certain than this.

Another set of reasons for rejecting the USS hypothesis comes into view when we focus on the peculiar indivisibility of a subject of consciousness and on how radical a change in a stream of consciousness a subject-switch would imply. But what must be brought into view can be accessed only from the first-person viewpoint. When I focus on what I find myself to be as the subject of the experience I am having at some given moment, I find that, though I can distinguish the different experiences (e.g., of seeing, hearing, thinking, etc.) I am having, I cannot even imagine any division of the subject having them. If I try to imagine or conceive of this subject having parts and of one "part" as the subject of the experience of hearing, then that experience just vanishes if I continue as the subject of the seeing and thinking. Whatever happens to the experience of hearing, it is no longer one of mine. Thus I did not conceive of my awareness being divided, but only of the elimination of one of its objects. When I think of myself as subject, I cannot think of myself as having parts.

Another way to see the partlessness, and hence the logical indivisibility, of the subject is to reflect upon the intuition we express in saying that no one can be only *partly* you or *partly* me, either now or in the future.[20] At this moment, as I think about the partlessness of a subject and perceive my surroundings, the experiences I am now having constitute only *part* of my *life*. But it would seem preposterous to claim that only part of *me* is having them. It seems incontestable that *I* am present in my *entirety* even though I am now living through only a tiny part of my life. Moreover, if someone in the future thinks a similar thought, that person would have to be either me or someone else. It seems clear that that person could not be only partly me and partly someone else. (As we shall later see, reductionist views of persons are committed to denying this.)

We see what a radical change a subject-switch would have to be when we reflect upon the deep difference between subjects. That this difference is deep seems clear when one takes the first-person viewpoint and reflects upon the relation one has to one's own experience in comparison with the relation one has to the experience of anyone else, even someone as similar as an identical twin. As you reflect upon the fact that you might have had an identical twin, you clearly see that even very close similarity does not blur the radical breech between your inner subjective states and those of your twin. You injure your foot and are in pain, but your twin doesn't feel it. The full depth of this breech become unmistakable when you reflect upon the possibility that (or, in other words, the possible world in which) the person who would have been your identical twin, if you had existed, exists *in your place*. Let us call this possible world "PW." This person in PW would be *exactly* similar to you, even more like you than an identical twin who might have existed along with you. For this "possible-world" twin who exists in your place would be exactly similar to you not only physically and mentally but relationally as well, i.e., your "possible-world" twin would bear all the relations to other people and things that you bear to them in the actual world.

Now the depth of the difference between you and your twin in PW becomes sharp, unmistakable, and of fundamental importance: if PW had been the actual world, you would not have existed! Your nonexistence would have been as certain and as complete as it would have been if the possible-world person existing in your place had not been like you at all. The difference between you and your twin in PW is "deep" or absolute, just as it is between you and every other person, whether similar to you or not.[21]

At this point the implications for the USS hypothesis become clear. The indivisibility of a subject of conscious states implies that a subject-switch could not occur gradually, in a part by part fashion. The switch would have to occur all at once and thus abruptly. Moreover, the deep difference between subjects implies that such a switch would be a radical change—so radical that its occurrence could hardly go unnoticed, especially in view of our immediate prereflective awareness of ourselves in having experience. The suggestion that such radical, abrupt changes of the very center of one's subjective life (in which one's deep identity apparently consists) are occurring unnoticed strikes one as wildly implausible, if not simply incredible.

Though the case for rejecting the USS hypothesis may already seem conclusive, one other important reason for rejecting it is certainly worthy of mention, despite the lack of space for more than a cursory treatment. The foregoing considerations are part of the case for concluding that a person has a deep, irreducible essence consisting of a unitary, noncomposite, indivisible subject of conscious states that endures through time while its states change. But in reductionist views of persons, a person is a composite entity—a highly organized, temporally extended collection of parts consisting of different parts at different times. And as we have noted, if a person is nothing other than this temporally extended collection, then the unappealing conclusion that person are perdurers would be impossible to avoid. Since none of the parts (whether physical or psychological) last for the lifetime of the person, the identity of the person over time would be the result of the apparently continuous though gradual manner in which some of the parts at any given time are being replaced by more or less similar parts. Thus personal identity over time would depend upon either the continuity of the body, or the continuity of memory and other psychological factors, or some combination of the two. But all such views face apparently insuperable difficulties—difficulties such as to render them either incoherent or so counterintuitive that they are virtually impossible to embrace.

In all the reductionist theories, whether physical or psychological, there is no noncomposite entity that endures for a lifetime. Persons are composite things consisting of enormous numbers of physical and/or psychological parts, each of which must satisfy the condition of entering at some time or other into that organized collection of parts that constitutes the person. Its being a member of that collection consists in its having the right sort of relation to the other members. This is the condition it must satisfy. Thus these theories imply that for some element in this collection, say an experience, to be one of mine it must satisfy the required condition—an implication that leads to absurdity.

The absurdity comes in view when we see that any such condition would have to mediate between my awareness that an experience (of which I am directly aware) is occurring and my awareness that it is one that *I* am having. Not only would this conflict with what we have previously noted to be the direct, nonobservational awareness I have of myself in having experience, but it entails the absurdity that I could somehow identify an experience of which I am directly (or noninferentially) aware without identifying it as one of my own. Clearly, I could not do that, whether the experience is presently occurring or is one that I am remembering (from the inside). To identify it at all is to identify it as one of mine.

Moreover, if there were a condition that an experience had to satisfy for me to see it as one of mine, I would be unable to be aware of myself at all. For I could become aware of myself only by having an experience, and I could become aware of that experience as one of mine only by seeing that it satisfied the condition supposedly appropriate for establishing that it belongs to me. But I could never know that the condition, no matter what it is supposed to be, was satisfied by an experience unless I could see that an experience satisfying it was one of my own. And this I could not see unless I were already, or independently, aware of it as an experience of mine. For without that awareness I would be unable to see that the condition is one whose satisfaction by an experience is appropriate for establishing that the experience belongs to me. Absurdly, my awareness of an experience as one of mine and my awareness that the experience satisfies the alleged condition would each have to occur prior to the other. Thus the fact that I am aware of myself implies that, contrary to the reductionist views, there can be no such condition.

Another major problem arises from the fact that, in reductionist views, personal identity over time consists in a relation that must be entered into by any physical or psychological element forming part of the "person stage" that the person is in at some given time. For any relation can be duplicated (i.e., have many instances, such as the relation *taller than*), thus implying the possibility of a duplication of the relation constituting the persistence of a person through time. But to affirm this possibility is to affirm the possibility that two or more persons existing at time t2 should turn out to be identical to a single person existing at an earlier time t1. Clearly, no single person can be *identical* to two or more persons. Whatever a particular person is, it is something there can be only *one* of.[22]

One of the best routes to an understanding of some of the other major difficulties confronting the reductionist begins with a focus on the unity of our minds, often called the unity of consciousness. As we noted earlier, this is a unity that you experience directly at any given time when you are conscious, but more conspicuously as you think about what happens when you are having a variety of different experiences (e.g., of seeing, hearing, touching, thinking, etc.) simultaneously. You then see that your mind is not a group of unrelated experiences (along with dispositions to have experiences) that are scattered over time. Your experiences are of many different kinds; and whether they are occurring at the present moment or are strung out over time, they display a unity that, though difficult to describe, is unmistakably present. Perhaps it is best expressed by saying that each is experienced by *you*. It is present not only in your presently occurring experiences, but it also extends across time to your experiences in the past. Your knowledge that this unity extends to the past is provided by memory. As you remember your past experience, part of what you remember (at least upon reflection) is that it displayed the unity that you presently find displayed in your presently occurring experience. But beyond that, your memory reveals that it also displays a unity *with* your present experience in that all are undeniably experiences of yours. It is in virtue of this unity, present at each time you are conscious, and also extending to your past experience that your various conscious states are unified to form a single mind—your own.

Though this unity is undeniably real, what is controversial is how it should be explained. Three types of views seem to exhaust the possibilities: (1) the unity is provided by one's body in that all one's experience are appropriately connected to that body; (2) the unity exists in virtue of the manner in which the experiences are connected or related to one another, and (3) the unity consists in the fact that each experience is had by a single, enduring subject. Though we have already encountered these views in other contexts, we will see them in a different light when we see how each must account for the unity of consciousness.

Views of the first type already may seem to be nonstarters, as we have previously found decisive reason to reject bodily theories of the person and of personal identity. But here we might mention two more reasons that appear in this context. First, the body cannot confer a deep unity on the mind, for it itself lacks any such unity or identity over time. Its identity over time is merely of the "loose" and "imperfect" type, as its material constituents are gradually but continuously replaced by others, eventually resulting in each constituent being replaced. Though eventual complete replacement seems to be a matter of fact, the matter of whether the very same body persists through complete replacement of its constituents is *not* a matter of fact.

Rather, it is a matter of how we have chosen to talk about the facts, i.e., it is a matter of our linguistic conventions. Thus if the sameness or identity of your body is the source of the unity of your mind, then the matter of whether certain experiences had in the distant past were experiences of yours is merely a matter of what we have decided to *say* about them, not a factual matter of whether they were had by you or by someone else.

Second, if your body is what makes possible the unity of your mind, then an experience is one of yours only if it satisfies the condition of being suitably connected to your body. This implies the absurdity that you would be unable to identify a presently occurring experience of which you are directly aware as one of yours without first knowing that it is suitably connected to your body. As we noted, this is absurd partly because you cannot identify such an experience at all without identifying it as one of yours. We also saw that if you could not identify such an experience immediately, without having to see that it satisfied some condition, you could not become aware of yourself at all. Thus, again, views of this type must be rejected.

Views of the second type would explain the unity of the mind as due to certain relations that experiences forming a single mind bear to one another. Some will be causally related, some will resemble each other, some will occur simultaneously or nearly so, and some will be rememberings of others. Although there seems to be no satisfactory account of precisely what these relations are, it is clear that in understanding the unity of the mind, there is no appeal to anything beyond the experiences themselves and their relations to one another. In particular, no appeal is made to a single subject to whom each experience belongs. Let us call this the relational account of mental unity.

The relational view may seem quite plausible when we think of how our memories, even those of experiences of a very long time ago, ground our conviction that we have existed for a considerable number of years. They disclose in an utterly convincing way that those experiences of long ago were our own, and thereby reveal not only our continuing identity through time but also the unity through time of a single mind, namely, one's own. Certainly any (non-memory based) evidence of the existence of one's body of bygone days has no such impact upon our convictions.

But closer examination of the relational view reveals great difficulties with it. We have just seen why it may appear that your memories, along with other less obvious relations that your experiences bear to one another, are what provide the unity of your mind and ground your conviction of your continuing identity through time. It seems natural to infer from this that what you are is your mind. But now the first difficulty with the relational view appears. For if you are your mind, then either you are a set of presently occurring experiences or you are that much larger set that includes not only your present experiences but all your past and future ones as well. But each alternative seems wildly implausible.

If what you are is that very large set consisting of all the experiences you have ever had or will ever have or are presently having, then only a *part* of *you* is present now. But this seems totally unacceptable. As we have noted, only a *part* of your *life* is present now, but *you* are present *in your entirely* at this moment and at any other time at which you exist. If, on the other hand, you are that set of presently occurring experiences, then you are only a few seconds old. For they change rapidly. Even if we add your personality traits and other (non-conscious) dispositions to have certain experiences, this alternative doesn't gain much appeal. For even your mental dispositions change gradually over time, apparently resulting eventually in their complete replacement by others. Given this consequence, we see that some of the reasons for believing that you cannot be your body show with equal force that you cannot be your mind. More specifically, if you are those experiences and mental dispositions that presently constitute your mind and all these constituents are replaced within ten years, then your belief that you have remained one and the same person for more than ten years is not grounded in some fact about you, but is merely the result of our linguistic conventions, i.e., of what we have decided to *say* about the facts.

Another problem comes into view when we wonder about what relation or relations to other experiences could possibly make an experience one of yours. If *relations* cannot do this, then it cannot be done, since in the relational view there is nothing else to do it. Of the relevant relations, the memory relation may strike us as the most promising candidate for this task when we think about how our memories convince us that past experiences we remember "from the inside" were our own. Our memories provide us with an access to our past experiences that erases any doubt about whose experiences they were. Thus it seems clear that if our present remembering of past experiences cannot be our relation to them that makes them experiences of our own, then *no* relation can.

But this is not what the memory relation does—it does not and cannot make an experience you remember one of yours. Though the experiences you remember are experiences of yours, neither your remembering them nor your ability to remember them is what *makes* them yours. Rather, they were yours when you had them, and your memory of them merely *reveals* this to you. It was *your having* them when they occurred that *made* them yours, not your subsequent memories of having them. It is because you had them in the first place that you can remember having them. What your memory of them does is reveal in a most compelling way that they were experiences of yours, and it does this by including a remembering of *your having them* when they occurred.

Although we now apparently have more than sufficient grounds for rejecting the relational view, there is another consideration that removes any remaining doubt by revealing conditions under which relational views imply what is either incoherent or patently false. What these views imply comes into view when we consider a thought experiment involving the bisection of the human brain. Thus some preliminary remarks about brain structure and function will be helpful.

The "higher" brain consists primarily of the two cerebral hemispheres— the portion of the brain largely, if not entirely, responsible for the existence of our consciousness. People survive as conscious beings in the absence of one of these hemispheres, thus revealing that each is sufficient for the continuation of conscious life. This has been shown by cases of actual people who have undergone the surgical removal of a hemisphere with only slight loss of function. Though in the case of most people each hemisphere fails to provide a duplication of the full range of functions provided by the other, it is likely that in a few people the hemispheres are equipotent and thus such that these people would not experience any change of conscious functioning with the loss of one of them. Let us suppose that you are one of these people.

Let us now suppose that you are one of three identical triplets and that the three of you are injured in an automobile accident. Your brain is unharmed but your body is so badly injured that you will soon die. The bodies of your two identical siblings, however, are uninjured, but their brains are so badly damaged that neither will ever experience any conscious life again. A decision is made to save two people by bisecting your brain, down the center between your cerebral hemispheres and placing half in each of the bodies of your siblings. Both operations are successful, two people survive; but what happens to you?

Before addressing this question, we should note that though this thought-experiment may seem quite bizarre, it is not incoherent. It expresses a metaphysical possibility. Perhaps each half of the lower brain and brain stem also more or less duplicates the functions of the other, in which case the operations yielding two people would be consistent with the laws of nature (i.e., would be naturally possible as well). But even if this is not the case, the *metaphysical* possibility of the situation described shows that the thought-experiment can be used to explore our views of what constitutes a person and, in particular, to reveal what they imply under bizarre circumstances. This is significant because a view that implies what is unacceptable is thereby revealed to be unacceptable itself.

With respect to what happens to you, there are three possibilities: (1) you do not survive the operations, (2) you survive as one or the other of the surviving offshoots, or (3) you survive as both of them. The first alternative, though expressing a possibility, is virtually ruled out because there can be no evidence in support of it. If you could survive the removal or destruction of one of your cerebral hemispheres, then there could be no reason why you would not survive if this hemisphere were not destroyed but placed in another. Nor can the third alternative be taken seriously, unless we are prepared to embrace an extremely radical revision of our concept of what a person is. As we noted, it seems incontestable that a person is a singular individual, i.e., something there can be only *one* of. Clearly, the second alternative is by far the most plausible: you survive as one or the other of the offshoots.

But the difficulty for the relational view becomes clear as we see that the second alternative cannot be embraced by the relationist. Since each of the survivors bears exactly the same psychological relation to you and since (in the relational view) there is no subject of conscious states whose continuing existence is necessary for identity across time, any grounds for claiming that you survive as one of them are grounds for claiming that you survive as the other. There can be no fact about one of them (e.g., the fact that you are the subject of its experience) in virtue of which you are *that* one and not the other. Once we know how the offshoots came about and how their experiences are related to yours, we know all of the relevant facts about them. There is no further fact (in particular, no deep, further fact that the continuing existence of a subject would provide) that would distinguish them and which could make it true that you are one of them rather than the other. Thus either you survive as both or you do not survive at all. But these are the highly implausible alternatives. Perhaps the possibility that you do not survive cannot be totally excluded, but the suggestion that you might survive as both strikes one as simply a non-starter, unworthy of further consideration. Yet the relationist cannot avoid it.

This thought-experiment brings into sharp focus an important difference between the relational view and the view that you are a subject of experience. As we noted earlier, the latter view is nonreductionist, implying that there is a deep difference between you and every other person, even someone exactly similar to you. This difference is sharp, radical, and absolute. There are no circumstances under which it could be even blurred, let alone erased. It is entirely unaffected by close or even exact similarity. Though the offshoots of the transplant operations are exactly alike, both physically and mentally, there is nevertheless a deep difference between them, a difference in virtue of which you are one of them and not the other. Your being one of them and not the other would be a deep, further fact. You are something extra, distinguishable from that organism with a series of interrelated mental and physical states—states that could be matched by exactly similar ones of an exactly similar organism.

Because of this deep difference between you and every other person, the question as to whether you survive the operations admits of a definite and correct answer: it is either that you do, or that you do not. We may not be able to *tell* which is correct (though *you* would if you survived), but such uncertainty is not relevant to the fact that there *is* a correct answer. For at no time can there be any indeterminacy or (ontological) ambiguity about whether you exist at that time. Your existence is an all or nothing matter. It cannot be obscured or rendered indeterminate by someone's being only partly you and partly someone else. For there can be no such person. If any experiences occurring after the operations are had by you, then you have survived, and in your entirety, even if only for a little while. If none are had by you, then you have not survived. But no survivor can be only partly you, just as no experience can be only partly yours and partly someone else's.

However, the relationist must deny all this. In her view, there is no deep difference between you and someone exactly similar to you (or, indeed, between you and any other person). Consequently, the question as to whether you have survived the operations is an empty one. Once we know that each offshoot has half your brain and that the experiences of each bear the same appropriate relations to your own (i.e., are related to your preoperative experiences in the way in which the latter are interrelated), we know all the facts about the outcome. There is no deep, further fact that must be known to know what happens to you. Though there are different ways to describe the outcome (e.g., that you have survived as both offshoots, that you would have survival as either if the other had not existed, or that the question of what happens to you is not intelligible under such circumstances), they do not imply different views about what the facts are. For these different descriptions are only different ways of talking about the fact, not disagreements about what the facts themselves are.

The relational view may strike us as wildly implausible, if not patently false, when we see that the facts are insufficient to settle the issue of what happens to you. For this view implies that the question of whether you exist after the operations has no definite answer. Your fate is an intrinsically indeterminate matter. We could say that you do survive the operations, but your continuing to exist would be merely a matter of what we have decided to *say*— a matter of our linguistic conventions, rather than a matter of what the facts are. Or we could say that you do *not* survive, and have an equally good case for saying that. But irrespective of what we decide to say about the outcome, your existence does not consist in a deep, further fact that would make true (or false) what we say about whether you continue to exist. Whether you do or not is *indeterminate*—a matter to be settled by convention rather than by discovery of fact.

It is important to understand the full implications of the view that there can be any indeterminacy in one's identity across time. The possibility of such indeterminacy implies the possibility of someone who is neither you nor someone else. It would be indeterminate as to whether you are that person. But this seems inconceivable, at least when one takes the first-person viewpoint and tries to imagine or conceive of the experiences of such a person. You can imaginatively project yourself into the future and imagine your having experience then. But what would it be to imagine the experience of someone who is only partly you—an experience that is only partly yours? What this could be, if anything, is completely opaque to the first-person viewpoint. But because the viewpoint of the first person must be accorded authority in this matter, such opaqueness indicates that there is no possibility to be conceived. In other words, determinacy is an *essential* feature of personhood. It is not even metaphysically possible for a person to be partly you, to be neither you nor someone else. This is not a metaphysically possible state for a person to be in. Thus if you are such that someone could be only partly you, then you are not a person. But you are a person if you are anything at all. Thus, incredibly, we reach the conclusion that if the relational view is true, you do not exist!

We have now completed our relatively extensive examination of the important issue about what a person essentially is. More precisely, the issue is about what it is without which a person could not exist and yet is all that is needed for the existence of the person. Consequently, the continuing existence after death of this core or essence is both necessary and sufficient for the continuing existence of the person.

Though there is, as usual, much more to be said about this issue, our investigation of it has revealed compelling reasons to reject all of the reductionist views of persons. The materialist views fail not only because they are reductionist, but for a variety of other reasons, not the least of which is that the mental states of persons are not physical states. As we noted, the conclusion that the mental is an immaterial reality seems unavoidable. Some reductionist views acknowledge that the mental is immaterial, but all imply that a person is a composite entity consisting of different parts at different times and that personal identity over time is a matter of how the parts are related. These "relational" views of the identity of persons over time take personal identity to consist either in bodily continuity or in psychological continuity, or in some combination of the two. But as we saw, such views must be rejected. Among other things, they imply that you are a perdurer, that your duplication (resulting in two or more of *you*) is a metaphysical possibility, and that it is metaphysically possible for there to be someone who is partly you and partly someone else.

Such difficulties, though apparently fatal to all reductionist views, do not arise for the nonreductionist who holds that there is a single subject of conscious states that persists throughout the lifetime of the person. For a subject is a unitary being, not a composite entity constituted of different parts at different times. Not only does the nonreductionist view have the great advantage of being able to avoid such difficulties, but it provides the most plausible account of our experience and of our awareness of ourselves.

As we noted, the existence of a subject must be acknowledged. The notion of a subjectless experience seems nonsensical. Moreover, our knowledge of it is direct, preconceptual and nonobservational. This absolutely fundamental knowledge is not inferred from or mediated by any other knowledge, and is the primitive, prereflective source of our self-knowledge. Without such knowledge of the subject, we could have no conception of ourselves or, indeed, be aware of ourselves at all. Thus our knowledge of a subject of conscious states could not have a more secure foundation.

We also saw that once the existence of the subject is acknowledged, as it must be, the conclusion that it persists through time as the selfsame enduring subject seems unavoidable. The suggestion that a subject might exist only momentarily before being replaced by another in a replacement process that goes on entirely unnoticed strikes one as wildly implausible. It assumes that the subject is not directly known, and seems to clash head on with the deliverances of experience-memory.

The conclusion of this rather lengthy portion of our study now seems clear: a (human) person is an embodied subject of conscious states—an embodied "soul," we might say. But the subject is an immaterial individual, distinct from its material embodiment, even if, as a matter of fact, it cannot exist without such embodiment to sustain it. Put somewhat differently, its continued existence after bodily death is conceivable, and thus metaphysically possible,[23] even if the natural laws of our world are such that its existence is causally dependent upon the existence and proper functioning of its body. That the subject (i.e., the conscious self) and the body are causally linked seems undeniable, but the nature of this linkage has not been established. More specifically, there remains the question about whether the self continues to exist when not causally linked to the physical body. But an informed answer to this question requires an investigation into not only what, in general, these links are, but also into what the causal relation itself should be understood to be. This is the matter to which we will now turn.

Mental-Physical Relations

The Causality Problem

We have just considered compelling, if not conclusive, evidence that a person is, in essence, an immaterial yet concrete individual that persists through time, normally throughout the lifetime of its body, and possibly longer. Since this will seem to many to be a provocative, if not simply incredible, conclusion, we should not be surprised to find that it has been heavily criticized, with most of the criticism centered on the problem of understanding how material and immaterial things can causally affect one another. It is true that several contemporary philosophers have questioned the intelligibility of the notion of an immaterial individual persisting through time and distinct from other such individuals exactly similar to it. But it can be shown that respect to such problems (i.e., the problems of understanding how a nonphysical individual can persist through time and be distinguished from an exactly similar one), physical objects do not fare any better than nonphysical subjects.[1] So our focus will be on the causality problem—the problem receiving the most attention and widely considered to be insurmountable for the view that the nonphysical self causally interacts with its body.

Once we acknowledge that the self and its mental states are distinct from its brain and body, the conclusion that it causally affects and is affected by the activity in its brain seems unavoidable. For we ordinarily assume without question that one's mental activity of choosing, say, to raise one's arm is the initial cause of one's arm rising, and that, for example, the stimulation of one's eyes by light reflected from a tree is the initial cause of one's visual awareness of the tree. Self and body (by way of its brain) causally affect each other, i.e., they causally *interact*. But now the causality problem comes into view. It arises from the concern that a nonphysical mental reality is so utterly different from the physical that either (1) we cannot even conceive of causal transactions between them, or (2) even if we can conceive of such transactions occurring, our current knowledge of the physical realm strongly indicates that this realm is a causally closed system in which no such transactions actually occur. The first concern or objection is conceptual, the second is empirical or factual.

We are experiencing the first concern when we wonder how a nonphysical self having neither mass nor energy and without either location or extension in space can move the molecules of the brain or be affected by them. We are exposed to the second concern when we note that neurology and brain science not only fail to mention any nonphysical causes involved in the workings of the brain but seem to have no place for them. The brain as it is conceived in science is an entirely physical system whose operations are physical processes with physical causes—causes which if known in their completeness would explain everything that happens in the brain. Clearly, each concern is important and must be effectively addressed in any view in which mental-physical causation occurs.

Another aspect of the causality problem is what we might call the *emergence* problem. If (as may seem obvious) the self and its mental states were not in existence prior to the existence of its body, it must have come about or have emerged in the process of bodily growth and development. Its apparent causal source is the body, and its mentality develops along with development of the brain. Furthermore, the mental appears in the world only in association with activity in a brain or some sort of nervous system. These facts amount to another compelling instance of the causal influence of the physical on the mental.

It is easy to see why the causality problem has led many thoughtful people to embrace some form of reductive materialism and to believe that, in the end, the mental will be seen as only some manifestation of the physical. But, as we have seen, this approach fails: the mental is an immaterial reality. Recognizing that materialism is untenable, some have argued that the nonphysical reality of the mental can be acknowledged by seeing the mental as a *characteristic* or *property* of certain physical things (more specifically, of some brain events or processes) that also have physical properties. But this view, which acknowledges only a dualism of properties and not a dualism of particulars or substances, faces apparently insurmountable difficulties.[2] What these difficulties are need not concern us here; for even if they could be met, one would be left with a property dualism that would have no place for an immaterial self or subject that is clearly not a mere *property* of something else. Rather, the self is a particular possessing properties of its own. Indeed, it is a substance, since it is a particular that endures through time.

Another dualist view that is shaped by the causality problem is called epiphenomenalism. It acknowledges the existence of mental particulars, which, of course, have mental properties, but it denies that any mental particular or property ever *causes* anything to occur. The mental is a mere epiphenomenon or byproduct of the workings of the brain, with no causal power to affect the brain or anything else. The mental would be like a shadow, having no effect on the object that casts it. Hence, the problem of how the mental can causally affect the physical does not arise for the epiphenomenalist. But the equally troublesome problem of how the physical can causally affect the mental is left untouched.

What makes epiphenomenalism almost impossible to accept, however, is its implication that our mental states have no effect on our brains or anything physical. It implies that we could have done everything we presently say or do (e.g., build cities, generate scientific theories, teach classes and philosophize about death) even if we had been utterly devoid of consciousness. If it were true, then even our claims that we have conscious states, or that they have a certain character, would be without foundation. For these claims would be causally disconnected from our awareness of having such states. Consequently, such claims could be justified only if epiphenomenalism were false.

It is important to see that property dualism is also exposed to this difficulty. Since the primary motivation to embrace property dualism is to mitigate the causality problem, the property dualist is led to maintain that only the physical properties of those brain processes that also have mental properties are the causally efficacious ones. The mental properties are causally inert. But this implies a (mental) *property*-epiphenomenalism that is no more attractive than the ordinary epiphenomenalism of mental particulars.

Mind-Brain Interaction

Since the attempts to deny the causal efficacy of the mental are unsuccessful, the conclusion that both the mental and the physical have causal power seems unavoidable. More specifically, brain states affect mental states and mental states affect brain states. Causation runs in both directions: there is mind-brain interaction or *dualistic* causation. Thus the causality problem remains unmitigated; and we must now address the two central objections to the view that mind (or self)-brain interaction occurs.

The first objection was that the nonphysical mind and the physical brain are so utterly different that we cannot even conceive of them interacting. But to evaluate this objection we must take a much more careful look at what causation itself must involve. As we do so, we should remind ourselves that since physical-physical causation is what ordinarily comes to mind when we think about paradigm cases of cause and effect, our focus on the physical realm is likely shaping our concept of causation in general. If causation requires spatial contact or a transfer of mass-energy between the causally related items, then no mental-physical causation can occur. We might think that causation is this restrictive if we were to suppose, quite understandably, that motion can be produced in a physical object (and thereby affect the energy distribution in its physical environment) only if its motion/energy is transferred to it by something already possessing what is transferred and capable of transferring it through spatial contact. Since a nonphysical substance lacks spatiality and motion/energy, and thus lacks not only what is supposedly transferred but also the means of transference through spatial contact, it cannot enter into a causal relation with anything physical. This supposition owes its appeal to the (apparently plausible) principle that if one thing *a* brings about *b's* coming to have some feature F, then *a* must already have F. *a* brings F-ness about in *b* by transferring to *b* an F-ness that *a* already has. But this principle (called the synonymy principle)[3] is false. To illustrate, a solid cylinder of clay (*b*) can be shaped into a solid rectangular bar (given the shape F-ness) by means of a cylindrical rolling pin (*a*) [that, of course, lacks F-ness]. Spatiality and mass-energy may be involved in every case of physical-physical causation, but we certainly do not *know* that they are requirements for all cases of causation. Indeed, we apparently lack a deep explanation of why any particular, mental or physical, should have the causal powers and liabilities (potentialities to be affected) that it turns out to have.

When we wonder how there can be any causal relations between the mental and the physical, we ordinarily and uncritically assume that physical-physical causation is unproblematic. But this assumption is false. We may be assuming that one physical object can affect another in virtue of its mass-energy and its being extended over some volume of space. But this supposition merely invites the further question of why its mass-energy and volume should give it the causal powers and liabilities we believe it to have. It will not do to say that it inherits its causal features from the causal features of the parts (e.g., the molecules) that constitute it, and that these parts get their causal features from those of even smaller parts, say its atoms. For such a process of attempting to explain why objects on the macro-level have their causal features by pointing out that the more fundamental objects on various micro-levels have them cannot go on indefinitely. At some point, such explanation must come to an end with the admission that certain physical objects simply have the causal powers and liabilities that we find them to have. They just have them. No further explanation is possible or needed. After all, we didn't make these objects or give them their fundamental features. The best we can do is find out what these features are; and, as we do so, we should not be too puzzled to find that some of them are causal, at least not after reminding ourselves that they had to have some features or other to be in the world at all.

But if this is the way explanations of the causal features of physical objects must end, there is no reason to suppose that the case of mental particulars should be different. If physical-physical causation is inexplicable, at least on the fundamental level, then we should not be troubled to find that mental-physical causation is also inexplicable. At the very least, we should not be led to conclude that mental-physical causation is unintelligible or impossible on the grounds that we are unable to understand or explain how the mental and the physical are able to causally interact. For such reasoning, if followed through consistently, would lead us to conclude that no causation is possible. So perhaps the best we can do in the end is to simply acknowledge that the mental and the physical do causally interact even though we cannot explain why this should be.

If, as seems incontestable, there is mental-physical causation, then mass-energy and spatiality are not essential to all cases of causation. But if they are not, then what *is*? In what does the causal relation consist? If we assume that there must be something that constitutes this relation, then either of two types of answers is possible: either causation is *reducible* to certain noncausal features of the items involved or it is *irreducible* to anything else. If each of these two possible answers is consistent with, if not supportive of, the intelligibility of mental-physical causation, any basis for the intelligibility objection will have vanished.

Causation Conceived as Reducible

Let us first consider the possibility that causation is reducible—that causal properties are possessed by things only in virtue of those things having certain noncausal properties and entering into certain noncausal relations. But what are these noncausal properties and relations? To what is causation reducible? The only plausible answer seems to be "natural lawfulness," namely, the reductive-nomological account. A causal sequence of events is an instance of a regularity in nature—a natural law. To illustrate with a mind-brain regularity, suppose that whenever a brain state or event of a certain type, B1, occurs in someone's occipital lobes the person experiences a mental event of type M1—an event that may be described as that person's seeing a roundish, bluish green afterimage. Events of type B1 always precede or are accompanied by events of type M1. Such a regular pairing of events of different types is an instance of natural lawfulness. Though these event types are rather narrow, subsumable under broader types, when the types are sufficiently broad we would likely use the term "law of nature." But in either case, causation is nothing more than the invariable pairing of event types.

The central point to note in this context is that this reductive account of causation provides no basis for believing that the causally related items must have spatiality or mass-energy. The fact that the mental event has neither is not problematic at all. Invariable co-occurrence or temporal pairing of events of different types is all that is required. The causal relation is an invariable temporal relation.

It may seem difficult to believe that causation involves no more than an invariable temporal connection between types of events. What has happened to causal power, or the causal necessitation of an event? Isn't there a necessary tie between cause and effect that we express when, given the occurrence of the cause, we say the effect *must* occur? Also, speaking of *the* cause of an event is too simplistic as many causal factors are typically involved in a causal process.

But the reductionist has a ready reply. In our mind-brain causation example, there is a brain event that immediately precedes or accompanies (but never follows) the mental event that is the effect. This is a case of direct or immediate causation in that no intervening events separate the brain event we are calling the cause and the mental event in question. But in most cases of causation many other events intervene between the events we term "the cause" and "the effect." Also, there are many contributing causal factors, each of which is needed for the effect to occur. More precisely, a cause or causal factor (C) of an event (E) is a member of a set of conditions or events (S), each of which is necessary for E to occur and which together are sufficient (all that is needed) for the occurrence of E. The occurrence of the entire set, S, is both necessary and sufficient for E's occurrence. Which member (or members) of S we call the cause depends upon the context and on our interests and purposes. We may choose the most conspicuous causal factor or the last to occur before the effect occurs. In any case, it is only a causal factor insufficient by itself to cause the effect.

Causal power and the causal necessitation of the effect-event are to be understood in these terms. To say that a causal factor (C) is *necessary* for the occurrence of an event (E) is to say that an event like E (more precisely, an event of the type to which E belongs) *never occurs unless* an event like C occurs. And to say that the set (S) consisting of all the causal factors is *sufficient* for E is to say that when a set like S occurs, an event like E *always* occurs. The necessary connection between cause and effect is nothing more than an invariable temporal connection. And to provide a causal explanation of E is to show that E's occurrence is in accordance with a natural regularity, which, in turn, is causally explained by showing that it is a consequence of a broader or more fundamental natural regularity. But this process of appealing to ever more inclusive or more fundamental regularities must end if the most inclusive or most fundamental regularities are reached—regularities that will not themselves admit of explanation since explanation of a regularity requires appeal to a more inclusive or more fundamental regularity. If that point is reached, explanation collapses into description of the regularities and an implicit acknowledgement that this is the way the world is.

Though there are serious difficulties with this account of causation, we need not now be concerned with what they are. For it is sufficient for our present purposes to note that there is nothing in this account suggesting that mental-physical interaction is problematic. Not only does the mind not need spatiality and mass-energy to interact with the brain, but their interaction in a lawful way may prove to be a fundamental law of nature, neither admitting nor requiring explanation. If their interaction is such a law, as the *direct* causality involved indicates, we would not be able to explain how or why the mind and brain affect each other. But we would know why we cannot explain this. For we would know that, on this fundamental level, all we should expect to be able to do is simply take note of and describe what we find to be the case.

Causation Conceived as Irreducible

Though the reductive account of causality indicates that there is no intelligibility problem with mind-brain interaction, that account may be false. Perhaps causality cannot be reduced to natural regularities constituting the laws of nature. It may be that reduction runs the other way—that natural laws are regularities in virtue of regularities in the exercising of the causal powers and liabilities of the causally related items. In other words, causal powers and liabilities may be intrinsic, irreducible properties of the things that enter into causal relations. They are to be understood as the irreducible properties of substances, rather than as reducible to laws of nature and then laws of nature to regularities of successions of events. In this view, natural laws are not simply matters of what regularly follows what, but regularities in the manifestation of the causal powers and liabilities of substances.

This view appears, initially at least, to bode very well for the intelligibility of mind-brain interaction (i.e., dualistic causation). Our previous investigations have led us to the conclusion that the self, understood as the subject of conscious states, is a substance. For it is not an event nor some property of a material entity such as the brain, but an entity having properties of its own (such as the property of being conscious) and enduring as the self-same entity through time. These are the noncontroversial marks of a substance. There is nothing else it can be that is consistent with our previous findings. It is the kind of entity that would have its own causal properties, and these may well be such as to make causal transactions with the brain a possibility.

But why should we think that this account of causality is true? And, even if it is true, why should we believe that the self has the causal powers and liabilities needed for it to causally interact with the brain? We will consider three important reasons to believe that this account is likely to be true, and, in any case, more plausible than the reductive-nomological account. A consideration of these reasons will also bring into focus the case for believing that the self has the needed causal properties.

Deep Causation

The impression of causal power, of *making* something happen, seems to be central to our commonsense conception of causation. Causes necessitate their effects. We apparently have an impression of a (causally) necessary tie between cause and effect that we express when we say that an event *must* occur, given its causes. Perhaps the source of this impression is our experience of (what we naturally take to be) the exercise of causal power in exercising our will. By willing to raise my arm, I can make my arm rise (or at least initiate the physical process leading to its rising). I experience what seems to be a "deep" causal connection between my act of willing and my arm's rising, as I seem to *make* that event happen. But this deep causal connection vanishes in the reductive-nomological account. In that account, causation involves nothing more than an invariable temporal connection between types of event. So if, in this account, I were to speak of my act of willing as what makes my arm rise, all I should be understood to mean is that my arm's rising invariably accompanies or closely follows my act of willing. This is a reductive or deflated causal connection compared to the robust or deep connection apparently implicit in our commonsense understanding of the matter.

Clearly, the view that causal relations are deep, that they are grounded in intrinsic irreducible properties of substances, is fully in accord with our sense of what is happening in our volitional acts. This sense or intuition sustains our conviction that the causal relation *accounts for* the regularity of successions of events manifested in a causal law and thus *not* something *constituted* by that regularity. This understanding of causation is also in accord with the view that the self is an immaterial substance possibly having the requisite causal powers and liabilities to causally interact with its brain.

The Directionality of Causation

This view of causation has the great advantage of doing justice to our sense of the directionality of causation. The causal process has an intrinsic directedness: it runs from cause to effect, not the other way around. Its directedness is the result of an asymmetrical dependence of one event upon another. The effect depends upon the cause, but the reverse is not true. This asymmetrical dependence, and thus the directionality of causation, is due to the intrinsic causal properties of the substances involved in the causal process. Given those substances with their causal properties, it could not have run in the other direction. This account accords well with our sense of the intrinsic directedness characterizing the connection between one's act of willing, say, to move one's hand and one's hand moving.

The reductive-nomological account implies, on the other hand, that directionality is not intrinsic to the causal process. According to that account, the direction of the causal process is due to the direction of time, and thus not to anything intrinsic to the process itself. For the invariable successions of events to which causation is thought to be reduced are intrinsically symmetrical. They could have run the other way, as they appear to do when a video is run backwards.

Intentional Causation

In considering the first two reasons for believing that causation is irreducible, we have already indicated how supportive the irreducibility of causation would be of our intuitions about the character and function of our volitional activity (i.e., the activity through which we exercise our "intentional" causality). Now we will examine further what these intuitions indicate about the character and function of the causal power that we seem to exercise in both the mental and the physical aspects of our lives, as well as note their contribution to our basic notion of causality. What will also become clear is the extent to which the reductive-nomological view fails to accommodate these intuitions.

An examination of intentional causation—what occurs when we intend or will to perform an action—reveals a compelling case for believing not only that causation is irreducible, but also that dualistic causation is intelligible. How should causation be understood if it is not reducible to regularities in nature (or, indeed, to anything else), and if, as now seems clear, neither spatial contact nor the transfer of energy is essential to it? Perhaps the answer to this question is to be found in our experience of intentional action, as illustrated when you raise your hand by willing to do so. This is an experience of being an agent exercising (or at least seeming to exercise) her causality as an agent by willing to perform an action. It is an instance of agent-causation. Intentional causation is agent-causation, since the agent is what does the intending or willing. To understand such causation is to have an understanding of ourselves exercising causal power.

Understanding intentional causation is central to our understanding of causation in general because the experience of being an agent bringing about an action by willing to do so seems to be our epistemic access to our basic notion of causality—of what it means for something to be a cause. For it is a direct access, rooted in experience, as opposed to the indirect route provided by inference and reflective thought. When I will to raise my arm, I thereby provide my intentional contribution to my act of raising my arm. I succeed in this if my arm is not constrained or paralyzed or impaired in some other way. But whether or not I succeed, my intentional contribution remains the same. It is my experience of bringing about an action by willing it—by my providing my intentional contribution to it—that gives rise to my intuitive sense of *making* that action come about. The action doesn't merely accompany or follow my willing it. Rather, I produced it. I made it happen. This experience is the source of the persistent impression that the causal connection is deeper than the reductive-nomological account can acknowledge it to be.

Perhaps the impression of deep causal connection is misleading. Perhaps our volitional activity and, more generally, all of our conscious activities are epiphenomenal, having no (irreducible) causal power to affect the brain or anything else. Though we have already noted reasons (and will look at more) to conclude that this is virtually impossible to believe, our immediate concern is with the intelligibility of dualistic causation. The central point to be made now is that our experience of willing or intentionally contributing to an action (and of being acted upon) removes any remaining basis for the suspicion that the notion of a substance possessing intrinsic, irreducible causal powers (along with liabilities to be affected by the causal powers of substances) is unintelligible. Our grasp of the intelligibility of dualistic causation could hardly be more secure, for it is grounded in the immediacy of our volitional experience.

Not only is dualistic causation intelligible but a consideration of intentional causation provides good reason to believe that the latter is best explained dualistically and that dualistic causation is in fact occurring. Given that a self or subject of conscious states is an immaterial substance possessing irreducible causal properties, the best explanation of our irresistible impression that we are agents making things happen in both the mental and physical realms is that this impression is truth-disclosing: the reality of this matter is as it appears to be.

Still, there is a final concern that we have not yet sufficiently addressed. A self may be an immaterial substance with irreducible causal powers and liabilities, and yet be unable to causally interact with a brain. For the two substances must be *causally accessible* to one another.[4] Recognizing this, a critic may ask, can we conceive of spatial and non-spatial substances being causally accessible to each other? But the route by which this charge may be effectively addressed is one we have laid out earlier. Even if certain spatial relations must obtain between two physical substances for them to be causally accessible to one another, we need not grant that such relations are necessary for causal accessibility in the case of *mental-physical* causation. As we noted earlier, such relations are not necessary for mental-physical causation, and thus not for causal accessibility, in the reductive-nomological account of causality. So we must question the assumption that they would be required if causality is grounded in the irreducible causal properties of substances. The burden of proof seems to be a burden the critic should bear.

But we can push the matter a little further. If, as now seems clear, we have good reason to believe that the conscious self is a non-spatial substance and also that it causally interacts with its body, then we have equally good reason to believe that spatial and non-spatial substances can be causally accessible to each other, even if we cannot explain precisely how such a causal accessibility relation is to be understood or what makes it possible. What we can do is point out that the causal accessibility relation between the self and its body is somehow realized through embodiment, even if we cannot specify what embodiment is apart from its causal implications.

That embodiment does provide causal accessibility to one's body seems undeniable in intentional causation. To experience intentional causation is to experience the causal accessibility of one's body. In first-person terms, I experience my causal access to my body in volition and the access that its causal powers have to me, as subject, in sensation and perceptual experience. The causal access I have to it is conspicuously absent in the case of every other human body. Sensory stimulation taking place in the body of another has no direct causal access to me as subject, nor do I have direct causal access to it in volition. Clearly, causal accessibility is realized through embodiment.

The conclusion to be drawn from our rather lengthy study of the important issue of whether the notion of dualistic causation is intelligible is now clear: it *is* intelligible. There is clearly no intelligibility problem if causation is reducible to natural lawfulness. For mental events are connected to brain events in lawful ways. It is difficult to see how, in the reductive account, free will can exist in any robust sense, but that is a different issue. In any case, we saw very good reason to reject reductive accounts and embrace the view that causality is irreducible, that things have intrinsic, irreducible causal powers and liabilities. And in this view, dualistic causation is as intelligible as physical-physical causation ultimately is. A critic may object that we cannot understand how something nonphysical can have the causal power to affect a brain or how a brain could causally affect such a thing. But this merely points to the ultimate mysteriousness not only of dualistic causation but of all causation. As we saw earlier, physical-physical causation is not any better off—we cannot understand in an ultimate sense why physical things, or at least the most fundamental ones, have the causal powers and liabilities that we find them to have.

Dualistic Causation and the Causal Closure Hypothesis

Though we have found no grounds for doubting that dualistic causation is intelligible and thus (metaphysically) possible, whether or not causation is irreducible, we have not yet addressed the objection that such causation does not actually occur. This objection is motivated by the view that the physical world is causally closed. In this view, an appeal to physical causation alone will prove to be sufficient (in a completed physical science) to fully explain all of the physical events occurring at any given time (to the extent that they admit of a causal explanation). No appeal to anything nonphysical is needed.

This view has been encouraged by the remarkable advance of physical science, though, of course, the claim that the physical world is causally closed reaches far beyond what physical science has established and probably beyond what it will ever establish. We will focus on two questions central to our concerns: (1) What are the grounds for believing that this claim is true?, and (2) What implications would its truth have for our understanding of ourselves and our causal role in what happens in the physical realm? Clearly, our answer to (2) will have a bearing on our consideration of (1). For some of these implications may be unacceptable, if not actually known to be false, and thus would constitute good grounds for rejecting the causal closure hypothesis.

Whatever grounds there are for believing that this hypothesis is true are to be found in the findings of physical science. This science explains the workings of physical systems in entirely physical terms. Its success is this endeavor has encouraged the generalization that all physical systems, including the brain, will succumb to purely physical explanations. No appeal to any nonphysical substance, property, or event will be needed to explain what happens in the brain.

Though many who subscribe to this hypothesis are materialists who believe that the natural world is devoid of anything nonphysical, we have seen virtually conclusive grounds for rejecting such a view of the natural world. Because, then, the nonphysical reality of the mental must be acknowledged, not even mental properties (let alone mental substances and events) could have a causal role in the outcome of physical events. Thus those who accept the causal closure hypothesis and also acknowledge the immateriality of the mental are virtually driven to some form of epiphenomenalism—a view we have already noted to be exposed to formidable difficulties.

Although we will later examine in more detail the difficulties standing in the way of accepting any form of epiphenomenalism, a closer look at the significance of what physical science has in fact established will be helpful now. The advance of physical science, including brain science, has been impressive, but we must wonder if this advance provides good grounds for the generalization that every physical system, even brains, will admit of a totally physical explanation. For brains are unique in nature in virtue of their intimate association with consciousness, and so this generalization might not hold true of them.[5]

There are a number of reasons for doubting that the brain is a casually closed physical system. Since the brain's causal impact upon the mental is not in dispute, and since, as we have seen, the mental is an immaterial reality, the brain is not entirely causally sealed off from the mental. That is, even if it is causally closed to nonphysical causal influence, it does stand in a causal relation to the mental. The fact that the brain is not causally closed in the physical-to-mental direction should weaken our confidence in the assumption that it is causally closed in the opposite direction.

Another reason to question this assumption comes into view when we wonder how the existence of an epiphenomenal mental reality might be explained in evolutionary theory. Why would it have arisen in conjunction with brain activity in the first place and then retained if it had had no causal influence and thus no survival value? Without causal influence, it could not give the creatures who possessed it any competitive advantage in the struggle for survival. There are animals possessing features having no survival value for their possessors. But their existence is explained if they are necessarily connected to features that have positive survival value. To illustrate, the fur coat of a polar bear is warm—a feature necessary for the bear to survive in its native habitat. But its coat is also heavy in weight, a feature that, in itself, would be an impediment to the bear, but is retained anyway because of its necessary connection to the warmth of the coat. The brain-mind connection, however, seems entirely different from this one. We have no insight at all into how a conscious state (whether understood as a state of an immaterial subject or of a brain process) could bear a *necessary* connection to brain activity. As was implicit in our earlier deliberations about the character of conscious states, it seems clear that the appropriate brain activity might have occurred in the absence of any consciousness, in which case there can be no necessary connection between the two. The fact that consciousness is causally connected to certain brain activities still strikes one as radically contingent, a brute fact of a fundamental kind that we simply acknowledge as such.

However, the most compelling reason to reject the causal closure assumption appears in full force when we reflect upon the implication that everything we do would have to be done by way of our physical organisms without causal influence from any of our conscious states. We build bridges and skyscrapers, we communicate with one another with complicated patterns of speech, we teach courses, write books, and generate complex scientific theories—all without the benefit of the conscious states (of understanding, planning, intending and desiring) that seem to be the source of such activities. Clearly, this would conflict in a most radical way with our common-sense assumptions about the causal efficacy of our conscious states. But even such a level of conflict does not reveal the full depth of the problem. As the philosopher, John Foster, has pointed out, our conscious states would have no causal access to the speech centers of the brain, in which case our speech could not be informed by our thought or brought about by what we intend to say.[6] Our thought would be unable to inform any overt discussion of epiphenomenalism or of our conscious states. Any introspective knowledge of our own conscious states could not be expressed in speech to which it cannot contribute anything. Though this view of the complete impotence of the mental to affect the physical expresses a (metaphysical) possibility, it is nevertheless self-refuting in that any (thought-expressing) claim that it is true could be made only if it is false. It must be false if I am now expressing my thought. For such a view to be acceptable, the evidence for it would have to be overwhelming.

Mental-Mental Causation

The hypothesis that our mental states have no effect on our brains seems impossible to believe. But the suggestion that none of our mental states have any effect on other mental states we have is equally incredible. As we shall see, mental-mental causation seems undeniable. And if our grounds for concluding that there is mental-mental causation turn out to be the very same grounds for concluding that there is mental-physical causation (i.e., that the causal closure hypothesis is false), then both are equally undeniable. Let us examine these matters more closely.

An example of one mental state affecting another occurs when one's awareness of the content of a sensory experience causes one to form true beliefs about that content. To illustrate, my awareness of a red and round expanse in my visual field when I am looking at a red ball causes my true belief that there is a red ball in front of me. Obviously, the same is true of the other senses. In each case, I am exercising a causal power to affect my mental states.

This power may be even more evident in our capacity to reason, especially in the conscious, reflective process of constructing and evaluating arguments. In first-person terms, as I formulate the propositions that are expressed in the premises and the conclusion of a valid deductive argument, or think through such an argument in evaluating it, I have a succession of thoughts about the logical relations among the propositions. This is a succession in which I manifest my power to direct my thought in a manner that would be impossible to understand without acknowledging the causal role of my *consciousness* of the contents of the propositions and of the logical relations holding among them. For it is only in virtue of my consciousness of what a proposition is about that I am able to become conscious of the logical implications of that proposition—a consciousness that supplements my consciousness of the logical implications of the other relevant propositions, as I proceed in a consciousness-directed consideration of the argument. It seems simply incredible that I could reason in this reflectively conscious manner if my propositional consciousness had no causal power to affect the reasoning process.

The conclusion that conscious states are not entirely devoid of causal power should now seem inescapable. The subject of conscious states has by virtue of these states at least the causal power to affect its own conscious states, if not its brain as well. But once the causal power of the mental to affect the mental has been acknowledged, its power also to affect the physical becomes even more difficult to deny. We have already examined compelling evidence that the mental causally affects the physical, but now virtually conclusive evidence drawn from immediate experience comes into view. As we looked at what happens in our experience of employing our reflective consciousness in thinking through an argument, we found irresistible the conclusion that we are exercising causal power over our own thought. The foundation for this conclusion could hardly be more secure, as it is grounded in one's immediate experience—in one's very experience of going through the process, in contrast to inferences we might draw as a result of it. But with respect to the immediate experience of causal power, reflective consciousness employed in reasoning is indistinguishable from willing to move one's body. There is no introspectively discernible difference in experience of causal power, whether one is directing one's thought in thinking through an argument or providing the intentional contribution needed for the volitional control of one's body.

These considerations are compelling, if not conclusive: in virtue of our (nonphysical) conscious states we do causally affect our bodies. Hence, the physical realm is *not* causally closed. This is a conclusion grounded in our immediate experience of willing to perform an action and would have struck us as virtually beyond question were it not in conflict with the causal closure hypothesis. But this hypothesis, by contrast, is highly theoretical and all-inclusive in scope, asserting that every physical effect, whether known or unknown, has physical causes sufficient for its occurrence. In view of the conjectural status of this hypothesis along with our less than adequate knowledge of the intricate workings of the brain, the conclusion that the physical realm is *not* causally closed seems to be the far more justifiable one to draw, at least as the matter stands at this time.

Paranormal Causation

Paranormal causation may be characterized in the broadest terms as the causation occurring when the self acquires information from, or acts upon, its environment (including other embodied persons) other than by way of its brain. A consideration of the possibility of such causation is relevant to our study because a deceased person who continues to exist would no longer have a physical body to enable her to communicate as she once did. A deceased person, whether disembodied or in a nonphysical body, would be unable to communicate either with the living or with other deceased persons if a physical body and brain is needed for any communication with another person. Thus if it were a fact that some deceased persons continue to exist, we could have no evidence of that fact unless some form of paranormal causation were not only possible but known to actually exist.

The forms of paranormal causation alleged to exist might be divided into two categories: extrasensory perception (ESP) and psychokinesis (PK). Extrasensory perception leads to the acquisition of information, either directly from the minds of others (i.e., via mental telepathy) or from clairvoyant apprehension (i.e., virtual perception) of the environment. In clairvoyant apprehension, the object of consciousness (i.e., the intentional object) is of something presently existing or occurring. Retrocognition occurs when the intentional object is some state of affairs that obtained in the past. If the intentional object of this sort of apprehension is some future event or state of affairs that will obtain, precognition occurs. PK (sometimes called "psi-action") is conceived to be the direct action of the self or agent upon the material realm, rather than its acting by the normal route of indirectly affecting some part of that realm by directly affecting its brain. The normal route is that by which it directly affects its brain, which, in turn, brings about bodily behavior by affecting the nervous and muscular systems of the body.

Though we will later look at evidence for the existence of paranormal causation in at least some of these forms, our immediate concern is to see what the findings of our study of normal causation imply about the intelligibility (and thus the metaphysical possibility) of paranormal causation. Given that normal causation is best viewed as grounded in the causal powers and liabilities of substances, and that the self has the required powers and liabilities to causally interact with its brain, all that would be required for the intelligibility (i.e., the conceivability) of paranormal causation is the conceivability of the self merely having more causal properties of the kind it would already possess. Since the self already has the causal properties needed to interact with such things as brains, namely, its own, there would seem to be no serious difficulty in conceiving of it having the further causal properties of affecting and/or being affected by a brain other than its own. With such properties, an embodied self could affect the mind of another self by directly affecting that self's brain, much as it directly affects its own brain. Similarly, it could be affected by some other self if that self could directly affect its brain. By such means, one embodied self could telepathically affect the mental states of another even though they remain entirely unaware of how they accomplish such a feat (or even *that* they do so). Though both cause and effect would be a self-having-a-conscious-state, it may be that neither self is aware of any telepathic interaction taking place.

The conceivability of clairvoyance may be revealed by similar reasoning. Some effects that brain activity have on the self consist in providing the self with information about the body and the external world. By way of certain processes taking place in its brain, the self comes to have sensory experience of its body and of the surrounding environment. In other words, the self has the causal properties needed to acquire information from physical states of affairs, namely, those obtaining in its own brain. But the mere extension of these causal properties to those needed to acquire information from physical states of affairs other than those obtaining in its brain seems easy to conceive. For we are conceiving of nothing more than increasing the size of the class of things from which the self can acquire information, without appealing to causal powers and liabilities other than those of the kind it would need to acquire information by way of its own brain.

The conceivability of PK is implicit in this account. The self, in its volitional activity, exercises its causal power to affect its body and thereby its environment by acting directly on its brain. The conceivability of PK is the conceivability of its acting on physical objects other than its brain. Thus its conceivability, like that of clairvoyance, is shown by conceiving of merely an increase in the size of the class of physical things the self can directly affect.

It has been suggested that ESP and PK might be occurring continuously in normal mind-brain causal relations.[7] More specifically, it might be that the self clairvoyantly apprehends the information it receives from its brain and acts upon its brain psychokinetically (perhaps by wielding psychokinetic force at the micro level of the workings of the brain where these workings are subject to the laws of quantum physics rather than those of classical physics). In this view, clairvoyance and PK would be normal functions; and what we ordinarily term clairvoyance and PK would be the same paranormal extension of the self's causal powers to things other than its brain. The evidence for the existence of these paranormal phenomena would be much less extraordinary and easier to accommodate in such a view.

Despite these reasons to believe that the conceivability of ESP and PK is unproblematic in any view in which a nonphysical self interacts with its brain, it may seem that a serious difficulty has not been taken into account. This difficulty comes into view when we wonder *how*, under highly unusual circumstances, the self can, in effect, interact with physical things other than its brain. Taken further, we might wonder *how* the self can interact with even its own brain.

Thought we have already noted the ultimate mysteriousness of all causation, whether mental-physical or physical-physical, this fact may seem not to provide a basis for an adequate response to the "how" question. For we do commonly ask how a cause leads to its effect when considering cases of physical causation. But in these cases we are inquiring about the chain of events occurring between cause and effect. The "how" question is about the intervening events. To illustrate, if I were to ask how a certain fertilizer causes the lawn to become greener, I am asking what takes place between the application of the fertilizer and the greening up of the grass. To learn about the complex chain of events beginning when the fertilizer is applied is to become genuinely informed and to have one's question answered. But such cases are cases of indirect or remote causation, since what we call the cause is causally remote from what we call the effect. The cause does not bring about the effect immediately or on its own, but is only a member of a chain (or chains) of events of which the effect is a later member.

But cases of mental-physical causation are not like this. They are cases of direct or proximate causation in which nothing intervenes between cause and effect. To illustrate such a case, consider your act of willing to raise your arm (or move your body in some other respect). This seems to be a case of direct causation. Presumably, you do this by affecting your brain which then initiates a chain of neural and muscular events that leads to your arm's rising. But once you have willed to raise your arm, there is nothing more you need to do (or, indeed, nothing more we can even imagine you doing) to initiate the physical process that begins with an event in your brain. Here no event intervenes between your willing and the relevant brain event—your mental act of willing directly affects the physical. Clearly, the mental must directly affect the physical at some point if it is to affect the physical at all. And this seems to be one of those points. To claim that there is no direct causation—that no cause is causally next to its effect—seems incoherent. But if direct causation must be acknowledged, then to ask how, in cases of direct causation, the cause leads to its effect is to raise a question in the absence of the only context that would make the question meaningful. Correctly understood, this question is about what intervenes when, by the nature of the case, *nothing* does.

Since "how" questions become unanswerable only in cases of direct causation, such cases may leave us with an impression of mystery, at least prior to our recognition of these cases for what they are. For they are inexplicable in the sense that explanation comes to an end with them. When our search for explanation implicit in our "how" questions can no longer lead to our discovery of intervening events but must confront an instance of irreducible and thus unanalyzable causal power, we apparently have reached the point at which any further understanding can be attained only by acknowledging that this is the way things are, and that any further explanation is neither needed nor possible. No further explanation is possible by way of further analysis or more complete description of what is involved in a direct causal link, whether of the mental-physical or the physical-physical kind.

Applying these considerations to paranormal causation, we should note that if instances of clairvoyance and PK are instances of direct causation, our questions about how they occur become unanswerable for reasons we understand. In that respect, their occurrence would not be as problematic as we might have thought. Still, a problem remains in understanding such causation. This problem comes into view when we ask how the self could have causal access to a brain other than its own or to any physical state of affairs external to its body. We noted that embodiment apparently makes normal mental-physical causation possible, but that would not help us understand how the self could have causal access to states of affairs other than those obtaining in its own brain. Our understanding is aided somewhat by reminding ourselves that the embodiment relation is a causal relation, not a spatial one. For this reminder leads us to wonder why spatial remoteness of another's brain and the remainder of the physical realm external to one's own brain and body should be considered to be a serious problem. Also, if the "embodiment" relation is only a name for a direct causal link that we must acknowledge to exist but cannot further specify or explain, then the infrequent appearance of other such links with the physical should not strike us as altogether unbelievable. As direct links, they would be no more inexplicable than the direct links we have already acknowledged to exist. At any rate, the existence of other such links is surely conceivable.

Though we have been focusing on the conceivability of paranormal forms of mental-physical causation, we did not focus our attention on paranormal mental-mental causation. Yet the latter merits some attention, not only because it is a route by which telepathy might be conceived but because apparently it would be required for persons without physical bodies to communicate with one another. But the difficulty in conceiving of this is no more serious than those involved in conceiving of the other forms of paranormal causation. Since, as we have seen, we have compelling evidence that mental-mental causation is occurring in our own mental activity, we can, without difficulty, conceive of its paranormal extension to other minds. We simply conceive of such mental-mental causation as not in every case restricted to a process occurring only in a single mind by conceiving of what happens when we affect our own mental states as affecting instead, or also, the mental states of another.[8]

We might wonder about what the circumstances are under which such extended causation might occur. But at least the question of how (i.e., by what intervening events) it might occur need not arise. If the self, by virtue of being in certain mental states, can directly affect a mental state in its own mind and, under some circumstances, in the mind of another, the question of how it does that should not arise in either case. As we noted, the immediacy of the causation involved would preclude the existence of intervening events.

In bringing these considerations to a close, we should remind ourselves that we have been trying to establish only the conceivability or (metaphysical) possibility of ESP and PK, and not to show that ESP and PK actually occur. As we shall later see, however, the evidence that they do occur is weighty and merits serious consideration. But since it is central to the overall case for believing that some persons have in fact survived bodily death, we will consider it then. Still, having established the conceivability of the causation that might be operative in ESP and PK is important, not only in providing the motivation to take seriously claims that they have occurred and that some deceased persons have communicated with the living perhaps by way of them, but also in understanding what might have occurred (and continue to occur) if any of these claims are true.

The Causal Independence of the Conscious Self

We have found compelling reasons to believe that the self is a nonphysical subject of conscious states that causally interacts with its brain and that conscious states are states of this nonphysical subject rather than brain states. But we have not yet explicitly addressed one important causal question: Is the conscious self (causally) dependent on its brain for its very existence— to bring it into existence and then to sustain its existence? Even though its states of consciousness are not brain states and it is (metaphysically) distinct from its brain, it would not survive the death of its brain if it is brain-dependent in this way.

The variety of ways in which its consciousness is causally affected by activities in its brain may seem to establish that its very existence is brain-dependent. The fact that its consciousness is profoundly affected by serious brain injury or disease may seem sufficient by itself to render this conclusion unavoidable. This fact may seem to imply that the conscious self emerged or came into being with the development of its brain and now depends upon the functioning of its brain for its continued existence. If the source of its existence is its brain, then the conclusion that the brain is needed to sustain its existence may seem impossible to avoid. It can be avoided however, as Hasker has argued. Though embracing an "emergent" view of the self, Hasker argues for the logical possibility of the continued existence of the self by pointing to cases of emergent realities (e.g., some intense magnetic fields) that continue to exist, apparently by holding themselves together by gravity, after the magnets generating them have been removed.[9] He appeals to the possibility that the emergent self is related to its brain in the way that such an emergent magnetic field is related to its supporting magnet.

Still, it may seem that though such a possibility must be acknowledged, its realization after death is not very likely. The numerous and weighty considerations supporting the view that the conscious self came into being with the development of its brain seem equally supportive of the conclusion that the self will not exist after its brain is destroyed. But there are other views in which the truth of such a conclusion may seem much less likely. So we must examine further the issue of how the self's dependence on its brain should be understood. As we shall see, there is an alternative conclusion that may better fit the full range of empirical evidence relevant to this issue and thus may be the more plausible one to draw.

According to the alternative view we shall consider here, the conscious self is not brought into or kept in existence by its brain, even though its consciousness of the physical world and its ability to affect that world would be severely diminished if not abolished altogether apart from its embodied condition. More seriously yet, even those conscious states not involved in trans-actions with the external world, for example, those by means of which it rea-sons and affects the course of its own consciousness, might be impossible for it if it were not embodied. As we noted earlier, our embodiment is deep, and any alternative view worthy of serious consideration must recognize and be consistent with our deeply embodied condition.

At this point, two distinguishable positions come into view. They dif-fer in what they imply about the condition of the conscious self apart from its brain. In the more optimistic view, the brain is a modifier (or, more pre-cisely, a selective dissociator) of the consciousness whose source is not dependent upon brain functioning for its existence. The function of the brain is not only to carry out its causal transactions with the physical realm and to support its consciousness in the ways that lead us to speak of its deeply embodied condition, but also to dissociate the brain-modified consciousness from the more expansive consciousness of the source as it is independently of its association with a brain. This source is the conscious self as it is in its expanded, brain-independent condition. As such, it is (identical to) the self having the brain-modified conscious states, even though when having them it is dissociated from what it finds itself to be in its fully integrated, conscious-ness-expanded condition.

The relationship between its diminished, dissociated condition and its fully integrated state may be compared to the relationship we experience as we awaken from a non-lucid dream (a dream in which we fail to realize that we are dreaming). As we awaken to our ordinary, more expansive waking consciousness, we remember the dream as only an episode in the much more extensive experience to which our waking consciousness gives us access. Though the dream was a conscious event for us, the much more expansive perspective of ordinary waking consciousness was not available to us then. In other words, when the dream occurred it was dissociated from ordinary waking consciousness into which it is rapidly integrated upon awakening.

The fact that we experience the transition in consciousness that we have just considered provides the empirical basis for our conception of a similar transition occurring after biological death. In the view employing this conception, death would (or, at least, could) be analogous to awakening from a non-lucid dream. If the analogy holds in some detail, then we might expect the post-mortem expansion of consciousness to include an awaken-ing-like experience of finding one's entire embodied life to be only an iso-lated episode dissociated from the more expansive viewpoint now available in one's fully integrated condition. It is also conceivable that we experience a clarity of thought and an enhancement of reasoning powers that transcend those of ordinary waking experience in the way that those of the latter transcend the confusion and the eclipse of reasoning powers often experienced in dreams.

In the second view, as in the first, the conscious self does not depend for its very existence upon its brain. But it is in a highly diminished condition when separated from its brain, or, more precisely, from the kind of brain functioning that supports its (intentional) consciousness. Now the role of the brain is that of an amplifier or enhancer, rather than that of a separator-dissociator. The deeply embodied condition of the self is not the result of its separation from the powers it has in its brain-independent condition together with its dissociation from any awareness of those powers. Rather, its present condition reveals what its conscious existence can be when supported by a well-functioning brain and body. Without that support it collapses, either abruptly with the sudden onset of irreversible unconsciousness or gradually with the gradual decline of the relevant brain functioning. In either case, it collapses into something that, while continuing to exist, has, in its diminished condition, only a non-intentional consciousness whose presence we could not remember. But why we should believe that such consciousness exists and how it might be understood is a matter whose consideration we will postpone at this point.

Though these views denying that the conscious self emerged out of its brain serve their purpose merely by being consistent with our deeply embodied condition, they might strike us as more plausible than the emergence views when we remind ourselves of the strange features of the conscious self—its peculiar uniqueness (which, unlike a physical object, is not the uniqueness consisting in uniquely satisfying some individuating description), the "deep further fact" implied by its existence, the unity of its consciousness, so unlike the contingent unity of composite things, and the essentially determinate (i.e., all or nothing) character of its existence across time. These features seem not only to be such that no physical object or system could have them, but also such that we might wonder what one could mean in claiming that a brain could bring into existence something having them, quite apart from wondering what empirical evidence could establish the truth of this claim. While we must acknowledge that, by virtue of its states of consciousness, it can affect and be affected by its brain, this fact falls far short of implying that its existence is brain-dependent. Moreover, we have found good reason to believe that the conscious self is a substance in that it is an individual that lasts through time and change of states. This is relevant since radically different kinds of substances (viz., physical and nonphysical) might causally interact even though neither could bring about the other if, as it seems, that would require the one doing this to do it by way of transforming some substance of its own kind.

Earlier we noted that conscious states or events seem to be radically different from anything physical—so different as to be comprehendible only as constituting a further category of reality, viz., the category of the (concrete) nonphysical. Here let us take note of only one kind of conscious state—the experience of remembering. A special consideration of memory is relevant at this point since it seems especially difficult to understand how memory could arise by way of physical process.

The fact that memory is directed upon the past, and thus upon what no longer exists, is the source of the problem. For the causal processes taking place in the brain unfold as they do at some given time by what actually exists at that time. Certain past events might have been causal antecedents but do not exist at the time of the presently occurring brain event that is taken to be the cause of a present experience of remembering. The directedness on a past that is intrinsic to such an experience might strike one as extraordinary and even inexplicable when compared to brain states and events as they are conceived in contemporary physical science. They are the effects of what is presently occurring in the brain and occur without any reference to or directedness on a past, in striking contrast to the intrinsic directedness of memory.

The burden of providing a materialist explanation of memory rests entirely with the trace theory. If this theory fails, so would the materialist attempt to explain memory. This theory has been well received, however. It strikes almost everyone as highly plausible, at least prior to careful reflection—so plausible as to make memory seem well understood. Present experience results in physical traces laid down in the brain, many of which last for quite some time after the experience has expired. When brain activity leads to the re-activation of these traces, the experience that occurs is a remembering of the experience that led to the formation of the traces.

Unfortunately for the materialist, the trace theory, whatever specific form it takes, suffers from deficiencies that are fatal to it. One problem is that no one has been able to identify any such traces, despite the considerable and lengthy effort expended in the attempt to do so.[10] Secondly, the determinate character of brain activity seems to rule out the possibility of memory being literally stored in the brain. It is well known that memories are often vague, incomplete, and apparently indeterminate or indefinite in themselves, at least with respect to much of the detail that may strike one as impossible to identify with any assurance. With respect to much of what is "before one's mind" in memory, the difficulty seems to be less of a matter of identifying what is (determinately or definitely) there but of there being no definite state of affairs to identify. In striking contrast, every physical state (at least above the quantum level), and thus every brain state, has some exact size, shape, location and energy distribution. It is absolutely determinate in itself, however difficult it may be for us to identify, in its various aspects, the determinate reality that it objectively is.

But the central (and apparently insuperable) problem for the trace theory is implicit in what we have already acknowledged to be true of memory—its intrinsic directedness on the past. There is nothing about a presently existing physical trace that could be directed upon what exists no longer. The fact that it is an effect of the past is of no help in addressing this problem. Even if the memory imagery that often attends the experience of remembering could be plausibly explained as the effect of a brain trace, the fact that this imagery is experienced as imagery *of a past* would be totally unexplained. Without this awareness of, or directedness upon, the past, there would be no memory. Our ability to remember is our ability to direct our awareness on the past and recognize it as such. But the trace theory simply presupposes that this ability is involved and thus presupposes what it purports to explain.

Even if we assume, despite the lack of evidence of brain traces, that the occurrence of an experience is associated with the formation of a trace in the brain, and that this trace when activated leads to a state of awareness similar in some respects to the trace-forming experience, we gain no understanding of why that state is an awareness of the past (i.e., a remembering). For the trace-forming experience is (ordinarily) not an awareness of the past, nor is the brain trace. The experience of remembering can enter this picture only by presupposing that it must have a place if the trace theory is to provide an account of memory. What now seems clear is that there *cannot* be a place for remembering in *this* picture—an assembly of presently occurring physical events, caused to occur by prior events and causing subsequent events, but directed upon nothing. Though it is clear that trace theories can offer no insight into the remarkable phenomenon of memory, what may not be clear is how their failure supports the view that the self neither emerged from its brain nor is kept in existence by its brain and body. Earlier we noted two variations of this view: (1) the brain is a separator/dissociator of consciousness, and (2) the brain is a consciousness-enhancer. In both variations, memory is intrinsic to the self, and thus dependent upon the self for its existence. The existence of the self is necessary (though perhaps not sufficient0 for there to be any remembering. In the first variation, the dissociation of the self from its past experience (i.e., forgetting) is an effect on the self by its brain. This eclipsing of the self's capacity to remember is not a permanent state, but a result of its present deeply embodied condition. In the second variation, the brain enhances the self's capacity to remember. But in both views, remembering is something done by the self, not by activated brain traces, even though brain activity affects the self's exercise of its capacity to remember its experience.

Now, the failure of the trace theory implies that we have no plausible materialist account of memory. Further, an understanding of why it fails, and indeed must fail, suggests that no such account is possible. Thus we should be led to seriously consider nonmaterialist accounts. For the views that take the ability to remember to be an intrinsic capacity of the self seem promising. When we reflect upon what we find ourselves to be as subjects of conscious states, acquiring knowledge of a world external to us as well as knowledge of our own experience, both past and present, it seems clear that a capacity to know and to remember is intrinsic to the kinds of beings we are. This capacity might be enhanced or otherwise affected by our embodiment, but not brought into being by the activity of our brains.

If it seems difficult to believe that a subject of conscious states should have intrinsic properties that, apparently, no brain or other physical system could have, we might remind ourselves that this is no more difficult to acknowledge than that the world should have included any subjects at all. For it seems easy to imagine the world as consisting only of material things. But given that the subject of consciousness must be acknowledged to exist and to last through time and change of state, it must have some properties or capacities intrinsically to have been anything at all. Moreover, what could be more central to what it is intrinsically than a capacity to be aware and to remember its experiences?

We have now completed our examination of the causality problem— the problem of determining whether a nonphysical self can causally interact with its body, and, if so, how such interaction might be understood. Though this problem is widely considered to be insuperable for the view that a person is essentially a nonphysical self interacting with its body, our rather extensive examination revealed that it is not really a problem at all, whatever one understands the causal relation to be. As we noted, dualistic causation (e.g., between a nonphysical self and its body) is not difficult to conceive whether one takes causation to be reducible to natural regularities or due to the nonreducible powers and liabilities of the substances involved in causal transactions. Nor are there grounds for doubt that such causation actually occurs, as there are no good reasons for believing that the physical world is causally closed to nonphysical influence.

After having noted that there is no good basis for the charge that a nonphysical embodied self could not causally interact with its body, we went on to consider whether a *disembodied* self—a self separated from its body by death—could continue to causally interact with other selves and/or the physical realm. We saw that such post-mortem causal interaction would be paranormal causation. But this is not problematic, for, as we noted, it seems clear not only that paranormal causation is quite conceivable but that the evidence of its actual occurrence is very strong. Indeed, it may be what occurs when an embodied self interacts with its brain. Finally, we took note of the strength of the case for concluding that, although the self is causally affected by brain activity, its very existence does not depend upon the existence of its brain. In summary, we did not find any of the putative causality problems to be sufficiently serious to threaten the view that a person is an embodied, nonphysical self who might continue to exist after biological death and to retain its causal powers in its disembodied condition.

General Considerations Supportive of Post-Mortem Existence

Theism and Revelation Accounts

In the first chapter, we noted that the coherence of theism (and thus of the concept of the theistic God) implies the coherence of the concept of an immaterial person. That this concept is coherent should now seem clear. Our extensive examination of the nature of persons has revealed not only its coherence but also that in fact it provides the best characterization of *us*, as we are essentially. We were led to the conclusion that though we are embodied, our material embodiment is not essential to our nature. Since our investigation was empirically grounded in our experience of having conscious states and then informed by careful, reflective thought about this experience, it provides apparently unassailable evidence of the coherence of theism.

While these findings are certainly congenial to theism, the truth of theism would be strongly supportive of post-mortem existence. For even though we found reasons to believe that the very existence of the self (as contrasted with the particular state it might be in) does not depend upon the continued existence of its brain and body, these reasons were far from compelling. The fact may be that, as a matter of natural law, we do not survive their destruction, at least without divine intervention. But if this is the natural law that describes our condition, it would be a law that God could (and perhaps would) suspend to keep us in existence after biological death. For a person would be something that God could keep in existence if, as now seems clear, one's identity as a person is distinct from the identity of one's body. Accordingly, the issue of whether theism is true is highly relevant to the overall assessment of the case for post-mortem existence.

The coherence of theism is necessary for its *possible* truth. But, of course, only its actual truth would imply the existence of a being having the power to keep us existing after death. Unfortunately, a proper consideration of the numerous and complex issues to be taken into account in assessing the overall case for the (actual) truth of theism is beyond the scope of this study. What

90

we can do, however, is determine how the likelihood of our continuing to exist after bodily death would be affected if theism were true. So for the sake of this purpose, let us assume that theism is true.

In assuming the truth of theism, we are assuming the existence of a God having the power to contravene natural law and thus to keep us in existence after bodily death even if the laws of nature are such that we would not continue to exist without His intervention. But why should we believe that God would intervene on our behalf in the course of nature, if indeed intervention is needed?

Many would claim that the best evidence for this belief consists in what God has revealed to us about His intentions. They might add that since God is perfect, He would not lie to us or break His promises. But such an assessment of the evidential value of revelation claims must bear up under critical examination. Christianity, Islam and other theistic religions do make claims that God has revealed certain truths to us. But there is much disagreement about what those truths are. Though we might sidestep the problem implicit in this situation, we cannot avoid the general problem with revelation claims. We must, of course, acknowledge as true what God has clearly revealed to us, but we should not acknowledge uncritically that what is claimed to be a revelation from God is indeed what it claims to be.

This is a general problem with revelation claims that affects all of them. We have reason to assent to what is claimed to be the revealed word of God only if we have reason to believe that God is the source of it. It would be of no help, of course, to point out that some claims taken to be the revealed word of God include the assertion that they come to us from God. For such an assertion, like any other revelation claim, may fail to be what it purports to be.

Revelation claims, then, give us reason to believe that God would keep us in existence after bodily death only if we have reason to believe that any of them are what they purport to be—communications from God. Thus their value in providing rational grounds for belief is limited. But there might be better reasons to believe that God would desire our continued existence. The God of theism is considered to have unconditional love and compassion for His creatures. Their great desire for continued existence in conjunction with His deep concern for their well-being would constitute good reason to believe that He would not let bodily death result in their permanent nonexistence. God's compassion and concern for our well-being would not imply that He would wish to satisfy all our strong desires. For in the case of many of them, their satisfaction may not turn out to be in our best interest. But the desire for continued existence seems not to be one of those. Since few, if any, are able to fully actualize themselves in this life, and since the full actualization of one's potential may well be the highest individual good possible for a person to attain, God's concern for one's long-term well-being would be what moves Him to extend one's existence.

Another motive the God of theism would have for extending our existence beyond death is His concern for justice. The theistic God is conceived to be the supreme upholder of the moral law and the dispenser of divine justice who will ensure that in the end all virtue is appropriately rewarded and all wrongdoing justly punished. Since there is no apparent lack of either, though wrongdoing seems especially prevalent and is sometimes the source of unspeakable harm, the God of theism would see much in need of moral compensation. A closely related moral attribute possessed by the theistic God that might well lead him to extend beyond death the existence of some of his creatures is divine mercy. A god of great compassion, deeply troubled by the enormous suffering endured by so many, would have ample motivation to prevent them from ceasing to exist without having experienced a more enjoyable existence.

The Deep Unity of the Self

The deep unity and essential singularity that our investigation has revealed a conscious self to have has implications for the possibility of its post-mortem existence. For if the self has such features, then it could not cease to exist in the way that a composite object can—by loss of parts. Composite objects are collections of entities, some of which exhibit a deeper unity than others. A heap of sand has very little; its parts are related only in a spatial way. A machine, such as an automobile, has a deeper unity, as its parts have functional as well as spatial relations to one another. Living things, even unicellular ones, have a yet deeper, organic unity. But all are wholes made of parts and so can be destroyed by loss of parts. Though they can retain their identity (but not in the absolute or strict sense) through the replacement of parts by similar ones, they are at every time throughout their existence necessarily dependent upon the existence of the parts constituting them at that time.

But the self is not like this. Composite objects are material things that occupy space and thus have different spatial parts in the different places of the space that they occupy. Since any finite amount of space is infinitely divisible, the logically necessary divisibility of a material thing into different spatial parts is a consequence of its occupying a finite region of space that is divisible. As we saw, however, claims that the self is located and extended in physical space seem nonsensical. Obviously, the same would be true of claims that it has spatial parts.

Still, it may seem that the self has experiential parts, if not spatial ones. It would have had its various experiences as "parts" of it if it had been a bundle or collection of experiences strung out over time, as in the relational view. As we noted, however, the relational view of the self must be rejected. Individual experiences are not independently existing entities which, when suitable bundled, make up a self. Rather, they are *states* of the self, having no existence apart from it. The self is the basic entity without which the experiences could not exist, though it could exist without any particular one of them.

The self, then, is not a whole made up of parts and thus is unlike the body or any collection of things. It has a different, deeper unity than that of any whole made up of parts, however intimately related the parts might be. The depth of our unity as persons come into view again, and in a convincing way, when we reflect upon what it is to have experience, whether presently occurring, anticipated, or recollected. The suggestion that one might be some collection of related parts then seems to be a nonstarter. As we noted in chapter four, claims suggesting that a self (or person) has parts seem nonsensical. In first person terms, nobody now or at any time could be only *partly* me. Nor could some experience be only partly mine. In other words, I could not have a partial existence in someone who is only partly myself. Nor is a partial survival possible for me. My existence at any time, before or after my biological death, is an all or nothing matter. Nothing could constitute my partial existence or partial survival because I have no parts. And the depth of my unity as a person comes into view when we see that it is not a unity grounded in a unity of parts.

This implies that the manner in which a composite thing is destroyed is not possible for persons. Lacking parts, persons cannot be destroyed gradually by gradual loss of parts. Their ceasing to exist would have to occur all at once and would be complete annihilation—an abrupt, perhaps instantaneous, reduction to nothingness. The significance of this fact begins to appear when we note that science does not provide examples of annihilation. The objects we encounter in perception are destroyed through dissociation of their parts. Physical science informs us that they are made up of smaller, invisible entities—molecules, which in turn are constituted of atoms—that go their separate ways. Destruction involves only separation and recombination, not annihilation. Even the atom may be split into subatomic particles, which, in turn, may be reducible to quarks, strings, or just energy. But this is only transformation of one form of matter/energy into another. The principle of the conservation of mass/energy tells us that there is no loss, no reduction to nothingness in these transformations. The abrupt vanishing into nothingness that would have to constitute the ceasing-to-exist of the self stands in stark contrast to this. It would be an event not encountered in everyday experience and apparently unknown to science. From these perspectives, it would be an astounding event.

Not surprisingly, the claim that the cessation of the self's existence would be an abrupt reduction to complete nothingness has not gone unchallenged. Kant argued that though the self, if a simple substance, would be devoid of spatial parts and thus could have no "extensive quantity," it might nevertheless have "intensive quantity" that it could lose by degrees. It might possess each of its faculties only in some "degree of reality" and thus could lose all by degrees. In particular, if it could lose its consciousness in this way along with its other faculties, it could cease to be by losing its powers in a gradual way, by "elanguescence."[1]

This objection is echoed on the contemporary scene. For example, the contemporary philosopher, Ernest Sosa, has advanced an important argument intended to show that the existence of a self could be a matter of degree.[2] If a self (or subject of conscious states) can exist only if it is conscious or has at least a potential for consciousness, then the question of whether it exists at a given time will be a question of whether it is conscious or potentially conscious at that time. But, he argues, both consciousness and the potential for consciousness admit of degree. Thus a self might cease to exist gradually through the gradual loss of consciousness and/or the potential to become conscious.

These arguments are flawed, however. First, they fail when applied to consciousness itself. It seems that the existence of consciousness does not admit of degrees, at least in its most primitive, nonconceptualized form. In that form, it appears to be one of the few really clear-cut cases of an all-or-nothing phenomenon. It can vary in quality of course, but apparently not with respect to whether it is present.

But the flaw that, by itself, is fatal to these arguments comes into view when we see that existence is an all or nothing matter, and thus not something that can be lost by degrees. There is no mean between existence and nonexistence; either something exists, or it does not. To assume otherwise, is (as the philosopher Chisholm has pointed out) like thinking that there is a path between nonexistence and existence, so that something moving along such a path can thereby acquire more existence. But clearly, this is a mistake. In Chisholm's words, "If something *is* on a certain path, then that something *is*. Or if it *isn't* yet, then it can't be on the path between being and nonbeing."[3]

Of course, something that exists can undergo gradual change. A sound, for example, may gradually diminish in intensity, but it must be in existence to be changing. It diminishes in its intensity but not in its existence.

One important source of this confusion about existence may well lie in our thoughts about how composite objects last through time, especially organisms undergoing a continuous replacement of micro-parts. As we noted earlier, all or almost all of the parts of such objects might be replaced after a certain length of time, thereby leading us to wonder whether the original object still exists. Whether or not it does may seem to be an indeterminate matter—not a matter that the relevant facts alone can settle. A similar problem arises with respect to persons if persons are bundles of experiences and thus composite entities. We noted that there could be conditions under which we would judge that the original person is only partly present, i.e., neither exists (in her entirety) nor fails to exist. Under such conditions we might be led to say that the original person is gradually ceasing to exist along with gradual replacement of parts. But no such problems can arise if a person has the deep unity that our investigation has revealed. Persons do not admit of partial existence or survival, whatever we choose to say about what happens to composite things over the course of time.

Though such considerations provide compelling reasons to believe that the ceasing-to-exist of the self or person would be an abrupt, if not instantaneous, reduction to nothingness, we have yet to assess the full significance of such a fact. Such an event is conceivable in that there is no logical contradiction in supposing it to happen. Apparently, it is metaphysically possible, but this fact leaves unanswered the question as to whether such an event is naturally possible, i.e., in conformity with the natural law of the actual world. The verdict of physical science seems to be that such events do not occur. But the verdict is tentative, of course. Besides, we might wonder if science can provide an authoritative answer to such a question—a question that seems more philosophical than one to be conclusively decided by empirical observation. Perhaps the best we can do is note that if such events do occur in the actual world, they would be inexplicable. Scientific explanation is largely causal explanation, with events being the causes and effects. An event of one kind (or kind) leads to an event of another kind (or kinds), which, in turn, leads to further events in accordance with causal (or natural) law. These causal chains extend indefinitely; they never lead to nothing. Nor does nothing lead to anything. An abrupt reduction to utter nothingness could have no place in such a process.

Do such considerations show, or at least provide good reason to believe, that if the self is as our investigation indicates it to be, then it will not cease to exist with the destruction of the body? If it cannot cease to exist in the way that the body can, namely, by decomposition or dissolution, then do we have grounds for believing that it will continue to exist without its body? As we try to answer this question, we might remind ourselves of a very widely held principle well expressed by Schopenhauer when he wrote, "Nothing can come out of nothing, and nothing can again become nothing."[4] Perhaps the most defensible answer, at least at this point, is that these considerations do contribute significantly to the overall case for believing that the self will continue to exist, whatever its state will then be, but do not, by themselves, provide sufficient grounds for this belief.

Non-Intentional Consciousness and the Self

We have seen reason to believe that the self or subject of conscious states does not depend for its existence upon the existence and proper functioning of its brain. But even if it does not, there can be no doubt that its conscious states are profoundly affected by the brain activity taking place in the cortex and might well depend upon this activity for their existence. Indeed, there are many empirically-grounded considerations (e.g., the apparent absence of consciousness following a powerful blow to the head, a massive stroke, or other severe brain damage) strongly suggesting that conscious states cease when the brain is destroyed. But if they do cease then, we must wonder whether the self could continue to exist without them, and, if it can, what sort of state it could be in. Clearly, consciousness could not be essential to its existence if it could exist under such conditions.

This situation suggests possible problems for the view that the conscious self could exist without its brain even if it would lack consciousness under such conditions. If consciousness is not essential for its existence, then what *is* essential? *Something* must be for it to exist at all—something to constitute *what it is*. Could it exist as something having a mere *potential* to become conscious—a potential realized only when it is causally related to a brain (or perhaps some other complex system)? Perhaps, but this leaves unanswered the question of what a self could be if it can exist without consciousness.

There are two plausible answers to this question. The first is that although the self can exist without ordinary consciousness, it cannot exist without consciousness of any kind. More specifically, it cannot exist without *non-intentional* consciousness—a form of consciousness that, unlike ordinary (i.e., intentional) consciousness, is not a consciousness *of* anything. Ordinary or intentional consciousness is always a consciousness *of*; there is always an object of this consciousness—the object upon which the consciousness is directed. You may now be conscious *of* music playing somewhere near you or thinking *about* going to the grocery store. This "of-ness" or directedness is what we referred to earlier as the intentionality of (ordinary) consciousness. But non-intentional consciousness is not like this: it is con-

sciousness that is not directed upon anything. There is no object of consciousness (i.e., no "intentional object," as it is called). It is consciousness
by itself, devoid of any intentional object.

In this view, the self is always conscious in a non-intentional way, and
thus non-intentional consciousness would be available as an essential feature of the self. So even if the destruction of its brain would leave the self
without any of the intentional consciousness that characterizes our waking
lives, it could go on existing as a conscious being in a state of non-intentional consciousness unless or until it again enters into an embodiment relation with a physical body (or a nonphysical one, if there is an afterworld in
which such things exist). This would be its state when disembodied if its
intentional consciousness ends when its brain is destroyed.

This view is intriguing, but its credibility depends upon there being satisfactory answers to two questions of central importance: (1) Why should we
believe that non-intentional consciousness even exists?, and (2) If it does
exist, why should we believe that it survives the destruction of the brain even
if intentional consciousness does not? In response to the first question, mystics the world over, from the various cultures and historical periods, attest
to its existence. A mystic is someone who has had mystical experience, and
a mystical experience of the deep, introversive sort is one claimed by the
mystic to occur after she has managed to get "behind the senses" and then
"behind the mind," transcending all sensory-intellectual consciousness, and
having eventually reached a state of "pure consciousness." This consciousness is without content; it is not *of*, or directed upon, anything. It is non-
intentional consciousness.[5] Though no intentional consciousness is involved,
implying that the self has no consciousness of having an experience, even of
the self having the experience, yet, paradoxically, the experience is later
remembered as had by oneself, not by no one in particular. And when the
mystic seeks another such experience, she seeks it not for something impersonal but for herself.[6]

What seems to be the same phenomenon is better explained in several
Eastern views, especially the role of the self in non-intentional consciousness. In these Eastern views, in which consciousness and self-nature are
treated in great depth and with the utmost care, the subject of conscious
states is held to exist and to know itself in a non-intentional way at all times,
even during deep dreamless sleep and other times when we ordinarily suppose, after awakening, that we were unconsciousness. We suppose this
because we have no memory of being conscious then. But, according to the
Visistadvaitins, for example, who hold that though the self or subject always
has a non-intentional consciousness of itself, it fails to remember what tran-
spires during periods of apparent unconsciousness because intentional con-

sciousness was not then revealing anything to it. During those times, the self is conscious only of itself and only in a non-intentional way. Though it returns to intentional consciousness with no memories of being conscious then, its continuous non-intentional consciousness of itself plausibly explains our sense of continuous existence throughout these periods.

Many of the important schools of Hindu thought (e.g., the Nyaya and Vaisheshika schools) held that although the self is a nonphysical substance and the source of (intentional) consciousness, such consciousness is not essential to it. Perhaps the most interesting one, at least for our investigation, is the Samkhya school, which has been hailed as "the most significant system of philosophy that India has produced."[7] In this view, the self is an ultimate subject, termed *purusha*. It is an entirely subjective, substantial entity, absolutely distinct from everything in nature (termed *prakriti*). Since even its intentional conscious states, i.e., all of its experiences, are part of prakriti, its existence does not depend upon them, or upon anything material in the prakritic realm. Consequently, it continues to exist throughout the periods of apparent unconsciousness that occur during biological life and also after biological death. Though it will have no intentional consciousness in the absence of its body, it will, as always, manifest its self-effulgent or self-shining nature, revealing itself to itself by its own light—apparently, the light of non-intentional consciousness. This light provides the unique epistemic access that the subject has to its own subjectivity. The Samkhya school was joined by several others in embracing this view.

Though this view is in striking contrast to the predominant materialist views of contemporary Western thought, it is a highly respectable view emerging out of a venerable tradition. It provides, at the very least, a coherent and plausible account of how the self might continue to exist as a conscious being after biological death, even if all of its states of intentional consciousness cease with the destruction of its brain. Moreover, this view is certainly not ungrounded philosophical speculation. It is a philosophic interpretation of the insights revealed in the Upanishads, at the core of which are reports of mystical experiences unsurpassed in depth and in power to move those receptive to them. Thus it is grounded in the experiences of mystics and purports to provide the most plausible interpretation of them. It provides an answer to the question of who or what is having these experiences and of how consciousness is involved in them.

Our evidence that non-intentional consciousness exists is not confined to such reports, however. Our own investigation has revealed its role in our coming to have a conception of ourselves. We acknowledged, in effect, that the self, or subject, must have a non-intentional awareness of itself when we noted that it cannot observe *itself observing itself* among the objects upon which it is directing its consciousness (i.e., among its intentional objects). We also noted that it could not acquire its self-awareness in such a manner even if it were a possible object of its own introspective observation. In first-person terms, even if the subject I was looking for in my introspective search were a possible (intentional) object of introspective observation, I would be unable to recognize it as myself unless I already had an (apparently non-intentional) awareness of myself that is logically prior to, and thus independent of, any such observation. If, as it seems, this logically prior and absolutely fundamental awareness is indeed non-intentional, then the conclusion that such awareness exists is inescapable.

In the course of answering our first question about whether non-intentional consciousness exists, we also have addressed the second question to some extent—the question of whether non-intentional consciousness survives brain death. The Eastern schools of thought that we considered insist that it does. In Samkhya terms, the brain is part of prakriti, from which the self (with its non-intentional consciousness) is absolutely distinct. And in mystical views generally, life, death, and the entire natural realm are claimed to have disappeared into an undivided unity—an absolute oneness in which there is no time, change or death. Yet, the mystic insists, consciousness is present. Perhaps what she experiences is a state of pure non-intentional consciousness.

Our own investigation of the self does not justify such a level of certitude about what death brings. Perhaps the self is completely destroyed when death occurs. That matter is left open. Still, if the self does survive as a conscious being, it is more likely to have non-intentional consciousness only, than to have both when not in association with a body. For the evidence that intentional consciousness depends for its existence upon brain activity is greatly weakened, if relevant at all, in the case of non-intentional consciousness. This evidence does not significantly diminish our grounds for believing that non-intentional consciousness continues throughout periods of dreamless sleep, coma, and other episodes of apparent unconsciousness, given that its occurrence then would not be remembered. It is also worth noting that non-intentional consciousness apparently is the ground from which intentional self-consciousness arises, and thus could exist even if the latter did not.

The importance of non-intentional consciousness to the survival issue should now be clear. Earlier we explored conceptions of the mind-brain relation in which consciousness does not depend for its existence (as contrasted with its quality) upon proper brain functioning. More specifically, we considered the conception of the brain as a consciousness inhibitor and then as a consciousness enhancer. We might now regard that discussion as about the possible relations between *intentional* consciousness and the brain. Thus the importance of non-intentional consciousness comes fully into view when we see that it opens up a third possibility—the possibility that the self continues to exist as a conscious being even if its intentional consciousness is destroyed by bodily death.

PART II: OSTENSIBLE EVIDENCE OF POST-MORTEM EXISTENCE

If any deceased persons have survived death and found themselves able to communicate to the living the fact that they still exist, one would think that at least some would try hard to do so. Of course, communication might be impossible for them, as it would be if, for example, they survived with only non-intentional consciousness. On the other hand, perhaps some have survived and managed to communicate. There are numerous, well-authenticated reports of strange occurrences indicating that such communication has indeed taken place. Moreover, there are people who have had near-death experiences that brought them to the threshold of death, giving them what they claim was a glimpse of an afterworld awaiting them. A study of persons and what happens to them when they die is surely incomplete without a careful assessment of such reports.

Our Investigation So Far

As we begin our consideration of these reports, we might remind ourselves of the relevance of our foregoing investigation—of how it provides us with a perspective from which to approach them. We noted at the outset that if a person is nothing other than the physical, or psycho-physical, organism that death destroys, then the continued existence of the person would be impossible. Clearly, one cannot survive the destruction of that which one is. Since there would be no question about what death brings, one embracing such a view of persons would be inclined to ignore reports indicative of survival or dismiss them as false without further consideration. Because we saw that the issue of what persons are is central to the survival issue, we spent much time and effort trying to determine the nature of persons. After examining various theories of the person, both physical and psychological, along with numerous other associated matters such as the immateriality of the mental, the "depth" of persons, and the question of how persons last through time, we reached the conclusion that what is essential to the existence of a self or person (indeed, both necessary and sufficient) is the existence of the *subject* of that person's experience. This subject is what we meant by the conscious self; and we noted that although the self is embodied in a physical organism, it is not identical to that organism. More specifically, it is a substantial entity—a different substance, though an immaterial one. Thus the destruction of that organism does not entail the destruction of the self. Still, the existence of the self might be *causally* (though not metaphysically) dependent upon the proper functioning of its brain, in which case it would perish with the death of its brain and body.

We also acknowledged that embodiment is a causal relation, not a spatial one. This led us to an investigation of how causation in general should be understood and then to explore carefully the alternative ways in which the particular causal relation between the self and the brain might be conceived. We saw that although the existence of the self might be causally dependent upon the activity of its brain, such a causal dependence is only one of the possibilities. Another possibility is that intentional consciousness depends causally upon brain activity for its existence, but that the self and its non–intentional consciousness do not. Then too, the brain might have a dissociative effect, perhaps in addition to other effects it might have on intentional consciousness, thereby allowing the possibility that the self survives with its intentional consciousness intact, or even expanded compared to what it had while embodied. Or the brain might be an intentional consciousness enhancer without being its source or that to which it belongs, such that the self survives with a greatly diminished intentional consciousness. There might be other possibilities as well.

Some of these possibilities might not seem very plausible, if not highly speculative. But the fact that there *are* several possibilities, no one of which is known to be the one actualized, has the result of leaving the survival question open. And its being open justifies our taking seriously well-documented reports of paranormal occurrences indicative of the continued existence of deceased persons, especially if we can conceive of how they might communicate with us even though they lack physical bodies. They would need to use paranormal means (e.g., mental telepathy) to communicate with us and with each other. But our examination of the causal connection between our minds and bodies in our normal, embodied condition revealed to us that there is no difficulty in conceiving of these causal powers extended in such ways as to include ESP and psychokinesis. Thus reports that deceased persons have survived death and have made contact with us are at least intelligible, whether or not any of them are true.

We are now poised to evaluate claims that some persons have survived death, recognizing that the truth of some is a significant possibility. We are in a position to have a clear conception of what the actualization of that possibility might well entail. Such awareness provides motivation to take such claims seriously, though, of course, not uncritically. These are benefits we gain from the rather difficult conceptual work we have done.

Near-Death Experiences

The near-death experience (NDE) is a phenomenon that recently has received a great deal of attention in the literature about whether persons survive bodily death. Because of advances in medical technology, we are now able to resuscitate people who otherwise would have died and thus, in the case of many, have enabled them to describe experiences they had while in a state of clinical death. The recent interest is quite understandable since at least in the best cases they are strongly suggestive of a continuing existence beyond death.

Death-Bed Visions

The early research occurring before many of the modern advances in medical knowledge and technology that enable us to rescue people on the brink of death was centered on the study of death-bed experiences, sometimes called death-bed visions. Though people who die shortly after a death-bed vision are, of course, unable to speak of it later, they are frequently able to describe it or otherwise indicate its content through their behavior before dying, often while it is occurring. Consequently, information about their experience comes to us second hand from the physicians, nurses, and relatives who were present. Still, they have evidential value worthy of our consideration.

Those who have such experiences typically claim, or otherwise indicate, that they have received a glimpse of an afterlife awaiting them, and are often in a remarkably lucid state at the time, despite considerable disorientation or incoherence prior to the vision. They claim to have seen and sometimes conversed with deceased relatives and friends who appeared with the apparent purpose of escorting them to the afterlife. With very rare exceptions, they did not doubt the reality of that which they had experienced, and their feelings were transformed as a result. They experienced serenity, peace of mind, and even elation, often after a period of fear, agitation, or depression. Though we might expect misery and gloom to prevail at the time of death, these people usually died in an elevated mood.

Some of the most remarkable of these visions that also have special significance for the survival question are those in which the dying person sees among friends and relatives coming to greet her a person whom she did not know had died. Quite understandably, her response is one of shock, disbelief or puzzlement at seeing such a person among the dead. Cases of this sort had motivated Sir William Barrett to begin the first systematic study of deathbed visions, a study that resulted in his book, *Death-bed Visions*, published in 1926.[1] He provides a vivid description of a young woman, Doris, who was dying after giving birth to her baby. She suddenly became intensely absorbed in a vision in which she saw her deceased father coming to take her with him. She was overjoyed in seeing her father and was elated at the prospect of going with him. Her baby was brought to her, perhaps partly to encourage her to live. Though she was torn between staying with her baby and going with her father, after some hesitation she explained to the attending physician, "I can't—I can't stay; if you could see what I do, you would know I can't stay."[2] Apparently, the vision was so compelling, so irresistible, that it overrode her powerful desires to be with her baby and to go on living. But the most extraordinary part of her vision took place when her sister, Vida, appeared with the apparition of her deceased father. This astounded her, for she assumed that Vida was alive. Because of her critical condition, she had not been told that Vida had died about three weeks earlier.

The significance of Vida's appearance becomes clear when we consider the skeptical view that Doris had a vivid but entirely subjective hallucination that provides nothing to indicate the continued existence of Vida or their father. For one must plausibly explain why Doris saw Vida among the apparitions, given that this was entirely contrary to any afterlife expectations she might have had. Of course, the correspondence between the appearance of Vida and the fact that Vida had died could have been simply chance coincidence; that can never be ruled out in an absolutely conclusive way. Also, there is the ESP explanation—Doris received the information about Vida paranormally, e.g., by mental telepathy from the living. But which explanation is the most plausible one? As usual, this is the central question. In trying to answer it, we must keep in mind our earlier deliberations about the nature of the self and the causal relation it has to its brain. For if, as these deliberations indicated, the self is distinct from its body (and thus its brain) and might not be causally dependent for its existence upon proper brain function, then the possibility that it continues to exist after biological death must receive serious consideration. And this possibility lends support for the view that the appearance of Vida is just what it appears to be—the still-existing Vida revealing her continuing existence and intentions to her sister in the form of a vision. How we might conceive of her doing this is something we shall consider later in a broader context, although our earlier discussion of indirect realism should indicate in a general way how we will then proceed.

Let us call the case of Doris a corroborative case, as Doris' vision includes content (the appearance of Vida) that can be corroborated by, or found in agreement with, objectively ascertainable facts (the death of Vida). Now we can point out that a single corroborative death-bed vision, or even a considerable number of them, can provide by themselves only a small amount of support for the survival hypothesis. Much more support might be found in other facts about death-bed experiences and more generally about NDEs of various kinds. The most support, however, might come from apparently paranormal phenomena other than NDEs (e.g., some mediumistic communications). In the end, our view about what will likely happen to us when we die should be based upon our best assessment of the amount of support the survival hypothesis receives from the various relevant sources (including our earlier more conceptual investigation) and then weighed against the very considerable amount of countervailing evidence that biological death will terminate our existence. But for now, we will take a closer look at the support that death-bed experience seems to offer.

More recent studies of death-bed experiences have utilized modern survey methods and computer analyses of results that were not available to Barrett. In 1959–60, the parapsychologist, Karlis Osis sent a questionnaire to 10,000 medical doctors and nurses in the U.S., asking them about the death-bed experience of their patients.[3] In this pilot survey he received 640 replies based on observations of over 35,000 dying patients and included over 1300 descriptions of apparitional experiences. 190 of the respondents were interviewed in considerable depth.

Because of concerns about possible influence by cultural factors (e.g., the Judeo-Christian background common for U.S. patients), the pilot study was followed by a cross-cultural survey carried out by Osis and Erlendur Haraldsson, a fellow parapsychologist.[4] Medical personnel were contacted in both the U.S. and in India. A great deal of important information was obtained, the highlights of which we can consider here.

One highly significant fact revealed by these studies as well as Barrett's is the great frequency with which "other-world" apparitions appear in death-bed experiences. Barrett had found that all the death-bed visions he examined involved only those relatives and friends who were already dead. And though the Osis and Haraldsson studies did show that apparitions of the living do occasionally appear, the frequency is low. In their studies, after grouping apparitions of the dead together with those of religious personages as "other-world" apparitions, they found that eighty-three percent of their U.S.

sample and seventy-nine percent of their Indian sample were made up of other-world apparitions. Those having "this world" significance constituted only seventeen percent of the U.S. sample and twenty-one percent of the Indian sample. In the words of Osis and Haraldsson, "This finding is loud and clear: *When the dying see apparitions, they are nearly always experienced as messengers from a postmortem mode of existence.*"[5] By contrast, people in normal health only occasionally see apparitions of people they recognize to be dead. In the Green and McCreery study, for example, only eighteen percent of the people in normal health saw such apparitions.[6]

Another remarkable finding of the surveys was that the apparitions of the dead and of religious figures were understood as having appeared primarily to escort the dying person to another mode of existence. This take-away purpose was apparent in about seventy-five percent of the cases involved in the surveys—a purpose with which the great majority of the patients, both American and Indian, were quite ready and frequently even overjoyed to share. Though apparitions of the living appeared in a small minority of the cases, not a single one of these apparitions in the pilot study was understood as having a take-away purpose. It is also of interest to note that death came more quickly in those cases in which a take-away purpose was expressed. Indeed, in many cases the patient died in accordance with the "call" of the apparition even though the medical prognosis was recovery. In some of these, the patient did not wish to die, vigorously trying to resist the call. As Osis and Haraldsson point out, "Such cases can hardly be interpreted as projected wish-fulfillment imagery...."[7]

Though it might seem quite plausible to suppose that the dying person really is encountering an afterworld, the skeptic will remind us that there are other interpretations to consider. The dying person might well be having an entirely subjective hallucination having no objective significance, perhaps due to drugs, psychological factors, brain injury or disease, or some combination of these factors. But Osis and Haraldsson found that this skeptical hypothesis is not in accord with the facts revealed by their studies. They found that only a small minority of the patients who had death-bed visions had received drugs having hallucinogenic effects. Furthermore, those who had received such drugs did not experience otherworldly apparitions with any more frequency than the others. Not only did their studies yield no evidence that drugs produce afterlife-related phenomena but that the same is true for brain disturbances caused by injury, disease, or uremic poisoning. They found that such factors either *reduced* the frequency of such phenomena or else did not affect it at all.

Osis and Haraldsson also took into account the possible effect of such psychological factors as stress and patient expectations. They found that evidence of stress manifested in anxiety or depression did not affect the frequency of other-world visions. Nor did they find any correlation between such visions and the patients' reported expectations with respect to whether they would die or recover. They tended not to see those people they had expressed a desire to see. Nor were their expectations reliable in predicting the content of their visions. An expectation to recover did not affect the likelihood of a take-away apparition appearing. In many cases the apparition seemed to possess a will of its own, even contrary to the expectation or desire of the patient, a fact suggesting that it was not merely a subjective creation of a dying mind.

The clarity of mind experienced by the patient at the time of the vision was also considered. In many cases (forty-three percent), the patient enjoyed normal clarity of consciousness—the mind was clear, rational and well-oriented. Clarity of consciousness was mildly impaired or fluctuating in forty percent of the cases and strongly impaired in seventeen percent. Such high incidence of normal clarity indicates that these remarkable experiences cannot justifiably be brushed aside as the fantasy of very ill, frightened people.

Since any study involving surveys and sampling techniques must pass muster on methodological grounds, it is important to note that these fare well. They have received some criticism: Susan Blackmore has questioned the representativeness of the responses received in the American study on the grounds that only 1004 questionnaires were returned out of 5000 sent.[8] But the list of 5000 physicians and nurses contacted was itself the result of a randomizing process carried out by selecting every seventh intern from an alphabetized list of interns in five north-eastern states. In addition, the investigators also checked to see if there was any relationship between attitude toward responding (as judged by speed of responding and need for repeated requests for a response) and phenomena reported that were supportive of belief in an afterlife, but found none. Finally, they carried out a spot check by telephone on those who did not respond and found that their attitudes toward the phenomena under investigation "were not substantially different from those of the responders."[9] These efforts to ensure the representativeness of the sample were not mentioned by Blackmore. Moreover, Blackmore's concern does not apply to the data on the Indian population, for that was based on face-to-face interviews with medical personnel.

Non-Terminal Near-Death Experiences

Though death-bed visions are had by people very close to death and thus, of course, count as NDEs, we shall now look at NDEs had by people who survived them and later described them in detail. Unlike death-bed visions whose content was revealed to investigators second-hand by way of the testimony of attending physicians, nurses and other witnesses, these people survived to provide first-hand accounts of their experiences. These NDEs became the subject of rather intensive scientific investigation carried out over the last three decades, largely by psychologists, cardiologists, and parapsychologists. In some of them, the subject reported information that was objectively verified and yet such that she could not have acquired knowledge of it by normal means. Moreover, some of this information was such that its possession by the NDE subject is apparently most plausibly explained as having its source in the continued existence of deceased persons.

NDEs possess one or more of several general characteristics. There is an overpowering sense of peace and well being, an impression of ineffability—as the experience possesses a richness and depth said to defy description—and a sense of timelessness, or else a feeling that time has become unimportant. The fear and anxiety often involved in dying is gone, and frequently replaced by an emotional distancing or detachment. There is an assumption that one is dead and an impression of being out of one's body (referred to as an out-of-the-body experience, or OBE), able to view it from a distance. A profound sense of reality pervades the experience and gives rise to the conviction that what transpired must be sharply distinguished from a dream or hallucination. Other phenomena reported are traveling in a tunnel, dark passageway, or black void, meeting others, becoming aware of a bright light sometimes revealing a "presence" or "being of light," viewing scenery of preternatural beauty, and reentering one's body. In a rather small proportion of cases, participation in a life review is reported.

Many NDEs are characterized by a progression or sequence of events that roughly fall into two stages. The initial stage begins rather abruptly as the person suddenly seems to find herself free of her body and of the pain and discomfort she was suffering. She is now at ease, able to view her body from a distance, usually from a viewpoint somewhat above it. She is able to observe items in the hospital room or other location at which her unconscious body happens to be. In the more remarkable cases, her apparent powers of observation enable her to observe events happening around her body: persons coming and going, their treatment of her body, the readings on instruments, etc. while her body is (behaviorally) unconscious or even clinically dead. Sometimes the view ostensibly provided by the OBE extends to regions beyond that of the unconscious body and has resulted in corroborated reports about the contents of those regions or about events occurring in them. But all of this apparent viewing is of "this-world" phenomena in the initial stage of the NDE.

The further stage is characterized by an apparent encounter with "otherworldly" phenomena. In this "transcendental" stage, there might be an apparent encounter with deceased friends and relatives, religious figures, a "being of light," a world of supernatural beauty, or a number of other phenomena suggestive of other-world encounter. This stage often begins with an impression of traveling along a dark passageway or moving through a black void, and then seeing a light at its end. Upon emerging into the light the NDE subject may encounter a "presence" or "being of light" with whom she might participate in a review of her life. Communication might be non-verbal—a direct conveyance of mental understanding—or it might take the form of a voice that she hears speak. At about this point she might become aware of being in an utterly new environment of supernal beauty and now might encounter religious figures, deceased friends and relatives, and perhaps others she cannot identify, but apparently never anyone still living at the time.

As the NDE approaches its end, there will be indications that the end is near. A boundary or barrier that must be crossed or surmounted might appear. It prevents her from going on, and leads to the awareness that if she were to continue, her journey would be irreversible and lead to death. At this point she will be informed that the experience is about to end and that she must "go back." Though the "presence" will likely appear to encourage her to decide for herself, deceased loved ones almost always inform her that it is not yet time for her to stay—that she must return. Though reluctant to return, she finds that returning is what happens. She regains consciousness in her physical body and now finds herself in the painful condition from which she was free during her NDE.

The aftereffects of the experiences usually are profound. The NDE subject often claims to have lost all fear of death. The experience remains etched in her memory and her life is often changed in the positive ways one might expect to result from a profoundly moving experience that usually leads one to reflect upon the moral quality of one's live and to reassess one's former values. One sentiment commonly expressed is a heightened appreciation of life, especially of the natural world and of other people, and a determination to live life to the fullest. There is often an increased appreciation of solitude, an emphasis on the importance of compassion, love, and generosity, and an enhancement of the capacity to accept others unconditionally. Another typical aftereffect is heightened reflectiveness, along with a desire to learn more about the implications of the NDE. In almost all cases, there is a sense of being spared for a reason, that one's life has been extended for some purpose—a sense that sometimes energizes one's life and alters its direction. The NDE subject usually emerges with a keener sense of what is important in life and a stronger desire to live in accordance with her understanding of what matters.[10]

Some qualification of my general description of the NDE is in order. I do not mean to suggest that there is some unified set of elements present in most, or perhaps even in many, of the NDEs studied. In most, only a few of these elements are present. Nor is the general sequence of events that I have described a characteristic of all NDEs. Some have argued that sequencing would appear in more NDEs if the NDEs not manifesting it had continued longer. In any case the earlier elements tend to occur more frequently, and the later less frequently. But the more important point to be made is that the elements in the general description commonly occur in NDEs, even though few individual NDEs contain many of them. Similarly, the description I have given of the sequence of events reflects a tendency rather than a form into which all can be fitted.

The frequency of occurrence of NDEs is worth mentioning, if only in passing. They apparently are more widespread than one might think. According to a 1982 Gallup survey, fifteen percent of the people responding claimed to have been near death and to have had an experience then. However, there is considerable controversy about the percentage of people who have a significant NDE when close to death and also about the kinds of NDEs that should be reflected in the percentage. Some have suggested that the great majority of patients near death simply lose consciousness and have no experience at all.[11] But some surveys place the percentage higher than Gallup's finding, viz., in a range from twenty to seventy percent.[12] Ring found a percentage in about the middle of this range. He found that forty-eight percent of his sample reported having some part of what he calls a "core NDE."[13]

There are good reasons to believe that many NDEs go unreported. There is abundant evidence that many people are reluctant to report having them for fear of ridicule or of being regarded as peculiar.[14] Also, it may be that many NDEs are not remembered. Apparently, most people fail to remember most of their dreams, and those who claim to dream rarely might be dreaming frequently but failing to remember them. Perhaps NDEs are similar in this respect. Clearly, a significant percentage of unreported NDEs would imply that the actual occurrence of these experiences is higher than the cited percentages suggest.

Though our central concern will be to evaluate the evidence that NDEs provide for the conclusion that persons survive biological death, the fact that at least hundreds of thousands of people close to death report having had an NDE is surely a relevant consideration. For it seems preposterous to maintain that all these people are simply lying or entirely deceived about the character of the experience they had. Thus such a route is closed to the skeptic: the fact that NDEs occur is undeniable.

Though NDEs do occur, they might fail to provide evidence that persons survive death. The issue of whether or not they do provide such evidence is, of course, the focus of our study of NDEs. There are two rather sharply distinguishable lines of arguments open to the skeptic who seeks to provide a plausible explanation of near-death phenomena without construing them as providing any good evidence of survival. One is the naturalistic or normal explanation. All the phenomena in question are to be explained in terms of the natural laws describing the physical and mental activity of human beings, either as these laws are presently understood or as extended by future discoveries. But any extensions are understood to be in accord with the basic conceptual framework within which the natural world is presently understood. The normal does not extend beyond the boundaries of this broad framework. The second line of argument has recourse to what we shall call "paranormal" explanations—explanations that attribute various psychic powers (viz., extrasensory, and possibly psychokinetic, powers) to some of the people having NDEs. Such powers go beyond what is normal, as previously specified. Someone taking this line of argument would provide naturalistic explanations for most of the near-death phenomena and resort to the paranormal explanation only for the remainder that cannot be plausibly explained naturalistically. We shall examine the naturalistic explanation first.

Naturalistic Explanations of NDEs

The central naturalistic argument is that NDEs are entirely subjective hallucinations having no objective significance. Because they are claimed not to refer to anything beyond the subject's own mind and its contents, they have been called *non-referential* hallucinations. Naturalistic explanations differ largely with respect to what is supposed to cause these hallucinations. The ones that seem to be most widely held would have us believe that NDEs are non-referential hallucinations brought about by physicochemical changes occurring in the brain. These changes, according to some accounts, are due to anoxia (a deficiency of oxygen) or to hypoxia (too much oxygen), according to others. Still other accounts appeal to the effect of anesthesia, hallucinogenic drugs, or temporal lobe impairment.

We might begin our critical evaluation of explanations of this kind by noting that people who have had NDEs typically insist that their experiences were *not* mere hallucinations, and that at least some of these people certainly seem capable of telling the difference. A psychotherapist with a professional's knowledge of hallucinations as well as dreams provides this report of his NDE:

> The experience I had was totally real, it was definitely not anything like a dream, nor was it like the detached feeling you get during a hallucination on LSD, where there is a dream-like quality of watching yourself, but not really being part of what is going on.[15]

Other professionals have cited other differences.[16] Both Sabom and Ring, for example, found that their respondents who reported having had both hallucinations and at least the core part of an NDE (which Ring defines as that "common set of elements" present in NDEs) could clearly distinguish between them.[17] Certainly, the testimony of so many who possess experiential knowledge of both phenomena must be accorded significant weight.

One main argument for rejecting these explanations is that most people having NDEs are not under the influence of anesthesia or drugs at the time, nor were they in states that would provide any indication that they were suffering from any of the other cited physical conditions. We should also remind ourselves of the results of the Osis and Haraldsson studies. They checked specifically for the possible effect of medicine deemed to have hallucinogenic properties and found no relationship between their presence and afterlife-related experiences. In their words, "Whatever these drugs did, *they apparently did not generate deathbed phenomena suggestive of an afterlife.*"[18] At any rate, the great majority of those who had visions (eighty percent) had had little or no drugs known to influence the mind, and, as we noted, a great many of them were considered to be clearheaded at the time of the vision. They were normally conscious to all appearances, and certainly gave no evidence of suffering from anoxia or hypoxia.

Other studies have confirmed these findings. Moody, Sabom and Ring all found that some respondents in their studies had core ND experiences without having received any anesthetics, and, in some of these cases, had received no medical treatment whatsoever. Whatever influence drugs and anesthetics have on core ND experiences, these agents are clearly not causally necessary for their occurrence. What this also implies is that even if core NDEs do at times occur when these agents are present, they cannot be causally sufficient for core NDE occurrence. And what is neither causally necessary nor sufficient for the occurrence of a phenomenon cannot be used to causally explain why that phenomenon occurs.

With respect to the cerebral anoxia hypothesis, it obviously fails in the case of the Osis and Haraldsson patients, but Moody also rejects it, citing cases of patients in his study who had core NDEs while normal flow of blood to the brain (and thus a normal oxygen supply) was maintained. Morse and Perry, too, reject it, finding that their medical records pertaining to the lack of oxygen in the blood gases revealed no more oxygen deprivation in the NDE subjects than in the control group who did not report having NDEs.[19]

But even if this hypothesis can plausibly explain some elements of some NDEs, it could provide no understanding of how someone could have in an NDE an apparent encounter with a deceased person whose (often recent) death was unknown to her. As will shall see, this inability to offer any plausible explanation of afterlife-related phenomena is a general, and apparently fatal, deficiency of all the naturalistic explanations.

In addition to suffering from the general deficiency, the cerebral hypoxia hypothesis would lead us to expect that NDE phenomena would be in general accord with the hopes, desires, and expectations of the patient. But again, this conflicts with the findings of the Osis and Haraldsson studies that revealed no significant correlation between these psychological factors and the contents of the NDEs the patients had.

The hypothesis that NDE phenomena are due to temporal lobe impairments, more specifically, seizure-like neural firing patterns, succumbs to similar difficulties. Though such neural activity might generate phenomena bearing some similarities to some core ND phenomena, there are also many differences between the two, as Sabom has pointed out.

The other main argument for rejecting this kind of explanation comes into view when we see that NDEs, including those had while behaviorally unconscious, are not essentially like the hallucinations brought about by such conditions as anoxia and hypoxia, the release of endorphins, brain malfunctions such as temporal lobe seizures, the effect of anesthetics, or the influence of hallucinogenic drugs. As Paterson aptly puts this point, "[These explanations] sound as if they were essentially directed to explaining some different kind of experience."[20] Consider the influence of endorphins. Not only are they not potent hallucinogens, but their known analgesic effects are of much longer duration than the seconds to minutes duration common to NDEs.[21] Admittedly, some of these conditions or agents can bring about phenomena bearing some resemblance to some of the elements frequently occurring in NDEs. Ether anesthesia can bring about visions of lights; and drug-induced hallucinations can produce memories and visions of lights and tunnels, as Siegel has argued.[22] But none of them bring about anything like the phenomena suggestive of an afterlife, especially visions of deceased friends and relatives. The Osis and Haraldsson study found that over eighty percent of the dying subjects who had NDEs had visions of dead relatives or friends and that eighty percent of these deceased persons expressed a take-away purpose. By contrast, in only about twenty percent of the drug-induced hallucinations did deceased persons appear, and expressions of any purpose, let alone a take-away purpose, were virtually absent. Moreover, even if significant similarities had been found in support of Siegel's position, we should not infer, as he does, that "neither is survival-oriented." As Becker has pointed out, we might draw the opposite conclusion instead.[23] It might be that what both NDE subjects and drug-hallucinators have in common—their being very close to death—is what explains their both having afterlife encounters.

We noted earlier that naturalistic theories interpret NDEs to be non-referential hallucinations; and we have just examined those in which the causes of these hallucinations are claimed to be neurophysiological changes occurring in the brain. Though theories of this kind have not been success-ful in providing a plausible explanation of NDEs, other naturalistic theories appeal to psychological factors. In these theories, the NDE is explained as a defensive psychological reaction to an awareness of the threat of death. Dif-ferent theories of this type differ in what is supposed to constitute the defen-sive reaction or in how it is manifested. Some of these theorists speak of the denial of death as the psychological factor motivating the NDE,[24] and oth-ers as a basic dread of catastrophe.[25] The NDE is commonly referred to as a "defensive fantasy" motivated by a desire to survive death, usually supple-mented by a system of beliefs that largely supply the content of the fantasy.

In some of these theories, the defensive reaction is more extreme, result-ing in the experience of depersonalization, characterized by a loss or blur-ring of one's sense of identity and of one's reality as an individual self. A psychological detachment from one's body is part of this phenomenon. Noyes may be the most notable expounder of this view.[26] Other theories appeal to mental illnesses such as schizophrenia[27] and others that tend to generate hal-lucinations.

Perhaps the first question we should raise about psychological theories is whether they introduce any genuinely new considerations, i.e., any causative factors that are not ultimately reducible to and expressible in purely neurophysiological terms. Although we have seen virtually conclusive rea-sons for accepting a mental-physical dualism, many, if not most, of the pro-ponents of psychological theories have materialist orientations that would pose problems for them however the reducibility issue gets settled, if it ever does. For if (in a completed science) the referents of psychological terms turn out to be nothing but complexes of referents of neurophysiological terms, then psychological theories do not provide accounts distinct from neurophysiological ones. If the reducibility issue gets settled in the other direction, then thoroughgoing materialist theories could not be sustained. But we can leave this problem after simply noting it, as it does not arise for the mental-physical dualist.

It might already be clear from our earlier observations that psycholog-ical theories do not fare well at all. A very serious, if not fatal, difficulty for all of them arises from the fact that some ND subjects were apparently unaware of the life-threatening condition they were in until after the NDE had begun or even, in some cases, after it ended.[28] Some did not fear death prior to their NDEs—another fact difficult to reconcile with the view that NDEs are defense mechanisms. In addition, each psychological theory suggests or implies that NDEs have a character very different from what they actually have. As we noted earlier, the Osis and Haraldsson studies have shown that NDEs are often in radical conflict with the desires, beliefs and expectations of the people who have them. More generally, no significant correlation between them was found. The cross-cultured studies revealed remarkable uniformity in core ND experience, despite vast differences in religious and cultural background.

The depersonalization theory does not fit the data any better. In this theory, in which the NDE is theorized to be an ego-defense mechanism, depersonalization is manifested in a feeling or sense that one is not an individual person. There is a crumbling or loss of the ordinarily sharp distinction between oneself and the rest of the world. But the typical NDE, in contrast, is characterized by a feeling of total reality of self.

Osis and Haraldsson found that NDEs suggestive of an afterlife tended to be of relatively short duration and quite clear-cut in contrast to those involving this-world phenomena. Thus this finding indicates that at least those NDEs involving afterlife-related phenomena are quite different from the hallucinations of schizophrenic patients, which tend to be long and drawn out. Further, the ND visions though ephemeral, tend to be in full color, in contrast to the monochrome display frequently characterizing the schizophrenic's hallucination."[29] It is equally important to note that though hallucinations are typically had by people with a history of hallucinations, very few of the NDE subjects had such histories.

Many NDEs are reported to have occurred when the state of clinical death of the patient was such that no consciousness whatsoever should have existed if any naturalistic theory implying that consciousness depends upon a properly functioning brain were true—an apparently universal implication of the naturalistic theories. There are reports of NDEs having occurred during periods when heartbeat was absent, periods extending forty-five minutes or more in some cases. Patients reported watching their inert bodies from a distance and provided detailed recollections of what had transpired during these periods, recollections that were corroborated by those attending to the body.[30]

Perhaps even more difficult for the naturalistic theories to accommodate are reputable reports of NDEs occurring while all measurable electrical activity in the cerebral cortex has ceased. Although cortical activity is usually not monitored while medical efforts are directed at saving the life of the patient, there are cases in which, for one reason or another, EEG activity is being measured at the time. The cardiologist, Fred Schoonmaker, is reported to have found, in a study of 1400 near-death experiences gathered over an eighteen-year period, fifty-five cases of patients who had NDEs while displaying a flat EEG reading, sometimes for periods as long as three hours. Some reportedly had vivid memories of events that had transpired while their EEGs were flat.[31] Similar reports are provided by the Dutch cardiologist, Pim van Lommel, who created quite a stir when he published, in 2001, his study of near-death experiences in *The Lancet*, a leading journal of medical research.[32] He too reports finding that patients were often able to describe precisely events that happened during cardiac arrest and absence of detectable electrical activity in the cortex. In responding to the charge that some brain function is still occurring, he writes:

> When the heart stops beating, blood flow stops within a second. Then, 6.5 seconds later, EEG activity starts to change due to the shortage of oxygen. After fifteen seconds there is a straight, flat line and the electrical activity in the cerebral cortex has disappeared completely. We cannot measure the brain stem, but testing on animals has demonstrated that activity has ceased there as well. Moreover, you can prove that the brain stem is no longer functioning because it regulates our basic reflexes, such as the pupil response and swallowing reflex, which no longer respond.[33]

The truth of what these reports assert or imply would show that consciousness can continue to exist in the absence of a properly functioning brain and thus would be fatal to all the naturalistic accounts. Given that the data are as reported, the defender of the naturalist account has two options: (1) to show (or provide good reason to believe) that the NDE did not occur at the very time that no detectable cortical activity was occurring, or (2) to show that at the time of the NDE there was undetected brain activity occurring sufficient to generate the experience. But the prospects for success in pursuing either option seem dim. Accounting for the subject's corroborated reports of events occurring while detectable brain activity was absent would require the defender to claim that the NDE actually took place while the subject was being resuscitated and brain activity was being restored.[34] But since the corroborated reports are of events occurring prior to the time of resuscitation, an explanation appealing to the paranormal (viz., precognitive or retrocognitive) powers of the subject would seem to be required, i.e., a nonnatural or *paranormal* explanation.

The other option may seem more promising. The defender of a naturalist explanation could argue that no detectable brain activity does not imply no brain activity at all. Perhaps very low-level brain activity was occurring. Though this possibility cannot be excluded, we must wonder how plausible it is to claim that such activity is of the right kind and quantity sufficient to generate the high-level, full-blown experience that an NDE usually is. But even if one were to maintain that very low brain activity might be responsible for such high-level experience, another formidable difficulty would remain. As we shall see, there are credible reports of NDE subjects reporting distant events whose occurrence was independently verified by others, even though these subjects were displaying flat EEGs at the time. They also reported other information that would not have been accessible to their senses even if they had been normally conscious. A plausible naturalistic explanation of this too would be needed. Given that reports of such NDEs can be substantiated by further research and that the view in which the subject is doing nothing more than exercising paranormal psychic powers proves to be untenable, we would here have compelling evidence that the conscious self can function, for at least short periods of time, independently of its brain. At the very least, the burden of proof must be borne by the defender of such a claim.

Our examination of naturalistic theories, though certainly not exhaustive, seems adequate for the basis of a fair assessment of them. Perhaps the most charitable assessment of them is that research to date has shown the truth of any to be unlikely. If we put aside certain general considerations that, as we have noted, seem to weigh heavily against all of them, then we can acknowledge that some offer a plausible account of some NDE phenomena. But that, clearly, is not sufficient. In the words of Ring in summing up his own assessment, "A neurological interpretation, to be acceptable, should be able to provide a *comprehensive* explanation of *all* the various aspects of the core experience."[35] None has come close to doing that. Nor has any psychological theory. Indeed, such theories seem even less likely to achieve such a goal.

Paranormal Theories: ESP and Super-ESP

To appreciate the motivation to abandon naturalistic explanations and turn to a paranormal one, let us look more carefully at the NDE phenomenon that is the most difficult one for these theories to explain—a phenomenon that might well lead someone to abandon all such theories, perhaps even without much knowledge of their other difficulties. This phenomenon, present in some NDEs, results in the acquisition of information by the NDE subject that she apparently could not have acquired by any normal method.

Some of these involve apparent encounters with deceased relatives, but most are reports of surgical and resuscitation procedures carried out along with other events occurring around the patient's body while it was giving no signs of any consciousness. Though most of these reports are rather vague, they are virtually free of error. And some are remarkably precise and detailed, apparently revealing a clear and accurate recollection of events taking place in the patient's room, some of which could not have been accessible to their senses even if they had been normally conscious. They sometimes provide an amazing amount of detail, subsequently found to be accurate, about such facts and events as the people who entered and left the room, some of whom they had never seen before, how they were dressed, what they brought with them, precise observations of the instruments used along with readings on their dials, what was said and done, the window and door locations and general layout of the room, and features of the floor, ceiling, and curtains, often from a viewpoint above the body. Sometimes they provide such descriptions of relatives who arrived unexpectedly and were anxiously waiting in a different location in the hospital complex.

Some NDE subjects have accurately described in great detail events transpiring far from the location of the comatose body. In one remarkable case, a young girl, Katie, had nearly drowned in a pool. A CT scan revealed massive swelling in her brain, and an artificial lung machine was needed to keep her breathing. Her chances of survival were thought to be very low. But after being in a profoundly comatose state for three days, she recovered completely and told an astonishing story. In addition to providing details about the various hospital rooms she was taken into, the people attending to her, and the medical procedures they carried out, she spoke of being able to "wander" through her family home (while comatose in the hospital), going on to report in minute detail such matter as the toys her brother and sister were playing with, meals her mother prepared, and her father's reaction to the crisis situation. She provided detailed descriptions of the clothing they were wearing and their positions in the house, mentioning that one of her brothers was pushing around a GI Joe toy in a jeep and that one of her sisters was combing the hair of a Barbie doll while singing a popular rock and roll song. When Katie's doctor, in checking out the accuracy of all her reports, relayed her story to her family members, they were quite shocked at the accuracy and detail of her apparent observations of them while lying comatose in the hospital.[36] Other equally impressive cases similar to this one could be cited.

Another striking case of an NDE subject revealing highly detailed knowledge she apparently could not have acquired in any normal way was reported by Kimberley Clark, a professor at the University of Washington's School of Medicine and critical care social worker at the Harborview Medical Center in Seattle. A migrant worker, Maria, a victim of a severe heart attack which later resulted in cardiac arrest, had a NDE in which, among other observations, she seemed to be looking down from the ceiling at the doctors and nurses trying to resuscitate her—something they accomplished rather quickly. When Clark came to interview her on the very day of her reported NDE, she was anxious to tell her story of "the strangest thing" that had happened to her. Though her detailed description of what the doctors and nurses were doing and wearing were later corroborated, Clark was not greatly impressed by them, judging that Maria could have constructed her story out of information acquired earlier in a normal way since she had had the opportunity to observe much about the hospital before her cardiac arrest. What did pique Clark's interest was Maria's further account of how her attention was distracted away from the resuscitation activities to an object on the third-floor ledge around the corner of the hospital building she had entered and presently occupied—a building she had never been in before. After having "thought her way" up there, she was able to get a very close "look" at the object which turned out to be a very large blue tennis shoe. She reported that the shoe had a worn region in the little toe area and that the lace was stuck under the heel. At Maria's request to have the shoe found and thereby validate her NDE, Clark begins to search for it. Finding it proved to be no easy task. It could not be seen from outside the building by looking up, nor was there any nearby building high enough to provide a view of it. Moreover, the third floor window of the patient rooms were so narrow that even after squeezing her face to the screen, Clark could barely see the ledge, let alone a shoe on it. However, she finally found a room from which, by pressing her face against the glass, she was able to see the shoe below her but not the details that Maria had reported. She found no perspective from which she could see them. In her words, "The only way she [Maria] would have had such a perspective was if she had been floating right outside and at very close range to the tennis shoe."[37] When Clark was later able to retrieve the shoe, she found it to be just as Maria had described it. Before actually showing it to Maria, she held it behind her until Maria described it one more time.

NDEs had by the blind constitute another kind of case equally difficult for naturalistic explanations to accommodate. Kübler-Ross reports cases of people who, though having been blind for years, were nevertheless able to describe accurately the colors of the clothing and jewelry of the people present during their NDEs. Testing after the experiences verified that they were still blind.[38] Many such cases of the blind having NDEs enabling them to describe visual details of their surroundings have been reported.

In view of the accumulation of credible reports of such cases in which the percipient acquires information that cannot be explained by appeal to brain capabilities, at least as presently understood, many with extensive knowledge of NDEs have been led to embrace a paranormal explanation of them. Of this group, some contend that the most plausible explanation of these cases is provided by the ESP hypothesis (which, as we shall see, must amount to a super–ESP hypothesis).[39] According to this hypothesis, all of the knowledge acquired in such cases was paranormally acquired by means of ESP on the part of the living. We need not resort to the survival hypothesis to arrive at the most plausible explanation of it.

Given our previous findings that the self is logically distinct from (though possibly causally dependent on) the body, we must interpret the ESP hypothesis as denying the existence of any good evidence that the self survives biological death. Still, it implies that the self has psychic powers (i.e., ESP and probably psychokinesis as well) that are brain-independent, even if the self's existence is not. One might wonder about the credibility of claiming that it has these brain-independent powers even though it presumably is causally dependent upon its brain and body in all other respects.

But the serious problems for the ESP hypothesis lie elsewhere. First, an OBE is not like ESP as ordinarily understood. A person having OBE, whether part of an NDE or not, seems to herself to be out of her body, viewing her surroundings from a viewpoint outside her body and sometimes far from it. The subject's body is perceived as though it is the body of someone else. This feeling is not characteristic of the clairvoyance postulated by the ESP hypothesis. Besides this feeling, it is typical of OBEs having veridical content that the subject could not have acquired in normal ways that she describes her surroundings as they would appear only from the viewpoint of an elevated position above the body. This is not typical of clairvoyance. In addition, the OBEs typically display a perceptual clarity and accuracy that greatly surpasses what has been verified in any non–OBE case of clairvoyant apprehension. Of course, the OBE subject is also having perceptual experience that is "extrasensory" in that it is not brought about by stimulation of the sense organs. But unlike clairvoyance, the OBE has a perceptual character supporting the claim that the OBE subject actually has separated temporarily from her body and is having perceptual experience causally independent of it.

Secondly, there are many cases of verified effects brought about by the OBE subject in the place where he experiences himself to be during the OBE— effects that are indicative of his presence there at the time. Perhaps the cases most indicative of the OBE subject's presence are the "reciprocal" ones, that is, those in which these effects include an apparition of the OBE subject. Clearly, an apparition of the OBE subject viewed by others at the place where that subject seems to himself to be while the OBE is occurring would be persuasive evidence of the subject's presence there. Apparently, such cases are not extremely rare. In 1954, Hornell Hart published a study of OBEs yielding knowledge that the subject could not have acquired in any normal way. Of the 288 published cases he found in the literature, he determined that 99 were evidential in that the paranormally acquired knowledge was reported in detail by the subject prior to learning of its truthfulness. And at least 55 of the 99 evidential cases were reciprocal.[40]

More recently, carefully designed experiments have been carried out on subjects who could induce OBEs voluntarily. They have resulted in OBEs during which verified physical effects occurred at the place where the subject seemed to himself to be, or was tying to reach, while his physical body at some distant location was being observed throughout the experience. As we shall see, such an OBE seems very difficult, if not impossible, to explain plausibly without granting that the subject separates from the body and enters into a causal relationship with a physical object other than its brain. Perhaps the most remarkable of the fairly recent experiments designed to test whether the subject (or at least something) leaves the body during an OBE was the Osis-McCormick investigation with Alex Tanous as subject.[41] Tanous was instructed to visit a designated target area while he was in a voluntarily induced OBE. The target area was a shielded enclosure equipped with strain-gauge sensors placed in front of a viewing window of a visual image device that would display visual targets. Tanous' task was to identify the randomly selected target that would appear in the image device. He was unaware of the presence of the strain-gauge in the target area and was not asked to try to move anything.

Any physical effects on the strain-gauge sensors were registered on a Beckman polygraph. Blind measurements of effects were made immediately before and immediately after target generation in the case of each trial. The experiment consisted of 197 trials carried out over twenty sessions. It resulted in 114 hits and 83 misses, a remarkable success ratio. But of particular interest to us in this context are the effects on the strain-gauge sensors. During those periods when Tanous was trying to identify the target (i.e., the period immediately following target generation), the strain-gauge activation level was *significantly* higher for the trials resulting in hits than for those yielding misses. It was also significantly higher then than during the periods when the blind measurements were taken.

These results seem to provide strong support for the hypothesis that the strain-gauge sensors were activated by the presence of the subject in the target area when the hits occurred. The alternative paranormal hypothesis is that the subject does not separate from the body but rather identifies the target clairvoyantly and affects the strain-gauge sensors psychokinetically. This is a great stretch, however, as psychokinetic effects apparently are always intentional. As Almeder points out, there is an intentional component in all known or alleged cases of psychokinesis. In his words, "People do not produce effects consistent with action at a distance (or general PK) unless they have a deliberate intention to do so."[42] As we noted, Tanous was unaware of the presence of the strain-gauge and thus could not have had any (conscious) intention to affect it. Perhaps someone determined to defend the ESP hypothesis, without much regard for credibility, would argue that knowledge of the presence of the strain-gauge was acquired clairvoyantly and then employed psychokinetically to carry out an "unconscious intention" to influence the gauge. But this would be to resort to a super–ESP hypothesis of a particularly extravagant form.

The third, and apparently most serious, difficulty for the ESP hypothesis is its tendency, when extended to accommodate problematic cases, to become a highly implausible super–ESP hypothesis, postulating far more extensive psychic capacities than are independently evidenced to exist. As we shall see, paranormal experiences other than NDEs stretch the ESP hypothesis to include what is in effect an appeal to super–ESP. But we will now examine how some NDEs do this.

First, we might note that although many of the NDE cases involving detailed corroborated reports (e.g., of people, procedures, and instruments involved in the resuscitation effort) might be plausibly explained as due to "ordinary" ESP (mainly telepathy and, to some extent, clairvoyance), others are not as tractable. In the more tractable cases, the paranormally acquired knowledge was about the immediate surroundings of the unconscious body. But in the other cases (e.g., the Katie case and the case of Maria), a good deal more telepathy and clairvoyance would have been required. Moreover, even in the more tractable case, the ESP hypothesis does not explain why the NDE subject's body and other items in the room should be viewed from a point near the ceiling.

Even more difficult to explain on the assumption that the subject remains dependent on its brain while exercising ESP is how NDE subjects could report *anything* about what transpired when their cerebral hemispheres, at least, apparently were not functioning (as revealed by a flat EEG reading), let alone the detailed corroborated reports that allegedly have been gathered. Though the existence of such cases is controversial, the evidence seems to weigh on the side of their actually having occurred.

Perhaps the NDEs presenting the greatest difficulty for the ESP hypothesis are those in which the NDE subject encounters among the apparitions of the dead a recently deceased person whose death was unknown to him. The case of Cory, a seven-year-old boy dying of leukemia, is a good example. He had numerous visions during the dying period, many of which included visits to the "crystal castle" where he would encounter recently deceased persons. On one occasion, he mentioned to his mother that an old high school boyfriend of hers who had been crippled in an automobile accident had approached him. He told Cory about the accident and how he had spent many unhappy years unable to walk. He wanted to let Cory's mother know that he was now in the crystal castle and able to walk. Cory's mother had not seen this man in many years and had never mentioned him to Cory. After telephone calls to friends, Cory's mother learned that this man did indeed die on the same day that Cory had the vision of encountering him.

On another occasion, Cory told his mother of a vision of encountering in the "crystal castle" one of his best friends at the hospital. She thought that the death of that person was highly unlikely, as they had seen him only a week before. But when they returned to the hospital for more chemotherapy the next day, they learned that this friend had died unexpectedly the previous night.[43]

Kübler-Ross cites many such cases drawn from her extensive studies of dying children. One especially interesting case begins with a fiery automobile accident in which the mother of two boys was killed and the two critically injured boys were taken to different hospitals, probably because Peter, the older brother, required the special care of a burn treatment facility. It is highly unlikely that either son was told of the death of their mother, as a severely injured child is rarely given such information. Kübler-Ross mentions that before children die there is often a very clear moment when, after great pain and discomfort, they are very coherent, quiet, and at peace. She found the younger boy in such a state, explaining to her with the words, "Yes, everything is all right now. Mommy and Peter are already waiting for me." With a contented little smile he then slipped off into a coma and died. Though she had then planned to visit Peter, when she passed by the nursing station a call arrived from the other hospital to inform her that Peter had died a few minutes earlier.[44]

Kübler-Ross reports another case in which a child who nearly died during very critical heart surgery had an NDE in which she met a brother with whom she felt so comfortable that it was if they had spent their lives together and knew each other well. Yet no brother existed during her lifetime and she had never heard of one. Her father, however, was so moved by her account that he was led to confess to the existence of a brother who had died before she was born.[45]

Kübler-Ross sums up her experiences with dying children in the following passage.

> In all the years I have quietly collected data from California to Sydney, Australia; from white and black children, aboriginals, Eskimos, South Americans, and Libyan youngsters, every single child who mentioned that someone was waiting for them mentioned a person who had actually pre-

ceded them in death, even if by only a few moments. And yet none of these children had been informed of the recent death of the relatives by us at any time.[46]

Given that these reports and others like them provide an accurate description of what happened (and that, as it seems, an appeal to the possibility of coincidence as a general hypothesis is implausible), one attempting to explain such cases without conceding that they provide significant evidence for survival would have little choice but to succumb to the pressure to embrace a super–ESP hypothesis. The NDE subjects presumably would be unconsciously employing telepathically acquired information about the recently deceased to construct a life-like and utterly captivating apparition of the deceased person appearing to approach and sometimes communicate with them—subjects who have exhibited no paranormal powers prior to their NDEs. Their telepathic powers must be sufficient to give them access not only to the people who were aware of the recent deaths of relatives but also to those aware of the recent deaths of acquaintances and even total strangers (as in the case of Cory). The addition of clairvoyance to the explanation obviously would not diminish the amount of ESP needed.

Numerous other obstacles stand in the way of accepting the ESP hypothesis. It must account for the feeling, often amounting to a conviction, of NDE subjects that they are out of their bodies. In addition, it must plausibly account for the related fact, typical of OBEs having veridical contents whose acquisition was impossible by normal methods, that these subjects describe the environment as it would appear from the viewpoint of an elevated position above the body—a fact not at all typical of clairvoyance. One must wonder whether the ESP hypothesis, however expanded or otherwise altered, can offer a plausible explanation of such facts.

What must also be plausibly explained is the apparent evidence that the subject separates from the body during at least some OBEs. As we noted, one line of evidence consists of reciprocal apparitions, i.e., cases in which the apparition of the person having the OBE was viewed by others in the place at which the person seemed to herself to be at the time. This constitutes at least *prima facie* evidence that the person (or subject) was indeed there (i.e., having perceptual experience of the environment at that place) rather than exercising ESP from the location of the body. Another line of such evidence is provided by experiments in which unintended physical effects were detected at the place where the OBE subject experienced himself to be at the time of the experience. As we noted, the production of such effects via ESP exercised from the location of the body would require super–ESP.

There are other features typical of ND OBEs that fall into place in the view that the subject then separates from the body and in this sense are supportive of that view. The altered sense of time, sometimes expressed as a sense of timelessness, would be explained by the fact that the NDE subject, now separated from the body, would not be receiving the constant though subliminal stimulation from the various bodily processes that, in effect, serve to mark the passage of time. The feeling of being out of one's body would be explained by simply acknowledging that that is indeed what has happened. The absence of pain and physical discomfort would be explained by the fact that the nerve impulses arising from various parts of the body which, when received by the brain, result in the experience of pain no longer do so because the subject who would have experienced the pain is now separated from the brain and thus causally detached from it. Clearly, the disappearance of pain is a puzzle in the view that ESP is employed by the embodied subject. Why should the use of ESP make any difference if the subject remains embodied?

Two further points are relevant in this context. Despite the great variety of circumstances under which ND OBEs occur, the reports are essential similar. Such factors as race, culture, gender, age, religious belief, and type of life-threatening circumstance seem to make no relevant difference. This fact would be plausibly explained if they were reporting what actually happened—their having separated from their bodies and experiencing the effects. But since an embodied subject employing ESP would not be reporting what actually happened, accounting for the essential similarity of the reports despite great variability in the circumstances under which they are produced would be much more difficult. Second, the view that ND OBE subjects were reporting what actually happened when they experienced an apparition of a deceased relative or friend whose recent death was unknown to them provides the most plausible explanation of the emotional tone of these NDEs. The mood elevation of these NDEs is well illustrated by the previously cited case of the dying boy who, after seeing his mother and older brother, Peter, waiting for him, became very quiet, contented, and died peacefully. The ESP hypothesis is ill equipped to account for this. If the NDE subject's awareness of the recent death of a loved one was the result of telepathy from the living, one would expect a negative emotional response, certainly not the conviction that the deceased person is doing very well and the desire to go with that person.

The formidable difficulties confronting the ESP hypothesis that the embodied subject uses ESP to acquire the paranormal knowledge manifested in some NDEs should now seem clear. Not only are there cases of OBEs or ND OBEs that apparently force the ESP hypothesis to become an implausible super–ESP hypothesis, but certain features of others indicate that this hypothesis is simply the wrong kind of explanatory theory. If this hypothesis were adequate, it could serve to explain those cases in which all naturalistic theories fail and thus could serve in conjunction with those theories where they are adequate to eliminate the need to appeal to the survival hypothesis. As the matter stands however, the survival hypothesis remains plausible. But is the evidence supporting it sufficient to justify rational belief that it is true? Probably not, if we consider only the evidence provided by OBEs and ND OBEs—the evidence we are now weighing. Extraordinary beliefs require extraordinary evidence. The antecedent improbability of survival may seem too high, even given our earlier conclusion that the self or subject is metaphysically distinct from the brain and its activity. For the improbability in question (the improbability prior to an examination of apparently countervailing cases) is an estimation grounded in our awareness that we are deeply embodied and completed embedded in nature. An awareness that we are creatures of nature in conjunction with a wealth of detailed information about the ways in which our conscious states are causally dependent upon proper brain function might well lead us to find quite improbable, at least initially, the claim that the existence of the self is *causally* independent of its brain. Still, there is other evidence beyond what NDEs provide that might tip the evidence scale in favor of the survival hypothesis— evidence to which we will soon turn.

Before leaving this section, one further implication of our examination should be noted. As we saw earlier in examining the depersonalization theory, the typical NDE subject has a feeling of the total reality of self—a very strong sense of self surpassing that of her normal conscious state. She also retains her private memories, e.g., those enabling her to recognize and, in some cases, converse with deceased relatives. That such is the case despite the apparent absence of her functioning physical body is supportive of the dualist view of persons we arrived at earlier. In particular, it is in complete agreement with, if not a validation of, our conclusion that the essence of a person is the experiencing subject, or subject of experience, that happens to be embodied in a human organism.

The very strong sense of self typical of the NDE subject is significant in another respect. Not only does it fly in the face of depersonalization theories generally, but, more specifically, contradicts those materialist, reductionist views of the self, according to which the self is an illusion and is revealed to be such in the NDE. Perhaps the most widely known of those espousing this reductionist view is Susan Blackmore who attributes many of the features of NDEs to the breakdown of the self-illusion. In her words, "The brain can no longer sustain that usual illusion of self. It has begun to break down."[47] This breakdown results in "the real loss of the fear of death"[48] and a transformation constituted by "a completely new vigor for life: energy, openness, simplicity, joyousness and even compassion."[49] The "breakdown of time"[50] in the NDE is similarly explained. But such effects and such features typical of NDEs cannot be explained in this way, given the conviction of the evident reality of self. Rather, this conviction indicates that the continuance of an experiencing subject is central to personal identity and thus supports the view of the self that we arrived at earlier.

Apparitions

Although we have already referred to apparitions in our consideration of NDEs, we shall see that some apparitions unrelated to such experiences apparently constitute significant additional evidence supporting the survival hypothesis. We shall consider apparitions of the living as well as of the dying or recently dead, noting the features they share and evaluating views of how they should be understood. Though our focus will be on apparitions of the dead, we cannot properly assess their significance independently of some consideration of apparitions in general. We shall give special prominence to certain well-documented cases of apparitions of the dead that seem most plausibly interpreted as revealing the continuing existence of deceased persons.

Many of the important studies of apparitions were carried out around the beginning of the twentieth century, largely by members of the newly formed Society for Psychical Research (SPR). The important, "Report on the Census of Hallucinations," appeared in 1894.[1] Its primary purpose was to show that most of the apparitions of the dead appearing around the time of death of the person whose apparition appeared could not plausibly be explained in terms of chance coincidence. Then, less than ten years later, Frederick Myers' monumental work, *Human Personality and Its Survival of Bodily Death*,[2] appeared. After the extensive investigations conducted during that period, it was generally believed that little more would be gained from further work. Subsequently, comparatively little more empirical data about apparitions have been gathered, as psychical researchers have tended to focus their attention on other kinds of evidence of survival such as near-death phenomena. Accordingly, we cannot ignore these early studies in our own investigations. Though old, these studies were thorough, and high critical standards were maintained in assessing their significance as evidence for life after death.

The features of apparitions make difficult any attempt to arrive at an adequate understanding of their nature. Many features typical of them strongly suggest a psychological interpretation in which the apparition is a

129

mental or, more precisely, a mind-dependent phenomenon. Those extreme objectivist views in which each person has a quasi-physical (or "astral") body that sometimes appears as an apparition when it separates (either temporarily or permanently) from the physical body (with which it is normally congruent) is rendered highly implausible by the fact that apparitions almost always appear as wearing clothing and sometimes in possession of such paraphernalia as hats, canes, books and jewelry. For virtually no one believes that such mundane physical things possess astral bodies. Instead, they would be interpreted as mind-dependent images contributed by either the apparent (i.e., the person whose apparition is appearing) or the perceiver. But if so, consistency should lead one to draw the same conclusion about the human forms that appear.

Many other features of apparitions indicate that they are not physical objects, at least as such objects are commonly understood. Many normal perceivers in a position to perceive physical objects where apparitions are supposed to be cannot sense their presence. They tend to appear and disappear within closed rooms with locked doors, appearing in many cases to pass through solid objects. Unlike physical objects, they sometimes appear to be partially or totally transparent. Even when appearing to be opaque for some time, they may have gradually become visible and may later fade out of existence while being watched. Hands or entire human bodies may pass through them without resistance. They rarely cast shadows and leave behind no physical traces.

Yet they typically have an objectivity resembling that of physical objects. Though, as we noted, they are usually not visible to everyone in a position to see them, they are sometimes intersubjectively visible in that a number of different people can view them simultaneously from their different perspectives. In some cases, even animals seem to perceive them. They appear as occupying physical space and, like physical objects, they obey the laws of perspective: Not only are different perspectives on them available to different perceivers at different locations, but their movement provides new views of them to a perceiver. They disappear from view when one shuts or averts one's eyes, like a physical object in one's visual field, and are often still visible when one looks again. Sometimes they are reflected in mirrors, and, in at least one documented case, an apparition was correctly perceived in a mirror while another perceiver saw it directly.[3] They may appear as incontestably real as any physical object clearly before one's eyes (even though they may later vanish abruptly).

The question of how the apparent objectivity (or, perhaps, intersubjectivity) of some apparitions is to be reconciled with their nonphysical features is one we shall postpone until our examination of various theories about what apparitions should be taken to be. Let us now take note of other facts about these remarkable occurrences that are relevant to our understanding of them and to the support they provides for the survival hypothesis. They occur with a frequency that might seem surprising. Most surveys reveal that about 10 percent of the population report having perceived an apparition at some time in their lives. Most of these apparitions were unrecognized, however. But studies of *recognized* apparitions have indicated that a large proportion of them are identified by the perceivers as apparitions of deceased persons. Green and McCreery found in their survey that "about two-thirds of all recognized apparitions reported to us were of people or animals whom the subject knew to be dead."[4]

The proportion of death-related apparitions seems even more significant when apparitions of the dying are brought into consideration. The early SPR study already mentioned—the "Report on the Census of Hallucinations"— was an attempt to determine whether the frequency of apparitions of the dying could plausibly be attributed to chance. An apparition of a person had to occur within twenty-four hours of the death of that person to be counted as an apparition of the dying. Given this definition of an apparition of the dying, the authors found that such apparitions were occurring far more (about 440 times more) frequently than what the hypothesis of chance coincidence would lead us to predict. Moreover, this number might have been considerably larger if certain other factors had been taken into account, one of which is that the time period surrounding death could have been made much smaller without having to exclude many of the cases that were counted, as there were more clustering around the actual time of death than what the twenty-four hour period would indicate. Indeed, the "Census" revealed that most (over 60 percent) of such apparitions are seen within an hour of death— a finding confirmed by subsequent studies.[5]

Many apparitions, of course, are of people still living—a fact that may seem to diminish considerably any support that apparitions of the dead would otherwise provide for the survival hypothesis. For it may seem that if the living are responsible (perhaps by unconscious employment of latent psychic powers) for some apparitions that provide the percipient with veridical information that could have been acquired only by paranormal means, they are likely responsible for all. Though we will address this concern more fully in our examination of the super-psi theory, what we should note at this juncture is that the timing of apparitions of the living is importantly different from that of apparitions of the dead, thus indicating that these different kinds of apparitions have different causes. As we noted previously, most of the apparitions of the dead and dying corresponded closely in time (within one hour) to the confirmed deaths of the apparents at locations other than where the apparitions were seen. But the event that corresponded closely in time to the perceiving of an apparition of a *living* person was that person's dreaming or thinking of being at the location where his apparition was seen and doing what his apparition was seen as doing. In some cases, the living person was at the time "mentally trying" to be, or to be perceived, at the location where his apparition was then perceived. These remarkable and uniformly different sets of close temporal coincidences were revealed by the "Census" and supported by later studies.

It is tempting to suppose that these temporal coincidences are best explained as manifestations of underlying *causal* relations. More specifically, the supposition is that an apparition of a living person perceived to be at some distant place at a certain time is caused by that person's vividly dreaming or thinking intensively of being there at that time. Similarly, the apparition of a dying or recently deceased person perceived at some place distant from the dying or recently deceased person's body is caused by conscious states of that person occurring somewhat before, at, or somewhat after her death.

Reciprocal Apparitions

This supposition, at least with respect to apparitions of the living, gains support from cases of reciprocal apparitions—cases in which (as we noted earlier) the perceiver of the apparition and the apparent (the person whose apparition is perceived) seem to be aware of each other. In these cases, the apparent is living and, of course, not physically present where her apparition is perceived. A famous and well-documented case of a reciprocal apparition that was also collective (i.e., an apparition viewed by more than one person) occurred in 1863.[6] It involved three persons, Mr. and Mrs. S.R. Wilmot and Mr. Wilmot's friend, W.J. Tait. The two men were sharing a stateroom on a ship on its way to America from Europe. The weather had been bad and one ship had been reported lost. Mrs. Wilmot, who was in America and who had become very concerned about the safety of her husband, found herself lying awake on a certain Tuesday morning thinking about her husband until about 4:00 AM when she seemed to herself to go looking for him. She seemed to herself to be traveling across the Atlantic until she came to a low black steamship. She went up its side and traveled through its cabin until she came to her husband's stateroom. Upon reaching it she hesitated to enter, as she saw a man in the berth above her husband's looking intently at her. But soon she entered anyway, went up to the side of her sleeping husband's berth, kissed and embraced him, and then left.

On that Tuesday morning, both Tait and Wilmot experienced the apparition, though Wilmot's experience was by way of a veridical dream of his wife's presence. On Monday night, after a week of bad weather, he was finally able to get a good night's sleep during which, towards morning, he had a dream in which he saw his wife in her night-dress come to his stateroom. In his words, "At the door she seemed to discover that I was not the only occupant of the room, hesitated a little, then advanced to my side, stooped down and kissed me and after gently caressing me for a few moments, quietly withdrew." When he awoke, Tait said, "You're a pretty fellow, to have a lady come and visit you in this way." Upon asking Tait what he meant, Tait described what he saw while awake—a description that agreed with Wilmot's dream. When Wilmot arrived at his home, his wife asked, "Did you receive a visit from me a week ago Tuesday?" She went on to explain how she seemed to herself to have traveled until finding the ship, the cabin, and the stateroom, and to have done the things the two men seemed to see her do. She gave an accurate description of the stateroom and the peculiar manner in which berths were arranged, with the upper extending further back than the lower one.

A description of a more recent reciprocal case was sent to the American Society for Psychical Research (ASPR) by a Miss "Martha Johnson" in May of 1957. She was at the time a young woman of 26 residing in Plains, IL. She described a dream she had early in the morning of January 27, 1957, in which she experienced traveling to the home of her mother in northern Minnesota, 926 miles away. After describing her experience of traveling through "a great blackness" she spotted "a small bright oasis of light" that she knew to be her mother's small house. In her words,

> After I entered, I leaned up against the dish cupboard with folded arms, a pose I often assume. I looked at my Mother who was bending over something white and doing something with her hands. She did not appear to see me at first, but she finally looked up. I had a sort of pleased feeling and then after standing a second more, I turned and walked about four steps.

She awoke from her dream at 2:10 AM, which was 1:10 AM Minnesota time.

Her mother gave her account of her own experience that morning in two letters to her daughter. The following are extracts from that account.

> I believe it was Saturday night, 1:10, 26th of January, or maybe the 27th. It would have been ten minutes after two, your time. I was pressing a blouse here in the kitchen ... I looked up and there you were by the cupboard just standing smiling at me. I started to speak and you were gone. I forgot for a moment where I was. I think the dogs saw you too. They got so excited and wanted out—just like they thought you were by the door—sniffed and were so tickled. Your hair was combed nice—just back in a ponytail with the pretty roll in front. Your blouse was neat and light—seemed almost white.[7]

Martha Johnson later confirmed that she had indeed "traveled" fixed up in this way, with hairstyle and clothing as her mother had described. It seems difficult to avoid the conclusion that, at the very least, a paranormal transfer of visual information occurred in these remarkable apparitions. But do they have significance for the survival issue? In our earlier investigation of OBEs involved in NDEs, we noted that OBEs were involved in reciprocal apparitions. Let us now examine that relationship a bit more closely. An OBE occurs when a person experiences herself to be where her body is not. If the two coincide in the sense that the person having the OBE is conscious of being in the location of her apparition when another perceives it, a reciprocal apparition occurs. And if we were to express this a little differently and say that a conscious apparition (an apparition associated with the conscious states of the person whose apparition is perceived) appears in these cases, we can hardly avoid asking whether any *apparitions of the dead* are conscious.

This is a question addressed in Hornell Hart's important study. He carefully compared numerous apparitions of the dead and dying with reciprocal apparitions of the living in respect to 45 characteristic traits and concluded with the following words:

> With respect to the 45 traits most frequently mentioned in 165 apparitional cases, apparitions of the dead and dying are so closely similar to the 25 conscious apparitions of the living persons that the two types must be regarded as belonging to the same basic kind of phenomena.[8]

He goes on to speak of the similarity he had demonstrated as being so close that it "would not occur by mere chance once in 10 to the 150th power."

The significance for the survival issue of such a close similarity seems clear. In the reciprocal apparitions involving the living, the conscious state of the person whose apparition is perceived seems to be what causes the apparition, even though the causation is unintentional in many cases. In such cases, the person whose apparition is perceived is not aware that her apparition is appearing to others. But causation need not be intentional. A similar inference can be justifiably drawn in the case of the dying and recently dead, not only on the basis of Hart's study but also on the basis of the timing data that we examined previously: the conscious states of the dying person seem to be what cause her apparition to appear to others around the time of her death.

Still, a critic of this reasoning might point out that dying people may well have brain function capable of supporting conscious states and that someone classified as recently dead (as within an hour after death) might have caused her apparition to appear prior to the cessation of her consciousness.

Perhaps in some cases the causal process initiated by the apparent while still conscious required so much time to culminate in a perception of her apparition that she was dead when that culminating event occurred. Another possibility is that in some cases conscious processes were still occurring shortly after the time taken to be the time of death.

Though such criticism would have force when leveled against a study of the dying and very recently dead, the Hart study included cases of the long dead—people whose brains could not have been supporting conscious states. The full significance of the Hart study for the survival issue comes into view here. Given this evidence of a causal link between the consciousness of the apparent and the perception of her apparition, the study supports the conclusion that some long dead persons still have conscious processes.

The Naturalistic Interpretation

The naturalistic interpretation according to which apparitional phenomena provide no good reason to believe that any are the result of paranormal activity will not detain us much at this point. We can acknowledge that the great majority of apparitional experiences are easily dismissed as having no paranormal significance. Many reports of them are fraudulent and a great number are instances of delusion or non-veridical hallucination corresponding to nothing outside the hallucinator's own consciousness. But we have been dealing with the verifiable, experimental data and some well-documented cases of reciprocal apparitions, along with issues of how they are to be interpreted. In addition, our focus has been (and will continue to be) on cases of people in normal health and apparently free of alcohol, drugs and other such vitiating conditions, so as to reduce the likelihood of including non-veridical hallucinations among the apparitional cases we consider. Many of the difficulties in providing a naturalistic explanation of NDEs and ND OBES—difficulties we have examined earlier in some detail—also apply here.

In general, what the naturalistic hypothesis cannot plausibly explain, whether the phenomena in question are NDEs, OBEs, or apparitional experiences, is how the subject of any of these experiences could have gained by virtue of having them the detailed, verifiable information that she apparently could not have acquired by normal means. Numerous, well-documented cases of these kinds apparently require a move to hypotheses appealing to paranormal activities. As we shall now see, there are apparition cases that stretch even the super-psi hypothesis to the breaking point and render any naturalistic explanation of them a non-starter.

Paranormal Interpretations of Apparitions of the Dead

Among the numerous credible cases of apparitions of the dead, there are some that stand out in their resistance to plausible explanation other than by invoking the survival hypothesis. They are the ones on which we will now focus. Many if not most apparitions of the dead appear only once and then only to a single individual. The following is a representative example. A young woman had just finished her morning cup of tea. Upon turning to take the cup to the kitchen she sees on her settee the apparition of her grandfather smoking his pipe. He had been dead for thirteen years.[9]

Though such cases have some evidential significance, they fall far short of providing compelling reason to believe in the continued existence of the apparent. We might well grant that the perceiver did have an apparitional experience. But, as we noted earlier, the extraordinary nature of a claim requires extraordinarily secure evidence to justify rational belief. Thus such cases, though usually compelling for the perceiver, are vulnerable to the skeptic's charge that in view of the numerous, ever-present sources of deception, they are more plausibly explained as instances of illusion, perceptual error, or even non-veridical hallucination.

Stronger support for the survival hypothesis is provided by "group" or "collective" apparitions. We shall define such an apparition as one perceived by two or more persons who happen to be present at the same location. Alternatively, we might say that two or more of those present have (qualitatively) the same apparitional experience. Interestingly, a rather large proportion (viz., one-third to one-half) of apparition cases in which a second person was in a position to be a perceiver turn out to be collective. Both the 1886 "Census of Hallucinations" and the 1956 Hornell Hart study yielded results indicating this frequency of occurrence.[10] The following case involves two perceivers: Mrs. P. is lying in bed with the lamp on waiting to feed her baby when she suddenly sees a tall man dressed in a naval officer's uniform, leaning on the foot rail of the bed. She awakens her husband who also sees the figure. It then speaks reproachfully to the husband, who responds by leaping out of bed. It now moves away, momentarily blocking the light from the lamp, and disappears into the wall. Mr. P informs his wife that the apparition was that of his father who had been dead for fourteen years. She learned later that seeing the apparition had prevented her husband from taking financial advice that would have proved ruinous.[11]

Other things being equal, cases involving two people simultaneously perceiving the apparition from their different perspective are more resistant to the skeptic's charge or naturalistic explanation than those involving a single perceiver. Moreover, many cases of collective apparitions of the dead involve many more perceivers than two, thus decreasing the likelihood that all perceivers were victims of some sort of deception or united in a conspiracy to deceive us. Still, the evidential support they can provide for the survival hypothesis is not compelling. Even if we can rule out the possibility of intentional deception, there remains the possibility that a group of honest and intelligent people are mistaken in their interpretation of their experience, however rare mistakes may be for such groups. For their opportunity to observe is almost always limited to a single exposure which arrives unexpectedly and is usually quite brief. There is no opportunity to prepare. Groups of such people in agreement about what they saw have in fact turned out to have been mistaken, unlikely as this may seem. They have been deceived by illusions such as reflections and mirages, claiming, for example, that they saw oases in desert regions where there were none. Again the skeptic will remind us that extraordinary claims—certainly those as extraordinary as claimed sightings of apparitions of the dead—require extraordinary evidence, and that collective apparitions do not provide evidence sufficient for rational belief in personal survival.

Collective and Iterative Apparitional Experiences

At this point we might wonder whether there have been any instances of apparitional experiences of the dead that would prove to be highly resistant if not invulnerable to such skeptical doubts. But we have not yet considered the kind of apparitional experiences of the dead constituting the best evidence—perhaps the extraordinary evidence needed to match the extraordinary claims that the continued existence of deceased persons is revealed in certain apparitional experiences. Following Almeder, let us call these cases of *collective and iterative* apparitional experiences of the dead.[12] The weight of the evidence they provide for a paranormal explanation surpasses that of the other apparitional experiences. In these cases, unanimous claims about what was perceived are extremely trustworthy.

An old, but unusually well-documented case of this kind consisted of apparitional experiences of the deceased Mrs. George Butler. The original account of it appeared in a pamphlet entitled, *Immortality Proved by the Testimony of Sense,* written in 1826 by the Reverend Abraham Cummings, Baptist minister of a church in Maine and graduate of Brown University.[13] The apparition (or specter, as it was usually called) occurred in a village near Machiasport, Maine It appeared on many occasions, to different groups of people—some numbering as many as 40—over a period of several months. It appeared both indoors and out of doors, delivered extended discourses to the people witnessing it, and moved freely among them. It made accurate predictions of births and deaths that were to occur in the village and seemed to know many private details about the lives of the villagers. It revealed to one man in the group that his father had recently died in a distant town—information unknown at the time to him and to everyone else present. Cummings argued that, given the time and distance involved, no one in the village could have had normal knowledge of this death. On another occasion, Mrs. Butler's (still living) husband stuck his hand right through the apparition, as though through a shaft of light—an event witnessed by six or seven people who later provided sworn testimony about what they saw.

Cummings had the good sense to obtain at the time over 30 sworn affidavits from some of the 100 or more people who in the company of others had perceived the apparition at different times and under different circumstances. He was concerned about fraud or hoax, but rejected this possibility after he had very carefully examined the testimony.

What should we say about this case? If we can assume that no fraud was involved and can put aside possible concerns about whether Cummings was a sufficiently critical and unbiased investigator, we might well be impressed with the support it provides for the survival hypothesis, more specifically, for the belief that the apparition indicates the continuing existence of the deceased Mrs. Butler (given, of course, that it cannot be plausibly explained by appeal to super-psi powers of the living). For the likelihood of mass hallucination or perceptual error under these conditions seems effectively ruled out. The likelihood that the unanimous testimony of a sizable group about what they experienced on a single occasion is low. But when such testimony is repeated over an extended period of time by groups whose membership changes frequently, the likelihood that the testimony as to what was experienced is in error becomes negligible. Almeder makes this point in a cogent way: "As a matter of fact, the probability of a large group of people being mistaken in their perceptual beliefs about what they have seen when they testify to seeing the same thing repeatedly under different circumstances (both indoors and outdoors) over an extended period of time (many months) in which the membership of the group changes frequently is zero."[14]

Still, we might doubt that the most plausible explanation of this case must acknowledge the existence of paranormal events if it stood alone in its category. But there are many other cases of collective and iterative apparitional experiences. One of the most striking was described in a book by John Fuller entitled, *The Ghost of Flight 401*.[15] Compared to the Butler case, it is rather recent, beginning with the crash of Eastern Airlines Flight 401, which went down in the Florida Everglades during the night of December 28, 1972, killing all the crew as well as 101 of the passengers aboard. About two months later, crew-members and passengers on Eastern Airlines flights carrying or using salvaged parts from the crashed airplane began to have apparitional experiences of the Captain of Flight 401, Robert Loft, and of its second officer, Don Repo.

The crashed plane was #310, a Tristar L-1011, on its regular route heading from the JFK New York airport into Miami, a route subsequently flown by other Tristar L-1011s. The first apparitional experience was had in February of 1973 by Virginia P., a flight attendant, when she was in the lower galley of Tristar #318. Upon noticing something out of the corner of her eye and turning to look, she saw a hazy white cloud. She then saw quite clearly a complete face appear "with dark hair, gray at the sides, and steel-rimmed glasses."[16] It was the face of Don Repo, the flight engineer of the crashed Flight 401. She was shaken with fright and told no one about her experience until after other sightings had occurred.

About a month later another sighting occurred aboard the Tristar #318 when it was at the Newark, N.J., airport about to fly to Miami. The senior flight attendant found one passenger too many when checking the number of passengers with her flight list. She found the extra passenger to be a uniformed Eastern Airlines captain sitting in one of the first-class seats. Assuming that he was deadheading back after bringing another plane to Newark, she asked him if he planned to take the jump-seat later (the usual practice); but he stared silently ahead. She questioned him again, trying to find out whether he would ride in the jump-seat or be a first-class pass rider, but again he made no response. Nor did he respond when she brought the flight supervisor to question him. He seemed normal in every respect except for appearing as if he were in a daze.

The incident had now captured the attention of other passengers who were looking on with interest. Several regular first-class passengers were in the immediate vicinity of the unresponsive captain and thus very well positioned to observe what was happening. One of the attendants brought the pilot of the plane to assess the situation. As he leaned forward to address his fellow captain, he suddenly froze and exclaimed, "My God, it's Bob Loft!"[17] There was a moment of silence. Then, to the amazement of everyone watching, the apparition abruptly vanished before their eyes. The plane was thoroughly searched from one end to the other, but no trace of the mysterious captain could be found. Though the witnesses to this incident were quite stunned and perplexed by it, the plane did finally leave for Miami after a long delay.

Other sightings of Bob Loft followed. One of the vice presidents boarded an L1011 that was prepared to fly Flight 401 from JFK to Miami. He had boarded before anyone else and, upon entering the first-class section, saw a uniformed Eastern Airlines captain sitting in a first-class seat. He said "Hello" to the man and then recognized him to be Bob Loft. At that moment the apparition vanished. On another occasion, Loft was seen by the captain and two attendants. Subsequently, an attendant who knew Loft well was looking into an overhead locker in the first-class area when she found herself looking directly into the face of Bob Loft.

The sightings of Don Repo were more numerous and extended over a longer period of time. Many were in the lower galley of Tristar #318 where Virginia P. had her experience of Repo. On one occasion, a catering crew left the lower galley in confusion and refused to enter it again, claiming that they had seen there the flight engineer who had abruptly vanished before their eyes. In another incident, a flight supervisor reported the malfunctioning of an oven to the maintenance crew. Soon a flight engineer appeared, fixed the oven, and left. Later another flight engineer arrived and was amazed to find that the oven was already fixed, as he was the only flight engineer on the plane. When the attendant looked up Repo's picture, she immediately identified him as the flight engineer who arrived first and fixed the oven.

The Repo apparition frequently spoke to the people who saw it. It was a well-intended, helpful apparition that appeared in order to make minor repairs for the flight attendants, do flight checks, and warn the flight crew about potential mechanical problems. For example, a flight engineer reported that upon arriving at the cabin to make his preflight checks, he found a man in an Eastern Airlines uniform sitting in his seat. He was shocked to see that it was Repo, who said to him, "You don't need to worry about your preflight, I've already done it."[18] With these words, the apparition vanished. Later, a captain on a different flight reported having come face-to-face with Repo who said, "There will never be another crash of an L-1011. We will not let it happen."[19] This apparition was seen and either immediately recognized or subsequently identified by various people on at least two-dozen occasions by the end of 1973.

Though many if not most of the Repo appearances were witnessed by a single individual, others were perceived by two or more people simultaneously. An instance of the latter occurred when plane #318 was being prepared to fly from New York to Miami. A woman seated in the first-class section noticed that seated next to her was an Eastern Airlines officer in the uniform of a flight engineer who seemed very ill. She spoke to him, but received no response. She then asked him if he was ill and if she should notify the flight attendant, but again with no response. She summoned the flight attendant who agreed that he seemed ill and that he might need help. But when the attendant asked him if he needed help, he remained totally unresponsive as he had to the earlier questions. By this time, others nearby were looking on with interest. Then the man vanished, right before the eyes of those watching. Later the woman and the flight attendant picked out a picture of Repo, identifying him as the flight engineer who had looked so ill before disappearing.

An especially intriguing incident involving a group of people witnessing the Repo apparition occurred in February 1974 when plane #318 was being prepared for a flight to Mexico City. One of the attendants in the lower galley clearly saw the face of Don Repo as she looked at the window of one of the oven doors. She had known Repo and could readily recognize him. Rushing to the passenger cabin, she grabbed the first stewardess she could find to accompany her to the lower galley and check out what she saw. This person clearly saw the same face, which, they determined, was not a reflection of anything in the galley. The two women called the flight engineer who came very quickly and found himself looking at a face he recognized to be that of Don Repo. Repo spoke audibly to him saying, "Watch out for fire on this airplane."[20] Then he vanished completely. The plane flew to Mexico City without incident, but when its engines were turned over for the continuation of the flight to Acapulco, the engine on the starboard wing would not start. The difficulty with it was determined to be so severe that a full engine replacement was needed—something that could be done only at the Miami base. But when barely off the ground in its flight to Miami, another engine (of three) stalled and then rapidly backfired several times. Only the captain's swift action of rapidly discharging carbon dioxide into it prevented it from bursting into flames.

Another incident in which the Repo apparition was not only collectively witnessed but also revealed a potentially serious problem with the plane occurred when an Eastern Airlines captain encountered a flight engineer sitting in the jump-seat of his L1011 who warned him that there would be an electrical failure. Without even thinking about it, the captain ordered a recheck, which uncovered a faulty circuit. Later, after a second look, the cockpit crew identified the flight engineer in the jump-seat to be Don Repo.

Stories about the appearances of Loft and Repo spread rapidly among the crews of Eastern Airlines and soon spread to the crews of other airlines. But Eastern management dismissed the stories as unfounded rumors and denied that any of their employees had written any reports of such incidents. The flight log (in which, by FAA regulation, unusual incidents must be recorded) would include any such reports; but when some of the attendants decided to look at the flight log of plane #318, they found, to their surprise and dismay, that (contrary to general practice) the pages for all the dates when either Bob Loft or Don Repo appeared had been removed. Such efforts on the part of management to show that no such reports ever existed would be understandable given the widespread belief that sightings of the deceased aboard planes might be very bad for business. But management denials seem belied by the failure to release the flight log of plane #318 and by the order issued to ground maintenance crews in 1974 to remove all parts salvaged from the crashed plane #310 which had been built into other planes, primarily plane #318. When these parts had been removed, the sightings, which had been occurring for at least two years, did finally come to an end.

We see then that the "ghosts of flight 401" episode is an apparently well-substantiated and highly intriguing case of collective and iterative apparitional experiences. But do such phenomena constitute weighty evidence for survival, or can they be more plausibly explained by appeal to super-psi? We will now focus on that question.

The Super-Psi Hypothesis

"Psi" is a general term that can be used to denote any psychic power—telepathy, clairvoyance, psychokinesis, etc. Accordingly, we shall take the psi hypothesis to be invoked in any attempt to explain all apparitional phenomena (defying naturalistic explanation) by appealing to telepathy, clairvoyance, psychokinesis, or some combination of the three. These paranormal powers are assumed to be wielded by the living only, and so apparitional phenomena provide no reason to believe that they emanate from deceased persons who continue to exist. As in the case of NDEs and ND OBEs, we shall see that the psi hypothesis is forced into becoming the super-psi version when stretched in an attempt to explain apparitional phenomena, especially those of the collective and iterative kind. However, we should bear in mind as we compare its plausibility with that of the survival hypothesis that the latter also assumes the existence of psychic powers, as such powers would be what deceased persons employ in their efforts to communicate with the living and each other. The difference is that the super-psi hypothesis must posit the existence of psychic powers of greater strength and complexity.[21] The question of which theory offers the more plausible account of apparitions of the dead is primarily a matter of how much greater these powers must be in the super-psi theory.

We have already noted some facts providing support for the survival hypothesis. One emerges from the timing of apparitions of the dead when compared with the timing of apparitions of the living. The fact that most apparitions of the dead are seen within an hour of the death of the apparent indicates that the apparitions were caused by the apparents, some of whom were dead when their apparitions were seen. Stronger support emerged from studies of reciprocal apparitions. The essential similarity of such apparitions of the living to apparitions of the dead and dying is evidence that the apparitions of both groups were caused by the conscious states of the apparents, some of whom were long dead.

An explanation of these facts by appealing to psychic activities of the living cannot be conclusively ruled out, but it would have to be highly complicated. In some cases, knowledge that a person is dying or recently dead would have to be acquired telepathically or clairvoyantly, and then communicated telepathically so as to generate in the perceiver a veridical apparitional experience of the dying or deceased person, even if the telepathic agent had never met the deceased. Here the survival hypothesis seems much more plausible. Though telepathic powers possessed by the deceased would have to be acknowledged, a deceased person would not have to use psychic powers to learn of her dying or death. Moreover, she is likely to remember the physical appearance she had when alive and thus would possess the knowledge that an apparitional likeness of her would reveal. A veridical experience of what is recognizably an apparition of *her* would be easier to explain. Besides, she is the one most likely to have a *motive* to communicate, but this leads us to another point of comparison.

A number of studies have shown that, with the exception of haunting apparitions connected to a place, apparitions tend to exhibit motive or purpose in when and how they appear, and also with respect to the persons to whom they appear.[22] This finding is significant because the purpose displayed is one the apparent, but not the perceiver of the apparition, would be expected to have. The perceiver typically was occupied with unrelated matters and without any knowledge of the apparent's condition at the time. The apparent's having such a motive or purpose as displayed would plausibly explain why the apparition occurred. But these facts are very difficult to reconcile with the psi hypothesis if the apparent is deceased. The display of motives and purposes implies the existence of those persons who have them. According to the psi hypothesis, however, deceased persons do not exist, and so any motives or purposes displayed must be attributed to the living, however implausible such attribution might be. Presumably, a living person, without conscious purpose or intent and without even any awareness of doing so, can link up telepathically with someone else, who is also without any consciousness of what is happening, to work out the details of an apparitional figure of a deceased person that this (living) person (or, in some cases, both persons) will unexpectedly perceive. Such an explanation not only seems entirely *ad hoc* but also employs argumentation so convoluted as to strike one as highly implausible, if not preposterous. Clearly, the survival hypothesis seems to be the more plausible one, allowing us to take the displays of purposes to be what they appear to be, especially if (as our earlier deliberations indicate) the self is such that it (metaphysically) could survive bodily death and indeed would if its existence turns out to be causally independent of its brain.

It is true that, as we noted, the deceased self or person would also need psychic powers sufficient to generate in the experience of the perceiver an apparitional figure of herself, grounded in her self-conception and thus recognizable to others who knew her while alive. Though such psychic powers would need to be considerable, they would not have to approach the strength they must have to do what the psi hypothesis requires of them. Of at least equal importance, the apparitional figure of a deceased person would not have to represent a *third* party. That is, a deceased person generating an apparitional figure of herself in the experience of one or more perceivers would not only be producing a figure as *she* intended, displaying *her* purposes and *her* consciousness of its surroundings, but would be one party to an event to which there is only *one* other party—the perceiver or perceivers. By contrast, the psi theory requires three parties in many of its accounts of apparitions of the dead: (1) a living person who generates the apparitional figure in (2) a living perceiver (and perhaps in himself as well) of (3) some deceased person. This requirement puts the psi theory at a significant disadvantage, for there is (at least to my knowledge) very little independent evidence that by using psychic powers one person can generate in the experience of a second person (or second group of persons) an apparitional figure of a third person, whether this third person is alive or dead.

So far our comparison of the (nonsurvivalist) psi hypothesis with the survival hypothesis has given the latter the edge in providing a plausible explanation of apparitions of the dead. The difficulties for each increase, however, when we bring collective apparitions of the dead into consideration, though this increase appears to be much less damaging to the plausibility of the survival hypothesis. As we have noted, collective apparitions are not exceedingly rare, but rather constitute a sizable proportion of the apparition cases in which more than one person was in a position to perceive the apparition. They cannot be ignored. Nor should we be swayed by the skeptic's reminder that groups of people in agreement about what they witnessed have been mistaken. Such mistakes are uncommon, and there are too many evidentially secure cases of collective apparitions to dismiss them in this way. Besides there are many well-documented cases of *collective and iterative* apparitions of the dead—cases in which the probability of error in the essentials of the unanimous testimony about what was experienced is or approaches zero.

The Telepathic Theory

The central theoretical problem generated by collective apparitions of the dead is to account for the fact that the apparitional figure is seen simultaneously by two or more people from their different perspectives. The views of the different perceivers are interrelated in such a way that the laws of perspective are not violated. In some cases, a figure is seen in full face by a perceiver facing it, in right profile by a perceiver on its right, and in left profile by a perceiver on its left.[23] How is this to be explained? Either *something* is objectively out there, external to the perceivers, in the region of space where they perceive the apparition to be, or *nothing* is out there. In the latter case, what the perceivers experience is not the result of stimulation of their sense organs by some external entity, but internally generated sense impressions that are projected outward, as in the case of an ordinary (nonveridical) hallucination.

Suppose that the second possibility is the one realized. Apparitional experience would be telepathically induced rather than due to stimulation of the perceiver's sense organs by an external entity. According to the survival theory, the still existing deceased person would telepathically induce in the perceivers an apparition of herself. In the (nonsurvivalist) psi hypothesis, the telepathic agent would have to be a living person, even though the telepathically induced apparition is of a deceased person. But in either hypothesis, the telepathic theory of apparition generation faces formidable problems in accounting for the timing of the apparitional experiences and for the fact that different perceivers see the apparition from their different perspectives.

In the "Shotgun" version of the telepathic theory, the telepathic agent affects each perceiver independently yet affects all at the same time. If all perceivers respond at the same rate, resulting in their having their apparitional experiences simultaneously, the timing aspect of collective apparitions is explained. But the problem arising from perspective differences is left untouched. Besides, the telepathic feat to be accomplished seems enormous, requiring super-telepathic powers.

The two other versions have the advantage of requiring less telepathic power on the part of the telepathic agent. In both versions, the telepathic agent affects one of the perceivers, resulting in a process of telepathic contagion in which the primary perceiver affects another in the vicinity who affects another, etc., until all in the vicinity are similarly affected and have similar experiences. This is the "Infection" version. The third variation—the "Extravaganza version"—adds to the Infection version the claim that as each member of the series of infected persons creates his apparitional experience he "... does whatever is necessary to render it dramatically appropriate."[24] And it would be dramatically appropriate for him to infect other properly situated members of the group so that they too experience the apparition.

The formidable problems facing all versions are not difficult to detect. All assume what we might properly call super-telepathy, though they ascribe it differently. Perhaps more importantly, none can provide a satisfactory explanation of the timing of collective apparitional experiences. Since it has been established that different people respond at different rates to a telepathically received stimulus, we should infer that even if (as in the Shotgun version) a group of people received such a stimulus simultaneously, the experiences they had in response to it would almost certainly not be simultaneous. The other versions are even worse off. Since a process of telepathic contagion takes time, different perceivers will be stimulated at different times.

However, it is the perspective problem (i.e., that different perceivers perceive the apparition from the different perspectives appropriate to their different locations) that seems insuperable given the resources available within a telepathic theory. For a telepathically generated apparitional figure would not be influenced by the perceiver's sense organs. Thus the perceiver's location in his environment and his spatial relation to nearby perceivers with their different viewpoints would be irrelevant. One would expect these different viewpoints or perspectives from which a single physical environment might be viewed would be as irrelevant to what is seen as they would be if each person were dreaming of seeing the apparition. Supplementing telepathic powers with super-clairvoyant ones would help significantly. If the telepathic agent clairvoyantly apprehended the location and posture of each perceiver in the environment, he could then use super-telepathic powers in the creation of an apparitional figure in the experience of each perceiver that would appear to each from the perspective he would have on it if it were an objectively existing entity located among them. Perhaps, then, the view that an apparition is an entirely subjective hallucinatory entity can be sustained if the timing problem does not prove to be intractable and it is defensible to appeal to super-clairvoyant and super-telepathic powers exercised by the telepathic agent. But it seems difficult to believe that there isn't a theory that provides a more plausible account of collective apparitions.

The Objectivist Theory

We will now examine the other possibility—that when an apparition is experienced *something* is objectively out there, external to the perceivers, in the region of space where the apparition is perceived. Let us call this view the "Objectivist Theory of Apparitions." In this view of an apparition, the problems so difficult for the telepathic theory do not arise. Since the various perceivers in the vicinity are simultaneously perceiving the same objective entity, their apparitional experiences would occur simultaneously, i.e., there is no timing problem. Nor would any problem arise from the fact that the different perceivers perceive the apparition differently in accordance with their different perspectives. All this is in accord with the laws of perspective, as we should expect when differently located perceivers are viewing the same object from their different locations with respect to it. Rather, the problems for this theory arise in trying to understand what such an objective entity can be, in seeing how its objectivity should be understood, in understanding its relation to the apparent, and in determining how it comes about.

As we noted earlier, apparitions exhibit a puzzling mix of seemingly incompatible characteristics, some possessed by physical objects and others indicating that apparitions are nonphysical. Myers' thoughts about how apparitions of the dead might be understood, though expressed quite some time ago, are still some of the most instructive. Beginning with cases of reciprocal apparitions, he proposes that when a "projector" views a distant scene as though from a point within it or confronting it, there may be an actual modification of space in the region where the projector conceives himself to be (regions that he sometimes calls "phantasmogenetic centres"). This modification is not material but yet such that persons with a certain perceptual sensitivity would detect in that region of space an image approximately corresponding to the conception latent in the projector's mind of how he would appear if perceived there. If his latent conception of himself at that time included such accessories as a hat, a pipe, a cane, certain clothes, etc., then these too could appear as features of the apparition. There is in such cases "a real transference of something from the agent, involving an alteration of some kind in a particular part of space."[25] But this "something" is not a quasi-physical etheric body, much less a material object; nor is it what is directly perceived when the projector's apparition is seen.

Though Myers believed that the "local modifications of space" are modifications in a realm of being other than the physical world accessible to our senses, we would do well to follow Gauld in steering clear of notions of realms inaccessible to empirical investigation. But we might try to accommodate it to this extent: Such a realm, if there is one, intersects causally, if not spatially, with the physical realm at the place where the perceivers near it may see an apparitional figure corresponding to some latent conception in the projector's mind. In any case, there occurs an objective, and perhaps quasi-material, modification of that region of space where the apparitional figure is seen. This objective modification does not affect physical instruments and is perceptible only by persons having a certain "non-optical" (and presumably non-auditory) sensitivity. Several people in the vicinity of this region may possess the peculiar sensitivity and so may collectively perceive, simultaneously and from their different perspectives, an apparitional figure in the region. Others present, but lacking this sensitivity, may perceive nothing there.

What may result is the perception of an apparition that may or may not be collective. The apparition resembles physical objects in some ways, but not in other ways. Its physical features might be due to, or at least linked to, the objectivity of the modification of the spatial region where the apparition appears. The nonphysical features are at least consistent with the non-materiality of the "local modification" of the spatial region.

Though Myers' starting point in developing his theory was with cases of reciprocal apparitions, it is rather obvious that the theory applies to apparitions of the dead as well as of the living. A post-mortem apparition in which the apparition exhibits consciousness, purpose and other features of an apparition that a purposeful living projector may exhibit differs from the latter only in that its projector is deceased. Consequently, the deceased projector's latent conception of a physical body that influences the features exhibited by his apparition is of a body he no longer has.

It is not easy to specify the kinds of psychic powers required of the projector or agent. ESP is apparently involved in veridical apparitions, as in those cases information is acquired other than by way of the sense organs. But the production of the "local modifications of space" (whether or not this occurs via an initial modification created by the projector in a "metetherial" realm of being) would seem to require something else, presumably psychokinesis on the part of the projector. An appeal to psychokinesis assumes that an objective modification of space, not being a modification in some mind, would require psychokinetic activity by the projector to bring it about.

The respects in which this space is psychokinetically modified by the projector would seem to be a function of the latent conception in his mind at the time. For one would think that different latent conceptions lead to different apparitional experiences by way of different phantasmogenetic centers (i.e., different modifications of space). Perhaps in this way, apparitions turn out to be the indirect effects of the projectors' mental activities, rather than the effects of direct telepathic contact with the perceivers.

At any rate Myers apparently would reject such telepathic contact. He considers the telepathic theory of apparitions, but finds it unable to explain certain cases of collective apparitions in which no likely link is discernible between the distant agent and any of the perceivers. In his words, "If in such a case a bystander perceives the invading figure, I must think that he perceives it merely as a bystander—not as a person telepathically influenced by the intended percipient, who does not in fact perceive anything whatsoever."[26] This seems telling against the telepathic theory in all its versions. If the person with whom the agent is likely to be linked in a way conducive to telepathic interaction perceives nothing while a bystander apparently not so linked perceives the apparition, a plausible explanation of what happened will not appeal to telepathy, or at least not telepathy by itself.

Since the objectivist theory seems to be the more plausible one, we will focus on it as we return to the issue of whether the survival hypothesis provides the most plausible account of some cases of apparitions of the dead. We have seen that with respect to some cases, primarily of the collective and iterative kind, naturalistic explanations are not even in the running; but the psi hypothesis remains as a strong competitor when strengthened to its super-psi form. Indeed, it has been argued, perhaps most cogently by Steven Braude, that even the cases seemingly most supportive of the survival hypothesis are in fact more plausibly explained by appealing to super-psychokinetic (super–PK) activities on the part of the living. Convinced that the telepathic theory is untenable, he employs an objectivist theory is his argument.

He maintains that what is experienced in collective and iterative apparitions is most plausibly understood as similar to the materializations allegedly produced in the best cases of physical mediumship, namely, as material products of the psychokinetic activity of living persons. Even if the apparitions are only quasi-material, they fail to provide good reason to believe that any emanate from deceased persons.

His argument begins with a very thorough analysis of some of the best cases of physical mediumship and reaches the conclusion that these cases reveal the existence of psychokinetic powers of great magnitude, perhaps what we might call a super PK. With this conclusion, he argues that we must be open to the possibility that PK (or ESP) of similar magnitude is involved in the production of other paranormal phenomena. But his argument becomes much less plausible when he infers that to rule out appeal to PK (or ESP) as a legitimate explanation of a paranormal phenomenon is to unjustifiably assume in advance what the limits of PK (or ESP) are. He says that we should resist ruling out any explanation of a paranormal phenomenon "... on the grounds that it posits a psi performance of implausible magnitude." For "... we simply have no decent idea what (if any) magnitude of phenomena is implausible or unlikely, once we have allowed psi to occur at all."[27]

His argument, however, is problematic in several respects, as Almeder has pointed out in detail.[28] We can grant the *possibility* that PK and ESP exist in an unlimited way without implying that they are the cause of a paranormal phenomenon. Since this possibility may not be actualized, it is not only justifiable but required for sound practice to look for positive evidence that it is in fact actualized, i.e., evidence that unlimited PK or unlimited ESP is the actual cause of the phenomenon. But even if either did exist in an unlimited way, there would be every reason to believe that there would be events it did not cause and that the paranormal phenomenon in question might be one of them. Again, positive evidence as to what the actual cause is would be needed. Thus, contra Braude, we can reject an explanation appealing to PK or ESP without unjustifiably ruling out in advance the possibility that PK or ESP exists in an unlimited way.

Even if we were to put these considerations aside, we would have sufficient reason to reject Braude's position. For to accept it is to accept the implication that we could never be justified in rejecting the PK or ESP explanation for a paranormal phenomenon because our rejection of it would show that we were unjustifiably assuming in advance that PK and ESP have limits. And this apparently implies that no amount of empirical evidence supporting the survivalist explanation of a paranormal phenomenon would justify our taking it as expressing what is really happening, i.e., expressing the *truth* of the matter, and to reject the super-psi hypothesis as false, at least as applied to the phenomenon in question. In other words, the hypothesis that super-psi powers of the living are what bring about paranormal phenomena is unfalsifiable.

We have for some time been considering the issue of whether collective and iterative apparitions of the dead are more plausibly explained by the survival hypothesis or by the super–PK hypothesis that appeals to the causal activity of living persons possessed of super–PK powers. We were implicitly assuming that positive evidence in support of a hypothesis is at least relevant to the issue, if not the determining factor in how the issue might be settled. But Braude's position implies that that assumption is mistaken—that no amount of positive evidence supporting the survivalist explanation of collective and iterative apparitions of the dead should lead us to conclude that this explanation expresses the truth of the matter and to reject as false the claim that they are the result of super–PK powers of the living. Thus it now seems clear that for this reason (and especially in conjunction with those we considered previously) we should reject Braude's appeal to the super–PK hypothesis as providing the most plausible explanation of such apparitions.

In the objectivist theory of apparitions, the survivalist explanation too would likely have to appeal to PK powers of deceased persons. As we noted, it is difficult to see how a deceased person could bring about an objective modification of a spatial region in any other way. But if PK is required, the magnitude needed may well be less than an unlimited super–PK. The deceased person would likely be *motivated* to communicate, perhaps by way of an apparition, and, if so, would *intend to* appear by way of it. The unmotivated and unintended exercise of PK, as implied by the nonsurvivalist explanation, apparently would require PK of a greater magnitude. Besides, the postulation of unmotivated and unintended PK effects is implausible. As we noted, we have no evidence that PK functions unconsciously.

The survivalist hypothesis, then, has the edge in virtue of its more plausible view of how PK is involved in the production of an apparition of the dead. But it receives further support from a line of evidence pointed out by Meyers. He saw that his theory of apparitions was compatible with a non-survivalist explanation of veridical apparitions of the dead. For such an apparition could be generated (perhaps via super–PK) by a latent conception in the mind of a living person who is dwelling upon, brooding over, or grieving about some deceased person. But he reasons that such an explanation is not as plausible as the survivalist alternative. The generator of a veridical post-mortem apparition cannot (or usually cannot) be among the perceivers of the apparition. For a veridical apparition conveys accurate information unknown to the perceivers, seems to manifest interests and goals they do not consciously have in mind, and often represents someone with whom they are not acquainted. Thus if a living person is the source of the apparition, she must be at some place other than where the apparition appears.

But no such living person is to be found. Often there are not even any plausible candidates—no person turns up who had been highly motivated to try to generate an apparition of someone other than himself in some perceiver or perceivers who might well be unknown to him. This is not surprising, as such peculiar motivation would not be common. Nor is anyone to be found who was dwelling upon or grieving about the deceased with such intensity as to make plausible the belief that he might have been the unintentional source of the apparition. Though there are rare cases in which a living person has generated an apparition witnessed by others of someone other than himself, in each of these cases this person was among the witnesses or perceivers. Apparently, there are no cases in which the person allegedly producing the apparition was not among the perceivers, that is, no cases in which there is found a living person who, given Myers' argument, is a suitable candidate for being the generator of a veridical post-mortem apparition.

The Survivalist Explanation

As we bring our study of apparitions to a close, it may be helpful to come up with a brief assessment of how well the survivalist explanation has fared in accounting for apparitions of the dead. We noted that naturalistic explanations do not offer a plausible account of veridical post-mortem apparitions, especially those of the collective and iterative kind. Thus our focus was on comparing the survival hypothesis with the (non-survivalist) psi hypothesis. Though both require the existence of extensive psychic powers, the survival hypothesis seems to require significantly less. But the plausibility gained in requiring less may not be enough to outweigh the initial plausibility possessed by the non-survivalist psi hypothesis in not having to make the extraordinary claim that deceased persons have survived bodily death and have revealed their continued existence by exercising psychic powers.

Still, the survivalist explanation does appear to be the more plausible one when a variety of other consideration are taken into account. As we noted, it gains modest support from a comparison of the timing of apparitions of the dead and dying with that of apparitions of the living. More support comes from careful studies of reciprocal apparitions, indicating that these apparitions are essentially similar to post-mortem ones. Then too, the motives and purposes exhibited in post-mortem apparitions typically are those the apparent, but not the perceiver or other living persons, would be expected to have. The survival hypothesis allows us to interpret these displays of purpose to be just what they appear to be, in striking contrast to the convoluted, complicated, and sometimes tortuous explanations that must be invoked to attribute such apparitions to the living, who lack consciously held purposes of the sort displayed. Finally, the psi theory implausibly requires three parties in its accounts of post-mortem apparitions, the third party being the living person who allegedly generates in the presence of a perceiver an apparitional figure of some deceased person. Not only does this result in a more complex explanation but it clashes with the fact that there is very little if any independent evidence that such "third-partied" apparitions ever occur, whether of the living or of the dead.

All things considered, then, the survivalist explanation has fared well in the controversy about how apparitional experiences should be interpreted, emerging as providing the most plausible account of the best cases of veridical post-mortem apparitions. Though the level of support provided by such apparitions hardly justifies a robust belief in survival of death, it does constitute an important element in the overall case for concluding that the survival hypothesis is true. Given that our earlier deliberations about the nature of the self have revealed the (metaphysical) possibility of its existence beyond biological death, veridical post-mortem apparitions provide significant evidential weight adding to that provided by NDEs and certain other kinds of paranormal phenomena.

Reincarnation

Another kind of phenomenon deserving of some consideration in our examination of the survival issue is that which seems to show that at least some persons have reincarnated, i.e., have been reborn in the natural world and have in that way continued to exist after biological death. If, as our earlier investigation indicated, the subject of experience is what is essential to personal identity and is distinct from the body, then reincarnation would occur at that time after biological death when the subject enters into relation with another body about to be born. This might happen only once, or a great number of times resulting in many successive lives, but one must survive death at least once for it happen at all. The evidence that it happens consists in verifiable memories and skills that apparently could not have been acquired in any normal way during one's natural lifetime.

Though a belief in reincarnation or rebirth may strike many Americans and Europeans as peculiar if not fantastic, it is very widespread not just in Asia but also around the world. Even in England and America, a significant number of people hold this belief. A 1981 Gallop poll conducted in England indicated that 28 percent of the population then believed in reincarnation, and a similar 1982 poll conducted in America found that 23 percent of the population held this belief. Later surveys carried out in the early 1990s in Europe and America indicated even higher percentages of persons believing in reincarnation. In America the percentage was 26, in Great Britain 29, in France 28, and in Austria 29. The three great Western religions along with modern science discourage such belief, but have not affected it much in most areas of the world. In the words of Ian Stevenson, the leading figure in reincarnation research, "... nearly everyone outside the range of orthodox Christianity, Judaism, Islam and Science—the last being a secular religion for many persons—believes in reincarnation."[1]

The prima facie support for this belief is also widespread. The strongest support for it consists in the spontaneous memories of young children who claim to remember having lived one or more previous lives; and cases of such children have been found in a great many different cultures throughout the world. Stevenson, alone, has personally investigated cases in Alaska, Brazil, British Columbia, India, Lebanon, Sri Lanka, and Turkey. He has in his files hundreds of investigated and apparently authentic cases, many of which come from other places or cultures. He points out that his collection of cases includes a considerable number from the United States, Canada, and Great Britain even though the culture in these countries is hostile to reincarnation.[2]

Reincarnation vs. Possession Interpretations

The existence of hundreds of investigated cases from around the world of young children possessing verifiable memories, and often skills as well, that they seemingly could not have acquired in any normal way is a remarkable phenomenon. If, as one would think, the extremely widespread belief in rebirth has an experiential basis, it would consist largely in this phenomenon. As we shall see, however, the reincarnation hypothesis is very difficult to establish as the most plausible explanation even of the cases that seem to be the most supportive of it. Given that both the naturalistic and the psi explanations can be ruled out as highly implausible in a number of cases, reincarnation would not be the only plausible hypothesis remaining. The hypothesis of discarnate possession apparently would provide an equally plausible explanation. But even if the most one can expect to establish in a case strongly supportive of the reincarnation hypothesis is that the case is *either* one of reincarnation *or* discarnate possession, such a conclusion clearly would be central to our concerns. For either would be as supportive of the survival hypothesis as the other.

As in the case of our examination of NDEs and apparitions, the general alternative views are the naturalistic or normal, the non-survivalist psi, and the survivalist interpretation. Thus the general form of our critical examination will remain unchanged. What changes are the kinds of phenomena to be considered. Because of the difficulty in excluding the possession hypothesis in cases that we might otherwise deem are best explained by the hypothesis of reincarnation, some consideration of possession as supportive of the survivalist view is appropriate in this context. Accordingly, we shall look at an example of an apparently clear-cut case of possession, several cases in which possession and reincarnation provide equally plausible (though conflicting) explanations, and two cases that might seem more supportive of reincarnation than possession. Of course, we are now assuming that both naturalistic and non-survivalist psi explanations are highly implausible in these cases—an assumption that might prove to be unfounded. Given our space limitations, we shall consider these cases in no more detail than is necessary to make an informed judgment about how they are most plausibly explained.

The apparently clear-cut case of possession we shall consider came to be known as the "Watseka Wonder" after the Illinois town where it occurred. It includes a remarkable display of veridical memories that seemingly could not have been acquired in any normal way. Two girls were involved: Lurancy Vennum and Mary Roff. Lurancy was born in 1864 and was a little over one year old when Mary died in 1865 at the age of 18. Mary was troubled by frequent "fits" and was said to have been able to read closed books with ease. In contrast, Lurancy showed no signs of abnormality until 1877 when, at age 13, she began to undergo spontaneous trances. After one of these trances, she lost all memory of being Lurancy, claimed to be Mary Roff, and wished "to go home" and live with the Roff family.

A few days later she was allowed to go and live with the Roffs where she "seemed perfectly happy and content, knowing every person and everything that Mary knew in her original body, twelve to twenty-five years ago [i.e., the 12 years preceding Lurancy's birth] ... calling attention to scores, yes, hundreds of incidents that transpired during [Mary's] natural life."[3] At the same time, she had completely lost her identity as Lurancy, having no knowledge of anything that she had known as Lurancy. She failed to recognize any members of the Vennum family, nor any of their friends and neighbors. But after three months and ten days her identity as Lurancy returned, at which time she remembered nothing about the Roffs but had regained all of her memories of her life with the Vennums. She lived a normal life after that except for some occasions when visiting the Roffs the Mary personality would return for a brief period during which she would temporarily lose her identity as Lurancy.

This was clearly not an ordinary case of alternating personalities. By every test that might be applied, the personality that displaced Lurancy's was not a dissociated part of the whole, as in cases of alternating personalities, but that of a girl who had been dead for about 12 years at the time of apparent possession. The alternating personalities hypothesis seems to be a nonstarter when we reflect upon the evidence of possession available to the Roffs. In the words of the American philosopher, C. J. Ducasse, who studied this case intensively, "... the Roffs had three and a half months of day-long close observations of the behavior, tastes, skills, knowledge and capacity to make and understand allusions to intimate family matters, possessed by the personality which was expressing itself through the body of Lurancy during those months. And the Roffs testified that those traits were the very same as those which had together been distinctive of their deceased daughter Mary, whom Lurancy had never known."[4]

Perhaps a normal or naturalistic explanation of this case could gain some plausibility if the Roff and Vennum families were intimately acquainted with one another, but such was not the case. The Vennums did not live in Watseka for the first seven years of Lurancy's life; and when they did live there, their acquaintance with the Roffs consisted of only one brief call made by Mrs. Roff on Mrs. Vennum and of a formal speaking acquaintance in the case of the two men. It seems clear that the only alternative to acknowledging this to be a case of discarnate possession is to have recourse to some other *paranormal* explanation. That paranormal explanation cannot be reincarnation, however, since Mary died *after* Lurancy's birth.[5]

Cases of Responsive Xenoglossy

Some cases that seem to defy all naturalistic explanation are those involving *responsive* xenoglossy. Responsive xenoglossy is the capacity to speak and understand a foreign language that the speaker has not learned in any normal way. It is quite rare and is to be distinguished from the *recitative* kind that occurs when a person speaks and/or writes in a foreign language apparently untaught to her, but without knowing what the words mean or how to converse in that language.

The case of Lydia Johnson, which began in 1993 when Johnson agreed to be a subject in experiments in hypnosis, is one of responsive xenoglossy that lends itself to both possession and reincarnation interpretations. It is also a case of hypnotic age-regression, as she was in hypnotic trance at the time and instructed to go back in time. In one of these trances she began to speak, just words rather than sentences at first, partly in broken English and partly in a foreign language unknown to everyone present. Her voice had become deep, masculine, and earthy. Then from the mouth of this 37-year-old housewife came the astounding words, "I am a man." When asked his name, the reply was "Jensen Jacoby," which she pronounced in the deep voice, YEN-sen YAH-ko-bee.

With the same broken English interspersed with foreign words and in the deep, guttural voice she began to describe a past life, lived in a tiny village in Sweden about three centuries ago. This session along with the following ones were tape recorded and careful notes were taken. Swedish linguists were brought in to translate Jensen's statements which, in the later sessions, were almost exclusively in Swedish—a language entirely unknown to Lydia. The following conversation exemplifies what transpired. All the questions were asked in Swedish.

"What do you do for a living?" He was asked.

"En Bonde (a farmer)," he answered.

"Where do you live?"

"I huset (in the house)."

"Var ligger huset? (Where is the house located?)"

"I Hansen (in Hansen)."[6]

Jensen manifested a simple personality in accord with the simple peasant life he described. He revealed little knowledge of the world beyond his own village and a trading center he visited. He raised cows, horses, goats and chickens. His diet consisted of goat's cheese, bread, milk, salmon, and poppy seed cakes made by his wife, Latvia. He and Latvia lived in their own stone house that he had built. They had no children. He was one of three sons and had run away from home.

As Jensen, Lydia was able to identify a model of a 17th-century Swedish ship, correctly calling it a "skuta." She also identified other objects of that era with which Swedish people would have been familiar. In contrast, she did not recognize or know how to use pliers and other modern tools.

The experiments ended after the eighth session due to fear of permanent possession ensuing. Lydia was unhypnotized, resting with her husband, when, suddenly and unsummoned, Jensen reappeared. He had to be forced back and dismissed by the hypnotists. As a result, no further communications with Jensen were attempted.

The significance of this case does not depend upon whether we can verify the historical existence of Jensen and the claims about how he lived. Verification of these particulars would be very difficult if not impossible. Yet these claims are consistent with general knowledge of that culture in that era. The ability to identify objects of that era in conjunction with ignorance of modern tools is significant. But, of course, the fluency in the Swedish language along with the manner in which that fluency was manifested is highly significant. It was spoken in a voice and dialect completely alien to Lydia's normal speech habits, but quite in harmony with that of a Swedish man living a peasant's life in the eighteenth century. After a very careful study of all the evidence, Stevenson concludes that Lydia could not have acquired her fluency by normal means.[7]

Another case lending itself to both discarnate possession and reincarnation interpretations is that of Uttara/Sharada.[8] This remarkable case involving responsive xenoglossy differs from the Lydia/Jensen case in several respects. First, the Sharada personality emerged spontaneously, without hypnosis, though the original personality (Uttara) was almost certainly in an altered state of consciousness when it first appeared. Second, Sharada spoke fluently in Bengali, a language unknown to Uttara and her family who spoke the Marathi language of their region. Her fluency went far beyond the short phrases and rudimentary sentences spoken in the Lydia/Jensen case. Third, a substantial number of Sharada's statements (made in Bengali, the only language she understood) were verified, unlike the statements made by Jensen. A family corresponding to her claims has been traced to the region in Bengal where she claimed to have lived.

The essential facts are as follows, Uttara Huddar, the subject of this case, was born in 1941 in Nagpur, located in the Maharashtra region of India. She was well educated and served as a part-time lecturer in public administration at Nagpur University. When in her twenties, she developed several physical disorders, was treated as an outpatient for several years, and then admitted to a hospital where she was given instruction in meditation. In 1974 when 32 years of age and subsequent to her meditation practice at the hospital, the Sharada personality suddenly emerged. Sharada spoke fluent Bengali, but could not speak or understand Marathi, Uttara's native language. Nor could Uttara (like the other members of her family) speak or understand Bengali.

Sharada appeared at irregular intervals, sometimes remaining for only a day or two before the Uttara personality returned, but at other times staying for several weeks, and once stayed for seven weeks. She continued to appear intermittently until at least 1979.

Sharada's memories, attitudes and behavior were markedly different from those of Uttara. Although Uttara was (and perhaps still is) unmarried and not a shy person, Sharada dressed and behaved like a rather shy, married Bengal woman. She differed from Uttara in her comportment, her gestures, and even her gait. Her tastes in food were similar to those of Bengalis, and unlike those of Uttara's family. She regarded Marathi as a "harsh" language and refused to learn it. She did not recognize Uttara's parents or friends, behaved distantly toward the latter's parents, and shuddered when any male touched her, even the male members of Uttara's family.

Sharada provided a wealth of detail about her life in Bengal, giving names of many of her relatives and of the places in Bengal familiar to her. She far outdid Jensen in this respect. As noted earlier, many of her claims were verified. Bengali genealogical data, for example, included the names of many of the males she had cited as her relatives. Sharada's own name does not appear but these genealogies list only the male members of a family. The information she provided was sufficient to lead Stevenson and Pasricha, after a thorough investigation, to conclude (tentatively) that "... the data of the case are best accounted for by supposing that the subject has had memories of the life of a Bengali woman who died about 1830."[9]

Stevenson and his colleagues were especially concerned to explore the possibility that Sharada acquired in a normal way her fluency in Bengali. During their investigations in 1976, they spent much of their time trying to find someone who might somehow have communicated to Uttara the knowledge of Bengali that Sharada displayed. But they failed to uncover any evidence of Bengali-speaking persons from whom Uttara might have acquired such knowledge. They also point out that even if Uttara had learned Bengali from some such person, she would have learned *modern* Bengali, not the Bengali that Sharada spoke, as Sharada's Bengali was an English-free and Sanskritized Bengali that was spoken 150 years earlier. Accordingly, Stevenson and Pasricha were led to conclude that Uttara had not learned Bengali prior to the appearance of Sharada. And if she did not, then Sharada's fluency in Bengali does not admit of naturalistic explanation.

This case, like the one of Lydia/Jensen, lends itself to alternative interpretations, i.e., as either a case of reincarnation or one of discarnate possession. If the appearances of Sharada were taken to be periodic eruptions of prior-life memories expressed in the language the subject spoke in that earlier life, this case would be interpreted as one of reincarnation. Stevenson and Pasricha suggest this interpretation in referring to it as "An Unusual Case of the Reincarnation Type." But they seem to find the discarnate possession interpretation equally plausible. The responsive xenoglossy featured in it indicates that it is not a case of ordinary possession, but possibly one of "true"[10] or discarnate possession, in which case Sharada would be a subject who, after having lived and died in the early part of the nineteenth century, came to possess Uttara's body almost 150 years later.

Spontaneous Recall of Ostensible Former Lives

We will now turn to cases of young children reporting memories of prior lives. Unlike the hypnosis cases, these memories are spontaneous or non-induced. We will not examine any cases of recollections had by non-hypnotized adults of allegedly prior lives, for the most impressive case-investigations have been of young children having apparent prior-life recollections. Since they provide the most persuasive evidence of reincarnation, we will focus on them.

Before examining particular cases of this type, it might be helpful to take note of the features recurring in cases from all cultures studied. Cases lacking these features are less likely to be authentic.

1. Most of the subjects are between two and four years old when they begin to speak about their previous lives, i.e., about the time they first learn to speak, and stop talking about them between five and eight years of age.
2. Usually about ninety per cent of the verifiable statements made by the subject about her prior life are correct.

3. The subject is likely to be born within a few miles of the remembered person's home and to speak the same language. (We should remind ourselves, however, that the existence of the remembered person is less likely to be verified as the distance increases.)

4. It is very likely that the remembered persons met a violent death, often when still young. Events related to that death tend to be prominent among the subject's memories.

5. The interval between the death of the remembered person and the birth of the child with the memories is rather short, usually from 4 to 48 months, the particular average interval being connected with the culturally determined beliefs about its length. The average length among the Haida of British Columbia and Alaska is four months, and among the Alaskan Tlingits it is 48 months. In other cultures, the average lengths fall between these extremes.

Though these features help to define the class in which authentic cases are likely to be found, there are further features whose presence would render highly plausible the conclusion that a case displaying them is a case of reincarnation (or, perhaps, discarnate possession).

1. The subject provides a detailed description of the alleged prior life that includes not only the location of the home and the name of the remembered person along with the names and characteristics of that person's family members and relatives, but also some selective historical events that could have been known only by the remembered person.

2. The subject and her immediate family members are interviewed at great length, preferably before they have established contact with the remembered person's family. The subject is questioned about matters she could be expected to know if her claims about being the remembered person were true, and she supplies a considerable amount of information, some solicited by the questions and some provided spontaneously. Careful notes are taken of what transpired, and tape recorders might be present as well.

3. In addition to providing apparent memories of a past life, in many cases the subject displays behavior patterns, abilities, attitudes, and so forth that can be checked for agreement with those of the remembered person. In some cases, the subject displays certain specific skills (e.g., playing a musical instrument or fluency in a foreign language) that were possessed by the remembered person but apparently could not have been acquired by the subject in any normal way.

4. Investigators independently verify a very high percentage of the verifiable memory claims made by the subject, in some cases even those claims whose truth was known only to the remembered person. If some distinctive behaviors or attitudes are exhibited by the subject, they are found to be in accord with those the remembered person had displayed. When the subject is taken to the remembered person's home, she seems at home there, recognizing that person's family members, displaying

emotions that the remembered person would be likely to display, and, in some cases, conversing with family members about intimate matters. She seems familiar with the home and its surroundings, sometimes pointing (correctly) to changes that have occurred since the death of the remembered person.

5. The fraud hypothesis is extremely unlikely. The number of witnesses is large enough to make a conspiracy very difficult to carry through without detection, and many would stand to lose much by exposure. The opportunities for fraud are lacking, as is any apparent motivation for fraudulent activity. In many cases, neither the subject nor her parents have anything to gain either financially or in enhanced social status by her identifying with the remembered person.

The extent to which these features are exhibited in a case is a measure of the grounds for concluding that it is a case of reincarnation. If a case should exhibit all of these features in close to the detail suggested above, it would provide an ideal level of evidence for the reincarnation (or, perhaps, discarnate possession) hypothesis.

The Shanti Devi Case

This early case is an interesting one because, if it occurred as reported, it displayed the above described features as well as any and thus would rank among those providing the best evidence for reincarnation.[11] Shanti Devi was born in 1926 in old Delhi. When she was about three years old she began to speak of a former life in Muttra, a city about eighty miles away. She claimed that her name then was Lugdi, that she was married to a man named Kedar Nath, and that she died in 1925 giving birth to a third child. She provided a wealth of verifiable information about her former life as Lugdi, describing the relatives of Lugdi and of Kedar Nath, as well as providing a detailed description of the house (and surrounding grounds) where Lugdi lived with her husband and children.

When Shanti's family began to investigate her claims, her granduncle sent a letter to Muttra using the address that she had provided. The letter was received by a still grieving and quite astounded Kedar Nath who, suspecting fraud, sent his cousin to investigate. The cousin had lived near the Naths in Muttra before moving to Delhi and had known Lugdi well. Upon arriving at the Devi house under pretext of business, Shanti, then nine years old, opened the door and, screaming with delight, threw herself into the arms of the astonished man. Before the visitor could speak, she explained to her mother who was hurrying to the door that he was her husband's cousin who lived in Muttra until moving to Delhi and that he could tell her about her husband and sons.

After conversing with Shanti and her family, he was able to confirm the accuracy of the factual claims she had been making over the years. They agreed that Kedar Nath would visit the Devis, and when he arrived, Shanti greeted him just as would a beloved wife from whom he had been long separated, showering him with hugs and kisses, serving him biscuits and tea with the general demeanor of a wife, and responding correctly to his intimate questions about things only Lugdi had known.

When independent investigators eventually arrived, they took Shanti to Muttra at her request, having her lead them to Lugdi's home. When the train arrived in Muttra, she greeted excitedly and identified without prompting relatives of Kedar Nath who were waiting on the platform. After getting off the train she began to talk to and question them in the local dialect of the Muttra district, unintelligible to others from Delhi—a dialect to which she had not been exposed. She later took them to the Nath home and provided information only Lugdi could have known, correctly identifying the former locations of wells, outhouses, and caches of money. More specifically, when Kedar Nath asked her to locate some rings she had hidden before she died, she said they were in a pot buried under the floor of the old house where Lugdi and Kedar Nath had lived. Investigators later found them in the place where she had told them to look. It seems that all who had known Lugdi had agreed that she had been reincarnated as Shanti.

Though the methods of investigation employed in this case do not meet the high standards we have come to expect in the cases investigated by Stevenson, the case is nevertheless a very interesting one, rich in verifiable detail and worthy of serious consideration if the central facts were as reported. Fraud seems unlikely given the rather large number of people who would have had to cooperate in fabricating such a case with no apparent motive for doing so. Moreover, independent investigators witnessed Shanti's responsive xenoglossy—a xenoglossy that (unlike that of the Lydia Jensen case) was not induced under hypnosis.

The Case of Jasbir Jat

This case was carefully investigated by Stevenson.[12] In this highly unusual case, the remembered person had not died until *after* the birth of the person with the apparent memories. Even though cases of young children with ostensible memories of previous lives are generally considered to provide the best evidence for reincarnation, this one is strongly suggestive of discarnate possession.

In the spring of 1954 when Jasbir was three-and-one-half years old he was believed to have died of smallpox. But after a few hours he began to show signs of life and then gradually revived completely over a period of several weeks. Now able to speak again, he declares that he is Sobha Ram, a recently deceased young man from a nearby village. As Sobha Ram, Jasbir correctly described the circumstances of Sobha Ram's death (which occurred close to the time of Jasbir's apparent death), recognized Sobha Ram's family members and identified their relationships to Sobha Ram, and provided a wealth of details that corresponded closely to details of Sobha Ram's life, even though each family had no knowledge of the other. Stevenson's careful inquiries in both villages failed to turn up anyone who could have served as a normal means of communication of information from the family of Sobha Ram to Jasbir.

The behavioral features of the case underlined the strong identification of Jasbir with Sobha Ram. When Jasbir was with Sobha Ram's family (the Tyagis), he enjoyed himself greatly and was very reluctant to return to his own family where he felt isolated and lonely. He wished to stay with the Tyagis and visited them often, even though his own family discouraged this, primarily out of a fear of losing him to the Tyagis.

The Jasbir personality never returned. Years later, Jasbir insisted that his memories of his life as Sobha Ram were as clear as ever. When Stevenson asked him if he knew what happened to the mind or person that had occupied the Jasbir body prior to its affliction with smallpox, he claimed that he did not. Though reluctant, he remained with Jasbir's family and gradually adjusted to his situation.

The fraud hypothesis is extremely implausible in this case (as it generally is in the cases Stevenson checks out and then reports in great detail). Jasbir's father had tried to suppress information about his son's strange claims and behavior from leaking out in the village. Clearly, his claims and behavior were not encouraged by his family whose lives were disarranged as a result. He became alienated among his own people in his village. And though most of the people in both villages were aware of Jasbir's activities, Stevenson was unable to find anyone stepping forward to even hint at fraud or sources of normally acquired information. Thus this well-researched case certainly seems to require a paranormal explanation, with the discarnate possession hypothesis being at least initially the most plausible.

The Case of Swarnlata Mishra

In addition to being rich in verifiable detail like many of the Indian cases, this case has three unusual features that make it of special interest to our concerns. First, unlike most investigated cases of the reincarnation type, the statements made by Swarnlata were written down prior to attempts at verification. (The case of Imad Elawar of Lebanon also has this evidentially important feature.) Second, Swarnlata claimed to remember two previous incarnations (one of which is relevant to the interpretation of this case).

Third, Swarnlata exhibited recitative xenoglossy apparently requiring paranormal explanation and adding considerable strength to this case.

Swarnlata was born in March of 1948, the daughter of M.L. Mishra, assistant in the office of the district inspector of schools, Chhatarpur, Madhya Pradish. The family lived in various towns in the district of Madhya Pradish during the period that concerns us. When Swarnlata was a little over three years old and living in the city of Panna, her father took her and several other people on a 170 mile trip south to the city of Jabalpur, also in Madhya Pradish. When passing through the city of Katni (57 miles north of Jabalpur) during the return trip to Panna, Swarnlata unexpectedly asked the driver to turn down a road toward "my house"—a request that understandably was ignored. Later while having tea in Katni, Swarnlata told the group that they could get much better tea at "her" house nearby. These comments puzzled her father as neither he nor any of his family members had ever lived closer to Katni than about 100 miles. Swarnlata later told her siblings of a previous life she had lived in Katni as a member of a family named Pathak and thereby deepened the puzzlement of her father when he learned of this.

During the next few years, Swarnlata revealed fragments of her apparent memories largely to her siblings but to some extent to her parents. She revealed ostensible memories of a prior life as Biya, daughter in a family named Pathak living in Katni, and later married to Sri Chintamini Pandey of Maihar, a town north of Katni. In addition to her memories, she also performed for her mother, and later in front of others, unusual songs and dances that apparently she had had no opportunity to learn—a fact whose significance we will later explore. She still had her memories when in 1958 she met a lady from Katni (named Srimati Agnihotri) whom she claimed to recognize from her previous life there. This event prompted her father to write down some of her statements. Neither he nor any other member of the Mishra family had any knowledge of the Pathak family of Katni at this time.

In March 1959, Sri H. N. Bannerjee spent two days in Chhatarpur (where the Mishras then lived) investigating the case before traveling to Katni to learn about the Pathak family. He took with him to Katni nine statements Swarnlata made about the Pathak residence (e.g., that there was a girl's school behind the house and that lime furnaces were visible from the house), statements he used to find the residence and was able to confirm on arriving there. He also found that her statements were in close accord with the life of Biya, daughter of the Pathak family of Katni and deceased wife of Sri Chintamini Pandey of Maihar.

In the summer of 1959, members of the Pathak family and Biya's husband's family journeyed to Swarnlata's home in Chhatarpur. She recognized them even though they took considerable precautions to avoid giving her any cues and frequently tried to mislead her. Shortly after these visits, Swarnlata was taken to Katni and Maihar where Biya had lived. In Maihar, where Biya had lived much of her married life prior to her death there, Swarnlata recognized additional people and places, along with commenting on various changes that had occurred since the death of Biya. Sri Mishri (her father) made some written records of these recognitions shortly after they occurred.

Stevenson spent four days investigating the case in 1961. He interviewed Swarnlata and fourteen others from the three families concerned. For most of the interviews he needed no interpreter, as the main witnesses spoke English well. He had Bannerjee's notes at his disposal, which he carefully rechecked, and later the extensive notes of Professor P. Pal, who studied the case in 1963. This was the basis for his detailed presentation and analysis of the Swarnlata case—one of twenty in his acclaimed book, *Twenty Cases*. After he left, he kept in correspondence with Swarnlata, visiting her in November of 1971, at which time she reported that she still had her memories of her previous life.

Swarnlata's prior life memories were remarkably abundant and accurate. Though all of her verified memories resist naturalistic or normal explanation, some seem impossible to explain in that way. For example, she provided information about the structural details of the Pathak house (in which Biya spent the early part of her life) as it was years before she began speaking of a prior life, something very few residents of Katni would have known. That she learned this from some stranger from Katni who knew the Pathak family seems extremely unlikely, especially when one realizes how carefully the activities of young girls in India are controlled by their families. As Stevenson points out, "She was never out on the street unaccompanied and she never saw strangers in the house alone."[13]

She revealed highly personal information about Biya's husband, Sri Pandey, that only Biya and her husband could have known. She claimed that Sri Pandey had taken 1200 rupees from her box of money, a claim that he verified though contending that he had taken somewhat less than that. He also stated that only he and Biya had known about this incident. Another incident in which she revealed information known only to Biya and one other person was one in which she claimed to have once gone to a wedding at Tilora village with Srimati Agnihotri (previously mentioned), at which time they had difficulty finding a latrine—a claim Agnihotri confirmed. The clarity of her memories and the level of her convictions about having lived a prior life became evident in another incident involving Biya. She insisted that Biya had had gold fillings in her front teeth despite the efforts of one of Biya's brothers to deceive her by claiming (falsely) that Biya had lost her teeth.

Actually, Biya's brothers could not remember the details about Biya's teeth. They had to consult their wives, who verified Swarnlata's claims.

In addition to Swarnlata's astonishing memories, her behavior when in the presence of Biya's family as well as in the presence of Biya's husband was very much in accord with that which Biya is likely to have exhibited. She behaved like an older sister when with Biya's brothers even though they were forty or more years older than she. When with Biya's sons, she behaved toward them as a mother would. Like the members of the Pathak family, they completely accepted her as Biya reborn, though they did not believe in reincarnation before encountering her. She showed strong emotion and wept when seeing or parting from members of the Pathak family. Upon encountering Biya's husband, whom she recognized with no difficulty, she looked bashful as Hindu wives do in the presence of their husbands.

Of at least equal significance are Swarnlata's spontaneous and usually rapid recognitions of people known to Biya, particularly members of the Pathak and Pandey families. In all, she recognized twenty people in the presence of witnesses. Stevenson points out that most of these recognitions took place in such a way that she was obliged to give a name or state a relationship between Biya and the person in question.[14] No guidance or cues were permitted. Moreover, there were several serious attempts to mislead her or deny that her answer was correct—attempts that failed to block her recognitions. The significance of her recognitions of other people is heightened if, as Polyani has cogently argued, such recognitions are instances of tacit knowing comparable to skills in their tacitness and complexity.[15] For an appeal to extra-sensory contact with the living cannot plausibly explain the possession of skills.

The unusual songs and dances performed by Swarnlata before the age of five manifest a skill we have already noted but whose significance we have not yet explored. Professor P. Pal, a native of Bengal, identified the songs as Bengali, and later learned that two of them derived from poems by Rabindranath Tagore. The third song also was definitely Bengali. But Swarnlata had lived entirely among Hindi-speaking people. After a very careful and circumspect estimation of the likelihood that Swarnlata could have received sufficient exposure to Bengali to explain her performances, Stevenson concludes that they are "...paranormal components of the case and are among its strongest features."[16]

Interestingly, Swarnlata claimed that she learned them in a prior life that occurred between the death of Biya (in 1939) and her birth (as Swarnlata in 1948). She claimed that after she died (as Biya) she was reborn as Kamlesh in Sylet, Assam (now in Bangladesh) and that when about nine she died (as Kamlesh) and then was reborn as Swarnlata. She claimed to remember that in her life as Kamlesh she learned them from a friend (Madhu) who knew them.

Naturalistic Explanations

A general consideration to keep in mind when examining cases of the reincarnation type (or other types of cases suggestive of continuing existence after death) is that the plausibility of an explanatory hypothesis depends upon the particular case under examination. A standard approach to the case in question is to consider the fraud hypothesis first, and, if that fails, move on to other normal or naturalistic explanations (e.g., cryptomnesia). If all fail, then the next step is to try paranormal explanations of the non-survivalist (psi) type. If they too prove to be extremely implausible, then the survival hypothesis alone remains. But this must proceed on a case by case basis. If one case proves to be fraudulent, other cases are, of course, left unaffected. Different cases succumb to different explanations. As always, our central concern is to see if any case (s) is (are) best explained by the survival hypothesis.

The Fraud Hypothesis

Though the Vennum case occurred a long time ago, the concurrence of a number of facts make fraud very unlikely. It was widely reported in the newspapers of the time, and aroused much attention. It was examined by numerous outside investigators, including the painstakingly careful and highly critical Dr. Richard Hodgson. The accuracy of Dr. Stevens' account of it was attested to by both the Roffs and the Vennums; and the integrity of the two principle witnesses, Dr. Stevens and Mr. Roff, was vouched for in many testimonials. In addition, it was accepted by renowned philosopher, William James, himself a highly critical investigator, and included in his classic work, *Principles of Psychology*.

Though, as we noted, the methods of investigation used in the Shanti Devi case did not reach the high standards we have come to expect in the Stevenson investigations, possible fraud has not been the concern. Indeed, there are researchers who believe that it provides the best available grounds for belief in reincarnation. In the other three cases the principle investigator was Stevenson, whose case-investigations are very impressive. He was always concerned about the possibility of fraud, but found neither motive nor opportunity for it in any of the twenty cases (of which the Jasbir and Swarnlata cases are only two) that he describes in detail and critically evaluates in his *Twenty Cases*. These facts coupled with the large numbers of witnesses involved make the fraud hypothesis "extremely unlikely"[17] in these cases. The same could be said of the Sharada case. In the Lydia Jensen case, which is also well-documented and carefully investigated, the understandable concern is not fraud but the fact that it has not been possible to verify the historical existence of Jensen. Accordingly, the significance of this case depends upon whether there is some other normal hypothesis that offers a plausible explanation of Lydia's responsive xenoglossy. Cryptomnesia has been claimed to provide such an explanation.

Cryptomnesia

To appeal to cryptomnesia is to appeal to the theory that memories that seem to be of a past life arise out of normally-acquired information whose source has been forgotten, though the information itself might be recalled when the person possessing it is suitably stimulated. Though the person displaying cryptomnesia has acquired the recalled information in normal ways (e.g., from books, TV, lectures, newspapers, and parents), he has forgotten not only its source but also the fact that he had acquired it. Thus he is deceived in thinking that he has prior-life memories.

How plausible is the appeal to cryptomnesia? Stevenson finds it to be far more plausible than fraud in the cases that he publicizes after extensive investigation and analysis. Even so, he finds it highly implausible in these cases. In almost all of those included in *Twenty Cases* (as well as many later ones), the children lived in rural areas where newspapers and radios (let alone TV) were virtually unknown. Not only were there no printed or broadcast records of the lives and deaths of the persons ostensibly remembered (or of anyone else) but any such records, had they existed, would have been inaccessible to the children at the age when they first made their main assertions about their prior lives. Thus only a *person* could have supplied the child with remembered information. But the persons having the information were not available. In the Swarnlata case, for example, the Mishra and Pathak families had never lived within a hundred miles of each other and each denied having had any previous acquaintance with the other.

There is another difficulty with the cryptomnesia theory that by itself seems fatal to this theory in the rich cases. Though in these cases the families were unknown to one another prior to the child's assertions, a critic might argue that a brief, almost casual acquaintance between the child and some stranger might have sufficed to provide the child with the needed information that the child later seems to remember. But, as Stevenson argues, such communication could not have sufficed, for two reasons. First, the information the child provides is frequently rich in quantity, minute in detail, and, in many cases, includes items of a highly intimate nature about the previous-life family—items not likely to get revealed to a stranger. Second, and perhaps even more important, the mere conveyance of information could not account for the spontaneous, swift, and numerous *recognitions* by those children of people and places of the prior life. Such recognitions, especially of people, seem to require actual acquaintance with the person later remembered. Verbal descriptions fall far short of perceptual acquaintance in providing what is needed for recognition, a fact well attested to by the difficulty people have in positively identifying some person (e.g., some criminal from a line-up of suspects) on the basis of a verbal description or even a sketch or composite picture. In the words of Polanyi, "the identification of a person is such a delicate operation that even a genuine photograph may not suffice...."[18] As we noted earlier, he argues cogently that recognitions are instances of tacit knowing, like skills in their tacitness and complexity. Even extensive verbal description could not produce them.

Though the Lydia Jensen and Sharada cases did not include spontaneous recognitions of persons known to the subject in an apparent prior life, they seem equally resistant to explanation by appeal to cryptomnesia. There is no evidence that Lydia was ever exposed to eighteenth-century Swedish, even in a brief or casual manner that might have been forgotten by her and her family. But even if she had had such exposure, such a level would have fallen far below what would suffice to account for her ability to speak and understand this language of the past. In the Sharada case, Stevenson and his colleagues were unable to find any evidence of relevant exposure to Bengali, let alone the amount needed for the high-level fluency that Sharada displayed.

To be sure, there are weak cases that may be most plausibly explained by an appeal to cryptomnesia. This Stevenson readily concedes. But it fails in the rich cases and, in particular, in the Stevenson cases that we have examined.

Paramnesia

Stevenson takes paramnesia quite seriously, finding that in many cases an appeal to it is more difficult to exclude as a highly improbable explanation than is an appeal to cryptomnesia. Paramnesia denotes inaccuracies and distortions in the informants' memories. It might occur in the following way: When some young child begins to make some utterances about a previous life, the enthusiastic parents (who already may be inclined to believe in reincarnation) encourage the child to make more utterances, perhaps by asking leading questions, with the effect of giving them a fullness and a coherence they do not have. They may begin to search for the prior-life family to which they suppose their child was referring. When they come upon a family having a deceased member whose life seems to be more or less in accord with some of the child's statements, they explain to that family what their child has said. The second family (who might also be disposed to belief in reincarnation and is likely to be grieving the deceased member's death) uncritically agrees that the child's statements might refer to that deceased member. The families exchange information about the deceased person and the child's memories. The child is asked more leading questions, perhaps along with cues about what the answers should be. Thus by way of the enthusiasm and carelessness of the two families, they credit the child with having provided numerous memories of the deceased person whereas in fact she contributed only a few, and often vague, memories before the families met.

It is easy to imagine something of this sort happening, especially in cultures strongly inclined to belief in reincarnation. Stevenson finds it to be the best explanation for some cases. He points to the Druse culture as one in which the scenario described above might well occur. Still, some of the strongest cases have occurred in the Druse culture (e.g., the case of Imad Elawar of Lebanon).[19] And, as we noted earlier, many important cases have occurred in the United States, Canada, and Great Britain where the culture is hostile to reincarnation. Moreover, the paramnesia explanation is inapplicable to those cases in which someone had made a written record of the child's statements before they were verified and before the two families had met (as in the cases of Imad and Swarnlata). Though these cases are few in number (less than 1.5 percent of all cases), that number is not insignificant. In 1999, Stevenson had 33 such cases on his list.

Inherited Memory

In many of Stevenson's cases, the person with the ostensible prior-life memories is related to the prior-life person. In these cases, initially it might seem plausible to attribute the reincarnation experiences to genetic-based or inherited memories. The problem, however, is that there seems to be no acceptable independent evidence that memories can be genetically transmitted.[20] In any case, the remembering person is unrelated to the remembered person in about two-thirds of the cases. Finally, many of the subjects report memories of events that happened after the conception of the prior-life person's children (e.g., how that person died), thus revealing the impossibility of those memories having been genetically transmitted to the subjects who had them. Moreover, such memories are common. In Stevenson's words, "...the majority of the children of these cases remember—even when they remember little else—how the previous personality died."[21]

Paranormal Explanations

We have now considered the primary types of naturalistic explanation and have found that none seem at all plausible as attempts to account for the best cases of ostensible reincarnation. But their failure in those cases alone would be fatal to them. For the necessary condition of their explanatory success is that between them they must plausibly explain *all* the cases, not just a few or even a great many. Given our space limitations, our treatment of them was not as extensive as one might have hoped, or as one would expect in a book devoted largely to reincarnation, yet seems sufficient to show that none will prove to be successful in the best cases and that these cases will turn out to require a paranormal explanation.

The Psi Hypothesis

Of the three paranormal hypotheses to consider—reincarnation, possession, and the non-survivalist psi hypothesis—the latter has the highest antecedent probability, as it would account for all the cases (other than those succumbing to naturalistic explanation) by appealing to the psychic powers of the living. It has the initial credibility gained by not having to defend the view that persons have continued to exist after biological death. Yet, despite this initial advantage, the difficulties lying in the way of accepting it are so formidable that in the end the other paranormal hypotheses might seem quite plausible when compared to it.

One difficulty for the psi hypothesis is to explain why these children who supposedly use psi-acquired information to construct their "prior-life" memories hardly ever show, or have credited to them by their families, any psychic abilities independent of these memories. The evidence for the existence of psychic abilities indicates that they are *general* abilities, not likely to be exercised narrowly upon the life of a single deceased person. Though the range of targets is peculiarly narrow, the psychic ability itself would have to be great. In some of the cases, the information provided by the child was not known to any single living person. In the Swarnlata case, for example, the information would have had to have been gathered from two or more minds, as each possessed only a portion of it. The Pathak brothers knew about the changes in the Pathak house in Katni and almost all the other information Swarnlata provided about events at Katni. But they failed to remember that Biya had gold fillings in her teeth. And, almost certainly, they failed to know about the latrine episode, or about the money Biya's husband took from her. Thus Swarnlata's ESP must have been extensive to have given her telepathic access to each of the minds possessing the information she provided about Biya's life, yet focused in a remarkably narrow way in that the items she acquired from the different minds shared the feature of having been known by a single deceased person—Biya. Extensive paranormal powers to access information are combined with equally remarkable powers to *select* only the few relevant items from the broad range of items made available.

Another feature of reincarnation experiences making them difficult to explain by appeal to ESP is that they are had by the subject as *memories*. For ESP-acquired information typically is not experienced as something remembered. Nor would one expect them to be if the ESP hypothesis were true; for it implies that reincarnation experiences are not really memories at all. Rather, they are informed by ESP and *disguised* as memories. When we consider this implication of the ESP hypothesis in conjunction with the amount of ESP needed to explain the rich cases (e.g., that of Swarnlata) and the highly specialized way in which it exists in young children who show no independent evidence of psychic abilities, it seems clear that what is being postulated is a super-psi or, more specifically, a super–ESP. For such ESP would be of a magnitude and of a peculiar, specialized form that would set it apart from the "typical" ESP whose existence is indicated by evidence. Though its existence is logically possible and though it might in fact exist for all we positively know, there must be independent empirical evidence that it does exist in young children if an appeal to its existence to explain the cases of ostensible reincarnation is to amount to more than an interesting but unsupported conjecture. Perhaps such empirical evidence will be acquired. However, Hintze and Pratt have asserted that (at the time of their writing, of course) none had been found in children under the age of five.[22]

Closely connected with the fact that the child experiences the allegedly ESP-acquired information as something remembered is the fact that he remembers it as information about *himself* as he was in a previous life. In nearly all cases, the child remembers the events he describes as having happened to him and he remembers himself as an actor in them. He remembers them "from the inside" just as we remember our own past experiences. In other words, he seems to remember *having the experiences* of a certain deceased person and thus quite understandably identifies himself with that person.

The ESP hypothesis implies that this identification is, of course, a mistake. But we must wonder why in that hypothesis the mistake should have occurred in the first place, especially when we see that cases of young children (other than those of the rebirth type in question) identifying with strangers are almost or entirely unknown.[23] It would seem highly unlikely that these children, even given the super–ESP that they are supposed to have exercised, should have identified themselves with people whom they had never met and, indeed, had never known even to exist. For there is no reason to believe that their ESP-acquired information about what turned out to be events in the lives of certain deceased people would be presented to them in the first-person mode as events they remember having experienced.

There is, however, a deeper, more compelling reason to believe that ESP could not be responsible for reincarnation experience. Expressed in first-person terms, ESP might be able to provide another with astounding information about some experiences I have had or am having, but what it might provide is not the (epistemic) access to my experiences that I have. For I (and only I) have a first-person access to my present experience in the act of *having* this experience; and I have such access to my past experience in remembering *myself having it*. My *having* or undergoing my experience is what *makes* it mine. Thus it is (logically) inseparable from me, and logically impossible for another to have had it or to genuinely remember having had it.

Clearly, even a super–ESP could not provide another with a first-person access to my past experience. Yet it is this access to it that is essential to memory and is what reveals to me in the clearest possible way that I am that person whose past experience I am remembering. If I lacked this access to my past—if my memory of my past experience did not include a memory of *my having* that experience—my knowledge (if possible at all) that certain past experiences were ones I had would be indirect or inferential and thus much less certain than it actually is.

Now, there is no reason to doubt that a young child remembers his past experiences in the way we do, i.e., by remembering himself having them. He has a first-person access to them; and it is this access to the experiences of some deceased person that would render entirely understandable why in many cases the child's identification with a deceased person is so intense that he will not retract it even in the face of great resistance and hostility toward it by parents and relatives. But, as we noted, even a super–ESP cannot provide such access. Since such access is entirely consistent with the reincarnation (or the possession) hypothesis, it can provide a very plausible account of the child's often intense identification with a deceased person—something the ESP hypothesis cannot do.

ESP Plus Impersonation

Another, and perhaps unanswerable, objection to the ESP hypothesis comes into view when we see that the information conveyed by the child in the rich cases is organized in a pattern characteristic of the mind of the deceased person with whom he identifies. This pattern consists of information about persons, places, and events known to the deceased person while excluding information not known to that person. In addition to such informational patterns, the child (in the rich cases) displays patterns of *behavior* not normal for a child in his situation but comparable to those of the deceased person. These patterns, at least when taken together in the best cases, suggest than an entire personality has been transported to another body. Since the existence of such phenomena seems fatal to the ESP hypothesis alone, defenders of it have attempted to supplement it with a theory of subconscious impersonation (or, "personation," to use Stevenson's term). To properly evaluate this theory we will look more closely at these phenomena, beginning with the informational patterns.

We noted earlier in our study of the Swarnlata case that the total amount of information she provided about Biya's life was not known to any single living person, though each of several persons knew a portion of it. The ESP hypothesis might be able to offer a plausible account of this by supposing that Swarnlata was able to access telepathically the contents of several different minds. But the account appears quite implausible when we consider the extraordinary powers of selection and organization of information that Swarnlata would have needed to have accessed her information by exercising ESP. She provided no information unknown to Biya and no information about events occurring after Biya's death. Yet the several minds that she supposedly had accessed telepathically (or, perhaps, records she had clairvoyantly accessed) contained, of course, a great deal of information not known to Biya. It is one matter to account for the transfer of information to Swarnlata but quite another to account for precisely *what* got transferred and manifested in her mind as an organized body of information closely resembling that of Biya's mind. In Stevenson's view, ESP may account for the former but not the latter. His argument for this is persuasive, if not compelling:

> ... if Swarnlata gained her information by extrasensory perception, why did she not give the names of persons unknown to Biya when she met them for the first time? Extrasensory perception of the magnitude here proposed should not discriminate between targets unless guided by some organizing principle giving a special pattern to the persons or objects recognized. It seems to me that here we must suppose that Biya's personality somehow conferred the pattern of its mind on the contents of Swarnlata's mind.[24]

Biya's personality could not have done that via ESP, of course. For in that hypothesis, she did not exist when Swarnlata was born. Rather, the pattern continues because Biya continues to exist in Swarnlata, or so it seems.

As we focus our attention on the behavioral features of the rich cases, we should note that the child's (often very strong) identification with some deceased person is itself a behavioral feature and one that may seem to require the addition of a theory of subconscious impersonation to the ESP hypothesis if this identification is to be explained in a non-survivalist way. In this view, the child gains information about the deceased person by way of ESP, which he subconsciously integrates and personalizes so thoroughly that he comes to believe mistakenly that he is that person, who he then continues to subconsciously impersonate. Other behavioral features of the cases may then be attributed to subconscious impersonation.

The theory of subconscious impersonation merits serious consideration. As we noted, there is an integrated set of behaviors exhibited by the child that more or less matches or can be reasonably inferred from what is learned about the deceased person but quite unusual for the young child in her family situation. For example, when Swarnlata was alone in the presence of Biya's children, she relaxed completely and treated them as a mother would even though they were men much older than her. Similarly, she behaved like an older sister when with Biya's brothers who were 40 years or more her senior. She formed a strong emotional bond with all of them.

Clearly, it is highly unusual for a young child to behave in this manner towards people who (in the ESP hypothesis) are total strangers. But given her strong identification with Biya, the theory that her behavior is due to her impersonation of the deceased woman might seem quite plausible. Yet there are other considerations that render it doubtful, even if it cannot be conclusively ruled out.

We noted earlier that the ESP hypothesis fails to explain in a plausible way how the child might come to identify mistakenly with some deceased person. Does the addition of the view that the child is impersonating the deceased provide much help? It seems not. Since ESP-acquired information typically is not presented as memories, we must now wonder why it would get personalized. And even if it were presented as memories, the child would very likely seem to be remembering certain facts, events, places, and people. The child would very likely *not* seem to be remembering *having the experiences* of some deceased person. Yet it is only by seeming to remember having the experiences of a person that the child, or anyone else, would be led to identify with that person. Seeming to remember anything other than having the past experience of a person would not be sufficiently convincing of identity to account for the very strong identification witnessed in many of the reincarnation cases.

In addition to the difficulty in understanding how these children could come to confuse themselves with strangers even though (as we noted previously) children without reincarnation experience never or almost never do, there is a problem in finding any motivation they could have for impersonating someone for a lengthy period of time during which they are typically receiving a great deal of negative reinforcement for doing so. Their sustained identification with a deceased person complicates their lives considerably, frequently embroiling them in conflicts with their families with no compensating benefits. Sometimes they make themselves outcasts within their families, as was the case with Jasbir. Clearly, powerful motivation is needed on the part of these children. Yet Stevenson was unable to find any such motivation in most cases, including the strong ones.[25]

The addition of the subconscious impersonation supposition to the ESP hypothesis is of no help in accounting for the child's possession of the skills and much of the information that requires a super–ESP, if explicable at all by appeal to ESP. It does not help to explain the numerous, spontaneous recognitions, achieved by Swarnlata and other young children, of the relatives and acquaintances of the deceased persons with whom they identified. As we noted, recognitions are instances of tacit knowing, skill-like in their complexity and tacitness. If such skills are already possessed, impersonation may affect how they are exercised. But the supposition that the child is engaged in impersonation would not help to explain how she could possess such skills in the first place. Much less could it help to explain the *pattern* of all the recognitions achieved by a child. Swarnlata recognized spontaneously twenty of Biya's relatives and acquaintances, but no one unknown to the deceased woman. Such patterns seem inexplicable by appeal to ESP (with or without the impersonation supposition) for two reasons. First, a recognition of another person is like a skill and thus the sort of thing ESP-acquired information does not provide. There are no grounds for believing that skills can be acquired by ESP. Second, even if skills could be acquired by ESP, why would the set of people recognized by the child match, or at least fall within, the set of people known to and thus recognized by the deceased person with whom the child identifies? There is no independent evidence that such discrimination among targets is ever a feature of ESP-acquired information.

The possession of skills that the subject could not have inherited or acquired seems to be the single most difficult item to explain by appeal to the ESP hypothesis. To fully appreciate the difficulty this presents as well as to show that recognitions of people are manifestations of skills in the relevant sense, we should distinguish between propositional knowledge (i.e., *knowing that* something is the case) one the one hand, and *knowing how* to do something (i.e., possessing a skill) on the other. ESP might enable the subject to know many truths about the past (e.g., about events, objects, and people). Each truth known could be expressed as *knowing that* something was the case, e.g., knowing that Biya had gold fillings in her teeth. But such knowledge about a person would not enable the subject to *recognize* that person, even if the subject had more of this knowledge than we have independent reason to believe could be acquired by way of ESP. For recognizing seems to be a matter of *knowing how* to do something. It is a skill generated through perceptual experience, not a matter of knowing that something is the case.

Even if one should doubt that recognitions are sufficiently skill-like to render highly implausible any attempt to explain them by appeal to ESP, there are other instances of these subjects knowing how to do something (e.g., knowing how to play a musical instrument or knowing how to speak a foreign language) that clearly amount to skills. Swarnlata's performance of Bengali dances accompanied by her singing songs in Bengali (a language unintelligible to the people in the region where she lived) is an example. It is a case of recitative xenoglossy as she could not respond in Bengali nor did she know what the Bengali words meant. Perhaps more impressive is Lydia Johnson's *responsive* xenoglossy, manifested in her fluency in eighteenth-century Swedish. Though her xenoglossy was induced by hypnosis, this was not true of Shanti Devi's responsive xenoglossy. Nor was it true in the case of Sharada, whose responsive xenoglossy was especially well documented.[26] Skills other than xenoglossy and also not learned in the present life but possessed by the prior-life person are exhibited by Paulo Lorenz's skill at sewing[27] and more impressively by Bishen Chand's skillful playing of drums.[28]

The possession of such skills seems impossible to explain by appeal to ESP, at least in the form in which there is independent evidence of its existence. It would seem to be logically possible that a super–ESP (or, more generally, a super-psi) exists, with no inherent limits and capable of producing all reincarnation experiences. But we might add, this would be no more than a *bare* logical possibility, whose actualization would be extremely unlikely, since *practice* seems to be necessary for the acquisition of any skill. Communication alone is insufficient. In other words, skills are incommunicable in any normal way. Thus we should infer that they are incommunicable paranormally as well. In any case, because we have no independent empirical evidence that such super-psi actually exists, we are justified in rejecting an appeal to it as providing the best explanation of these experiences. As we noted previously, we do not (contra Braude) unjustifiably impose limits on psi when we quite defensibly require of an explanation that it appeal to a form of psi whose existence has been empirically confirmed.

Reincarnation and Survival

We have been guided by the principle that we should accept the survival hypothesis with respect to some phenomenon suggestive of its truth only after finding the normal and non-survivalist psi explanations incapable of providing a plausible account of that phenomenon. Though the survival hypothesis turns out to have at least the edge in the competition, we have not addressed the issue of which survival hypothesis—discarnate possession or reincarnation—provides the more plausible explanation of a given case. What is at issue is whether any of the cases of ostensible reincarnation are such as to exclude possession as a plausible alternative explanation.[29] This issue is very difficult to settle, given that it turns on when the subject enters into association with the human organism. If this happens between conception and full embryonic development, reincarnation occurs; if after such development, it is a case of possession.[30] Stevenson's own (tentatively held) view is that while some cases are best explained as cases of possession, reincarnation provides the best explanation of several others. But we need not pursue this issue since the truth of either hypothesis in even a single case would imply the reality of survival.

Reincarnation and the Subject of Conscious States

In bringing this chapter to a close, it might be helpful to note how the evidence for possession and reincarnation relates to our earlier conclusions about the nonphysical nature of the conscious subject and its centrality to personal identity. The latter provides an account of *what it is* that might come to possess a body or to reincarnate in one, while the former is evidence that this actually happens. Since the subject of a person's conscious states is what *has* those states and (arguably) is both necessary and sufficient for the person's existence, it constitutes the essence of that person. Thus its continued existence after death constitutes the continued existence of the person.

The importance of the subject to the conceivability of possession and reincarnation comes fully into view when we see that what survives death can hardly be a collection of memories and dispositions existing on their own, without anything to unify them into what we might refer to as a "collection." Memories are (ontologically) incomplete in that they cannot occur apart from a rememberer. They are always memories of *someone*—the one who remembers. The presence of the subject unifies the collection into a single mind by being that which *has* the memories and other experiences. It is that single entity to which all of them belong. The (defensible)[31] view of the subject as the essence of a person (i.e., of what is necessary and sufficient for the existence of the person) provides a cogent account of both the unity and the ownership of experience, and thereby provides coherence to the notions of possession and reincarnation by providing a persuasive account of what it is that does the possessing or the reincarnating. Thus this view defuses all those objections and unexpressed doubts grounded in the belief or suspicion that the notions of possession and reincarnation are incoherent or meaningless.

A related set of objections (usually directed to belief in reincarnation) stem from either the belief that a person in an entirely material being, identical to the human organism that perishes, or the belief that though persons have a nonphysical component, this component is brain-dependent. In a recent critique of Stevenson's case studies, Paul Edwards has argued that if these studies are evidence of reincarnation they are also evidence for a number of "collateral assumptions" that he finds to be "surely fantastic if not pure nonsense...."[32] He enumerates them as follows:

> When a human being dies he continues to exist not on the earth but in a region we know not where as a "pure" disembodied mind or else as an astral or some other kind of "non-physical" body; although deprived of his brain he retains memories of life on earth as well as some of his characteristic skills and traits; after a period varying from a few months to hundreds of years, this pure mind or non-physical body, which lacks not only a brain but also any physical sense-organs, picks out a suitable woman on earth as its mother in the next incarnation, invades this woman's womb at the moment of conception of a new embryo, and unites with it to form a full-fledged human being....[33]

Largely on the basis of this materialist view of reality, Edwards goes on to reject Stevenson's reports, contending that "even in the absence of a demonstration of specific flaws, a rational person will conclude either that Stevenson's reports are seriously defective or that his alleged facts can be explained without bringing in reincarnation."[34]

Edwards points out that there is "a formidable initial presumption against reincarnation." It is a presumption stemming from the materialist view of reality currently widespread among intellectuals. In effect, we (along with Stevenson) were acknowledging this presumption in treating an appeal to reincarnation as a "last resort" explanation to be accepted only if all normal and all non-survivalist paranormal explanations failed. Moreover, the initial plausibility of Edwards' argument is due to an implicit acceptance of the materialist view underlying this presumption.

Still, this presumption is no more acceptable than the materialist view of persons that prompts it; and that view is one we were led to reject for numerous reasons that became apparent throughout our study, particularly of the mind-brain relation. Edwards' claims lose their apparent force when we remind ourselves of the reasons for believing that the subject of conscious states (which is, as we saw, the essence of a person) is a nonphysical being without spatial properties and thus such that questions about where it is in physical space do not arise. We owe our conception of physical space to the deliverances of our senses, but the subject is known not by them but only *introspectively*. We also took note of the basis for thinking that though the subject while in a discarnate state would not have a physical body, it might well have a phenomenal one that appears to it not unlike the way our physical bodies now appear to us due to stimulation from our sense organs. The reasons we found for accepting an indirect realist view of perception led us to acknowledge the existence of a phenomenal realm that is what is immediately known to us in our perceptual experience and thus known to us in a way in which physical objects never are. From the perspective attained in this view, it is the physical world of matter, not the phenomenal realm, which must remain epistemically remote and known only indirectly by way of an inference to the best explanation of our experience.

Edwards seems to find it obvious that all conscious states are dependent upon a properly functioning brain and, consequently, no consciousness could exist after biological death. But we found that this is certainly *not obvious*. The amount and kinds of dependence of consciousness upon the brain that can be observed must, of course, be acknowledged. But we explored many different relations the brain might have to the conscious subject, each of which is consistent with these observations and implies that the subject survives brain destruction. Moreover, the failure of materialist accounts of memory, coupled with the reasons for thinking that no such account is possible, enhance the plausibility of the view that the ability to remember is an intrinsic capacity of the subject and so would be retained if the subject survives bodily death.

The upshot of all this is that the dependency issue is complex and far from settled, that the question of whether death brings complete nonexistence is still an open one, and that a willingness to dismiss reports of phenomena suggestive of survival without finding specific flaws in the investigation of them seems presumptuous and close-minded. In any case, our rather extensive examination of causality in general and the self-brain causal relation in particular should prove to be of considerable value in properly evaluating the views of those who have difficulty taking seriously reports of paranormal phenomena suggestive of survival because they have already ruled out survival as a possibility.[35]

Mental Mediumship

The last kind of empirical evidence of survival that we shall consider is provided by mental mediumship. This phenomenon involves a medium or sensitive (usually a woman) who serves as a link between the living and what appears to be deceased persons still in existence attempting to communicate through her. The medium voluntarily enters into a condition that may vary from a slightly dissociated state to one in which she is fully entranced, i.e., a sleeplike yet conscious state. Some of the most persuasive evidence of survival comes to us from mediums while entranced. Most of this apparent or *prima facie* evidence consists in the *content* of the communications. But some consists in the means by which they are expressed. The entranced medium gives out statements automatically, i.e., not willfully and intentionally as in ordinary speech or writing. If spoken, the tone, pitch and inflection of voice may be notably different from the medium's in her normal state. But whether written or spoken, the vocabulary, the manner of expression, the ways in which ideas are associated, as well as the informational content, are, in the best cases, strikingly different from what an observation of the medium in her normal state would lead us to expect. Moreover, they are often characteristic of and claimed to issue from a deceased relative or friend of someone sitting with the medium at the time (viz., the sitter). Of central importance to our investigation is the fact that in some cases the information received from these ostensibly deceased persons apparently could not have been acquired by the medium in any normal way.

Though there is an enormous body of relevant material that might be considered in an investigation, we will be able to direct our attention more narrowly without significant effect on the conclusions we would eventually be led to draw. Accordingly, we shall focus upon a couple of the most impressive mediums of the past, the significance of proxy sittings, the phenomenon of "drop-in" communicators, and the evidential value of what has been termed the cross-correspondences. A briefer account is justified here for two reasons: First, there have been very few if any recent studies of mediumistic communications. Perhaps this is partly because mediums of the stature of the two we will consider are exceedingly rare. Second, we are justified in focusing more intensively on the two paranormal hypotheses, as the normal or naturalistic account seems effectively ruled out in the case of the two mediums we will study and appears to be a non-starter in the drop-in communicator phenomenon, as well as in the cross-correspondences. Though we will not ignore the normal account, we will see reasons for believing that it does not merit the amount of attention we gave to it in our earlier studies.

The Mediumship of Mrs. Piper

Mrs. Lenore E. Piper (1857–1950) was one of the most important mediums in the history of psychical research. She was the source of mediumistic phenomena that seem inexplicable without appeal to a paranormal hypothesis. Her mediumistic activity was observed by careful and highly competent investigators for a period of over twenty-five years. Indeed, it is likely that she was studied for more years and more systematically and minutely by more competent investigators than any other medium. In any case, the records of her mediumship activity remain unsurpassed in quantity and detail. Some of the most elaborate precautions were taken to exclude the possibility of fraud on her part—precautions that sometimes amounted to an invasion of her privacy. Yet no basis for suspicion of fraud or dishonesty was ever found. Nor does any other normal explanation fare any better than the fraud hypothesis in the case of most of the communications received through her. As we shall see, the information communicated through her was not of a kind that could have been found in public records or received from persons with whom she had normal communication.

Of the early investigators of Mrs. Piper's mediumship, the efforts and conclusions of two seem especially important to our concerns: the American philosopher, William James, and his close friend, Richard Hodgson, a leading member of the British Society for Psychical Research (SPR) and one of the early founders of the American Society for Psychical Research (ASPR). James first encountered her in 1885 and remained interested in her mediumship until his death in 1910. Hodgson came to Boston, Massachusetts (where Mrs. Piper lived) in 1887 and assumed charge of the investigation of her mediumship. Both were critical investigators of the highest level of competence, very much concerned to determine whether the extraordinary information she provided by way of her trance communications was such that she could have acquired it in normal ways.

James' investigation of Mrs. Piper's mediumship activity began in 1885 when he and his wife attended one of her séances. They told her nothing about themselves and said nothing while she was in trance. But Phinuit, her "control" at the time (i.e., the personality replacing the normal one and claiming to be that of a deceased person), nevertheless revealed information about them that, as they were later led to conclude, she could not have acquired by any normal methods. Subsequent sittings with her when in trance confirmed and reinforced for James his initial conclusion. It was also confirmed by twenty-five other persons whom James arranged to have sit with her under pseudonyms so that any normal access to knowledge of their identities would be blocked. Fifteen of them received during their initial sittings with her information about their lives which it seemed improbable that she could have come to know in a normal way. Many belonged to James' own extended family. In his words,

> The medium showed a startling intimacy with the family's affairs, talking of many matters known to no one outside, and which gossip could not possibly have conveyed to her ears.... My own conviction is not evidence, but it seems fitting to record it. I am persuaded of the medium's honesty, and of the genuineness of her trance; and although first disposed to think that the "hits" she made were either lucky coincidences, or the result of knowledge on her part of who the sitter was and of his or her family affairs, I now believe her to be in possession of a power as yet unexplained.[1]

Subsequent investigation amounted to a virtual demonstration that no satisfactory explanation of Mrs. Piper's mediumship could be provided without an appeal to the paranormal. Hodgson's extremely careful and extensive study of her mediumship did by itself much to provide such a demonstration. Like James, he first encountered Mrs. Piper at a time when he was highly suspicious of all mediums. He was regarded as an expert at detecting fraud. When in charge of Mrs. Piper's mediumship, he took the most elaborate precautions to rule out not only the possibility of fraud but of any other normal explanation of the content of her communications. He drew sitters from as wide a range of people as possible and had them introduced anonymously or pseudonymously. Sometimes they did not enter the room until Mrs. Piper was already in trance and then remained behind her where she could not have seen them even if her eyes had been open. He arranged for the careful recording of all sittings and paid special attention to the first sitting with a sitter. For weeks he had both Mrs. Piper and her husband under surveillance by detectives to see if they were attempting to gather information about the sitters. But nothing even remotely suspicious was ever detected.

Hodgson and James arranged to have the SPR invite her to London where she could be studied with the assurance that she could have no normal knowledge of any sitter. There she was studied by F. W. H. Myers, Henry Sidgwick, Sir Oliver Lodge, and other distinguished investigators. They too were very careful to make sure that she would have no opportunity to learn anything about the people who would sit with her. Lodge met her when she arrived and took her directly to his home where extensive precautions were taken to eliminate any possibility of fraud on her part. Her luggage was searched, the few letters she received were opened and read (with her permission), and sitters were introduced under pseudonyms. Yet she continued to provide information that she could have not acquired by normal means, much of which was about the deceased relatives and friends of the sitters.

Though a paranormal explanation seems unavoidable, the non-survivalist psi explanation must, of course, be given careful consideration. In many cases, there is good evidence that Mrs. Piper's trance personality was using telepathy to access the mind of the sitter. But occasionally she also provided several verifiable details about the lives of deceased persons (and ostensibly from those persons) that were unknown not only to any of the sitters but also such that no other single living person knew more than a few of them. In these cases, only some of the items were known to one living person and some to another. To illustrate, at one sitting Sir Oliver Lodge had with her, her control spoke of Lodge's deceased Uncle Jerry who was ostensibly recalling (at Lodge's prompting) several trivial details from his boyhood days that he spent in the company of his brothers, Robert and Frank. Robert recalled some of these details but denied recalling others. Frank, however, had a clear recollection of what Robert could not recall, but failed to remember some details that Robert recalled. Together they were able to verify all the details provide by the Uncle Jerry communicator, though none were known to Oliver at the time of the séance.

A non-survivalist psi hypothesis appealing to telepathy from the living could explain such cases but not without postulating telepathic powers of a grand scale for which we have no independent evidence. Mrs. Piper's trance personality would have had to have accessed telepathically the memory stores of two widely separated persons, each of whom was entirely unknown to her, and then collated the results. It seems clear that in such cases a non-survivalist psi explanation must appeal to a *super-psi* hypothesis.

The investigators were well aware of the non-survivalist psi hypothesis (as well as its extension to super-psi) as an alternative explanation of even cases like this one in which the survival hypothesis might seem more plausible. It is interesting to note that Hodgson, though initially very suspicious of all mediums, eventually became convinced that Mrs. Piper's mediumship activity not only did not admit of any normal explanation but also that her controls and communicators were, at least in some cases, just what they claimed to be—surviving spirits (or persons)[2] once associated with deceased human beings. Hodgson became convinced of this during the period when her chief control was "PC" (the George Pellew Communicator).

George Pellew was a young man of philosophical and literary interests who had been killed in New York a few weeks before the PC personality began to appear as Mrs. Piper's control, eventually becoming the principal one and remaining so from 1892–1897. Pellew had had, under a pseudonym, one and only one sitting with Mrs. Piper about five years earlier and was known to Hodgson. PC first appeared at a sitting to which Hodgson had brought a close friend of Pellew's. At that time and thereafter, PC exhibited a remarkably detailed and accurate knowledge of Pellew's life, passing recognition and conversation tests that, it would seem, only Pellew could have passed. Out of 150 sitters introduced to him, PC promptly recognized twenty-nine of the thirty people known to Pellew, failing to recognize (but only initially) only one young person who had "grown up" after Pellew's death. PC spoke to them of experiences they had shared with him and responded to them in the "give and take" of conversation as Pellew would have. As Hodgson put it, in each case "the recognition was clear and full, and accompanied by an appreciation of the relations which subsisted between G. P. living and the sitters."[3] He goes on to explain how the conversational dynamics characterizing the numerous little incidental conversations he had with PC left him with a conviction of the actual presence of George Pellew that he could not convey by merely enumerating several verifiable statements that PC made.

After Hodgson's death in 1905, a personality claiming to be Hodgson became one of Mrs. Piper's controls. Interestingly, he had frequently claimed that if he should die while Mrs. Piper was still acting as a trance medium, he would return as her control and communicate with his friends through her. This prompted James to resume his investigation of Mrs. Piper's mediumship and to focus on the sittings in which the Hodgson communicator appeared. By early 1908, there had been seventy-five of these sittings. After studying the transcripts of them all, he remained unconvinced that they provided evidence for survival powerful enough to outweigh the evidence for the non-survivalist psi hypothesis. He reasoned that Mrs. Piper's knowledge of Hodgson was likely sufficient to enable her subconsciously to impersonate him, thereby creating a fictitious and dramatized entity, made more convincing by its possession of ESP-acquired information known to him.

James' skepticism reminds us that the non-survivalist psi hypothesis might seem more plausible as an explanation of some paranormal phenomena if the person employing psi is supposed to possess a subconsciously wielded capacity to impersonate certain deceased persons. We considered the hypothesis that both ESP and subconscious impersonation were being

employed by the person having reincarnation experiences, but found that
the additional supposition did little to enhance the plausibility of the non-
survivalist psi hypothesis in accounting for the reincarnation cases we considered. Let us see whether mediumship phenomena are quite different in
this respect.

James' conclusion about the Hodgson communicator is supported by
the fact that Mrs. Piper had many personal contacts with Hodgson when he
was in charge of her mediumship. Though Hodgson was very reserved by
nature and professionally schooled to refrain from revealing any personal
information to the mediums he investigated, Mrs. Piper could hardly have
failed to gain some knowledge of his personality—perhaps enough for the
dramatizing and impersonating powers of her subconscious mind to create
an imitation of Hodgson's personality that would seem remarkably authentic. But the PC communications do not lend themselves nearly as well to
such an explanation. As we noted, about five years before Pellew's death, he
had attended, though under a false name, one and only one of Mrs. Piper's
sittings. She could have had very little, if any, normal knowledge about his
life and certainly not enough to have provided the basis of a dramatic and
highly authentic impersonation of him. Any such impersonation would have
had to have been rooted entirely in paranormally acquired information about
him. If even a super–ESP could, in the absence of normally acquired information, have been the means by which such a task was accomplished, it
would have to have been a paranormal power far exceeding anything independently evidenced to occur.

But there is another more general and equally formidable difficulty that
diminishes the appeal of the ESP-plus-impersonation hypothesis as an explanation of some of the most significant mediumship phenomena. This
difficulty comes into view when we take note of the distinction between the
dramatic imitation of a personality, on the one hand, and the dramatic interplay between different personalities, on the other. A hypnotized person and,
presumably, a medium in trance might display a remarkable capacity to
dramatize and to dramatically imitate a personality of which they have some
knowledge. But some mediumship phenomena go far beyond what might be
characterized as dramatic impersonation or dramatic imitation of a personality. Instead they exhibit a dramatic interplay between *different* personalities (viz., of a sitter and the communicator) in the give and take of
communication. Mrs. Piper's communications contain numerous instances
of this, perhaps the most noteworthy of which are the PC communications.
PC conversed in an appropriate manner with each of the many persons he
recognized (and known by Pellew when alive), revealing an intimate knowledge of the affairs of each and of the various relationships he supposedly had

with them. As we shall see, this phenomenon was even more impressively displayed in the mediumship activity of another medium, Mrs. Willett.

Though the interplay between different personalities in the give and take of conversational dialogue is a mediumship phenomenon whose significance we shall explore later, some reflection on it now might be helpful. Most of us have seen a person in hypnotic trance believing herself to be some person known to her (perhaps some well-known politician or celebrity) and providing a very impressive and dramatic imitation of that person. We might suppose that the well-known person is deceased with no effect on performance. But it seems very unlikely that even an extremely good hypnotist could lead that hypnotized person to engage in an animated conversation with close friends of the deceased that would pass muster with them. The hypnotized person would apparently need extensive ESP-powers. But even with them the task would be enormously difficult if possible at all. How difficult the task would be comes into view when we reflect upon what we do when in lively conversation with someone well known to us.

When in such conversation, we find that typically we are able to come up with the appropriate items of information as they are needed in the conversation. When conversing with a friend with whom we have shared experiences, we find that when the friend alludes to something about one of those experiences, we immediately understand this indirect reference and respond appropriately. When the friend's emotional attitude shifts from, say, one of levity and merriment to one of seriousness, we shift accordingly. Such conversational dynamics were manifested in the lively conversations PC had with his friends.

But we have an enormous conversational advantage over PC if, as the non-survivalist psi theory implies, he is a fictitious entity created by Mrs. Piper's trance personality (PTP). For we don't have to impersonate *ourselves*! We effortlessly and spontaneously act in character, as we are, so to speak, in constant *rapport* with our own minds—our own memories, emotions, attitudes, personalities. But PTP would have had to have impersonated the deceased George Pellew in such a strikingly authentic manner that thirty of Pellew's friends came to believe that he was still in existence and conversing with them. Our own experience in animated conversation indicates that to achieve such an astounding feat, PTP must have been either reaching back in time retrocognitively so as to establish telepathic rapport with Pellew when alive or else establishing such rapport with some living person, most likely the sitter conversing with PTP. Since the first alternative seems wildly unlikely, if not simply impossible, the plausibility of the psi-plus-impersonation theory rests with the second. But the second, too, seems unable to withstand critical scrutiny. If telepathic rapport is what is needed to attain an accuracy of impersonation sufficient to seem unquestionably authentic to close acquaintances, then we might wonder how such rapport with any mind other than that of the impersonated person could provide what is needed. But suppose some other mind sufficiently knowledgeable of the impersonated person could provide this if the telepathically established rapport provided an access to that mind something like the access one has to one's own mind. This would be a case of PTP virtually borrowing or sharing the mind of another and thus would require telepathy of a grand scale—a super-telepathy for which we have no independent evidence.

It might be objected that PTP's telepathic access need not be nearly as complete as the normal access we have to our own minds. It might be much more piecemeal and limited than that. But the way in which even a lesser amount of telepathy would have to be wielded seems highly complicated and extremely difficult to achieve. PTP would have needed an astonishing capacity not only to acquire almost instantaneously, by means of ESP, information known to Pellew or knowledge of his character as these are needed in the conversation, but also to translate, instantly again, the items so acquired into the form of a dramatic and highly authentic impersonation of him as he would have acted in the give and take of lively conversation with a close friend with whom he had shared various experiences. Moreover, it would seem that the almost instantaneously acquired telepathic access to the needed item would have to be relinquished instantly after acquiring the item if PTP is to translate it instantly, by way of the entranced Mrs. Piper, into the dramatic form it must have in the Pellew impersonation. In addition to the great telepathic and impersonation powers that PTP would need, its telepathic access apparently would have to alternate instantly between being established and being relinquished to achieve successful impersonation.

Such reflections about how the PC performances might be understood if the non-survivalist psi theory were true greatly diminish the plausibility of that theory. They may well lead us to wonder why James didn't reach the conclusion about them that Hodgson reached. He must have known that Hodgson witnessed them as they unfolded and studied them carefully. After a careful study of the Hodgson-control (that appeared soon after Hodgson's death), James concluded that it might well have been a fictitious entity and apparently thought the same of PC. If so, he overlooked one very important difference between PC and the Hodgson-control. As he notes, Mrs. Piper had many personal contacts with Hodgson before his death and could have been using this exposure as the basis for a subconscious impersonation of him. But she had virtually no opportunity to acquire normally any knowledge of Pellew. This fact is highly significant as there is no independent evidence that anyone can accurately impersonate someone she has never met.[4]

Mrs. Willett's Mediumship

A dynamic interplay between different personalities was perhaps even more impressively displayed in some of the Willett communications. Another intriguing aspect of these animated conversations is that the trance personality manifested considerable knowledge of philosophical issues and skill in philosophical argumentation in defending positions on them. This was in striking contrast to the interests, skills, and knowledge of Mrs. Willett in her normal state.

"Mrs. Willett" is a pseudonym. Her married name was Mrs. Charles Coombe-Tennant. Her two main communicators claimed to be the surviving spirits of Edmund Gurney and F.W.H. Myers. Gurney had died in 1888 and Myers in 1901. Both were classical scholars who were members of the SPR and had devoted much of their lives to the study of mediumship and other psychic phenomena. Both were highly interested in philosophy, very well read in philosophy and psychology, and had made significant contributions to the area of psychical research. Myers' monumental work, *Human Personality and Its Survival of Bodily Death*, still stands as a classic in its field. And Gurney, though dying young at the height of his powers, still managed to collaborate with Myers and F. Podmore in the important work, *Phantasms of the Living*.

Mrs. Willett's first communicator claimed to be Myers. A few months later this communicator stated that Gurney would be joining them. The first person they wished to have sit with her was Sir Oliver Lodge, perhaps because he had worked with Gurney on a number of psychical research projects. After many sittings with him, the Gurney communicator (GC) requested that G. W. Balfour come to sit with her—a request that was highly significant for a couple of reasons. First, Gurney had been a close friend of Balfour, and the two had worked together in their psychical research. He would have a very good understanding of Gurney's views about psychic phenomena. Second, GC stated that he wanted Balfour as the sitter because Balfour would be interested in the processes involved in communication rather than its products. And the sittings with Balfour did deal primarily with the nature of the processes involved in communication.

The Balfour-GC discussions provide outstanding examples of dynamic conversational give-and-take that make an appeal to an ESP-plus-impersonation explanation seem highly implausible. In these discussions neither Balfour nor GC passively accepted the views expressed by the other. Instead, there was continuous conversational give-and-take. Balfour would go over at his leisure his notes from a sitting, making critical comments, suggestions, and noting what was obscure. Then, at the next sitting, he would offer suggestions and ask for explanations of what was unclear. GC would answer his criticisms and try to clarify what was obscure, sometimes accepting and sometimes emphatically rejecting Balfour's suggestions. The dramatic form of these conversations was such as to suggest that Balfour was engaged in animated philosophical discussion with a highly intelligent and learned friend who shared his extensive knowledge of psychical research and who, though not physically present, was nevertheless able to communicate by using the entranced Mrs. Willett, somewhat like a person still living might use a telephone or a computer.

Though GC was the primary communicator during these Balfour sittings, the Myers communicator (MC) had at least as prominent a role in Mrs. Willett's broader mediumship activity. They spoke at considerable length about the processes involved in their communication through Mrs. Willett, providing an account on the level of complexity and sophistication that one might have expected if they really were who they claimed to be. For, as we noted, Myers and Gurney were scholars, widely read in the areas of philosophy, philosophical psychology and psychical research. They had studied mediumship and other paranormal phenomena at great length and had struggled to understand them. They were very intelligent, critical thinkers, accustomed to drawing subtle and significant distinctions, and, if necessary, to coin new terminology to express them.

Whatever we take MC and GC to be, it is evident that the Willett communications from them are the product of an intelligent mind or minds, gifted with a capacity for high-level critical analysis and highly informed in the subject areas in which Myers and Gurney had special interest and expertise. In particular, they reveal a thorough acquaintance with the ideas and terminology of Myers' book, *Human Personality and Its Survival of Bodily Death,* even that portion of its terminology that is found *only* there.

Before comparing the two relevant paranormal explanations of these phenomena (viz., the survival and the non-survivalist ESP-plus-impersonation hypotheses), we should note, if only in passing, that any normal explanation of Mrs. Willett's mediumship activity seems highly implausible. As in the case of Mrs. Piper, not even the slightest basis for any suspicion of fraudulent or deceptive behavior was ever found. At any rate, she had a great deal to lose from detection of any such activity, as she played a prominent role in public affairs. Among her many public service accomplishments, she became the first woman to serve as justice of the peace for Glamorganshire and was later appointed by the British Government as a delegate to the assembly of the League of Nations. That the other normal explanations are equally implausible will become evident in our examination of the ESP-plus-impersonation hypothesis.

Let us begin our evaluation of the ESP-plus-impersonation hypothesis as an explanation of the mediumship phenomena produced through Mrs. Willett by noting that an appeal to it in an attempt to account for the Balfour–GC discussions is even less plausible than it was in the case of the PC performances (in the Piper mediumship). All the difficulties that arose in the attempt to understand the latter by appeal to it also arise here. In this case, the Willett trance personality (WTP) would have been exercising an enormous ESP power to acquire the information that GC expressed in the discussion. Some would have been known to Balfour. But is it plausible to suppose that the content of the views expressed by GC when flatly in disagreement with Balfour also came from Balfour? And even if it could have come from Balfour, why would it have been expressed in the form of an emphatic disagreement with him?

However, it is when we try to account for the *impersonation* as well as the ESP that the difficulties for this hypothesis seem insuperable. For the impersonation to be explained is (like the PC case) not one of mere dramatic imitation of a personality but one in which the impersonator (viz., WTP) is engaged in conversational give-and-take with another person. More specifically, the ESP-acquired information would have had to have been translated into a dramatic, highly verisimilar impersonation of Gurney (and also of Myers, who, purportedly as MC, figured prominently in numerous other conversations with Balfour) as they would have acted in the give-and-take of dialogue—an impersonation so well done that it seemed to their friend Balfour to be natural and convincing. Apart from the amount of ESP required to accomplish this feat, the probable manner in which the ESP would have been wielded staggers the imagination. Since WTP is an entity distinct from the donor (or donors) of the ESP-acquired information, it would seem that the selecting of the proper donor and establishment of telepathic rapport with that person would have to occur almost instantly as some particular information is needed in the conversation—information whose receipt is followed, almost instantly again, by a relinquishing of this rapport so that the acquired information could be translated instantly into the dramatic form needed for the highly successful impersonation. As noted earlier, this almost instantaneous alternation between the making and breaking of telepathic rapport apparently would have to continue throughout the dialogues.

It seems clear, then, that a successful impersonation of a person as that person would have acted in the give-and-take of conversation with a close friend would be extremely difficult if not impossible to achieve, even if the impersonator knew the person rather well. But Mrs. Willett had never met either Gurney or Myers. Consequently, WTP would have had to create her completely successful impersonations of them entirely by means of ESP. Moreover, she would have successfully impersonated them, not by merely creating a dramatic imitation of their personalities, but by modifying her creations instantly as needed to produce highly authentic impersonations of them in conversational interactions with Balfour, who knew them well enough to detect any flaws in her performances. In other words, her creations would have been of the highest level of difficulty to achieve, if humanly possible at all—successful impersonations of people in conversational interaction with a close friend—and to achieve this without ever having met the impersonated people! Such a feat would be a breathtaking achievement and would go far beyond what is independently shown to have occurred, either experimentally or in spontaneous cases.

Even after reflecting upon these apparently insuperable difficulties to which the ESP-plus-impersonation hypothesis is exposed, we still have not seen the full extent of the case for rejecting it. For we have not yet considered the content of the conversations—its subject matter in conjunction with the high-level critical analysis and sophisticated philosophizing that characterized it. MC and GC were engaged in philosophical discussion with Balfour about various philosophical matters, primarily those involved in psychical research. The communicators not only displayed an expert's knowledge of these matters but were philosophizing well about them. They were holding their own with Balfour who was himself gifted with a keen philosophical mind. In brief, MC and GC were displaying a *skill*—a skill consisting in knowing how to philosophize well. The significance of this is something we have already noted when, in our study of reincarnation experience, we looked at cases of young children or adults revealing language or musical skills that they apparently had no opportunity to acquire in their natural life. As we noted then, the possession of skills that were not acquired in any normal way seems inexplicable by appeal to ESP, even an ESP of grand-scale proportions.

The charge that Mrs. Willett might have acquired the skill exercised by MC and GC has little to commend it. Though Mrs. Willett was intelligent and well educated, her interests led her not to a study of philosophy and psychical research, but to take a prominent role in public affairs. MC and GC expressed views on such philosophical issues as the mind-body relation and the nature of the self, making subtle philosophical distinction, all in a language abounding in technical philosophical terminology. But normal Mrs. Willett was neither knowledgeable of nor interested in such matters. Nor was WTP, whose attitude toward the communications may be accurately described as one of boredom and bewilderment. At one point when GC was discussing some complex philosophical matter she did not understand, she exclaimed, "Oh, Edmund, you do bore me so!"[5] And again, "I can't think why people talk about such stupid things. Such long stupid words."[6] Similarly, when the philosophical scripts were shown to Mrs. Willett for the first time many years later, she found them incomprehensible and said that they left her utterly bored and bewildered.

Given these considerations, it is difficult to believe that Mrs. Willett had any specific knowledge of the subject matter of the conversations. But even if we suppose, contrary to all the known facts, that unbeknownst to everyone she had acquired some such knowledge, it would have fallen far short of what she would have needed to have engaged in the high-level, sophisticated philosophizing of MC and GC as they interacted with Balfour. As Broad and others intimately familiar with the Willett mediumship phenomena have attested,[7] the high-level philosophical discourse displayed in the exchanges between MC, GC, and Balfour could not have been attained without years of study and solid practice in the area of the subject matter and in philosophic thought, more generally. We know that Myers and Gurney had more than put their time in, as these topics had been the primary interests in their lives. We have equal assurance that Mrs. Willett had not.

These reflections about the extensive preparation needed to have carried out the philosophical exchanges with Balfour serve as a reply to a possible objection to a survivalist interpretation of this case. For they remove any grounds for doubt that a genuine skill—the skill of knowing how to philosophize well—was being exhibited by MC and GC. A proficiency that requires years of study and practice to acquire apparently would have as much claim to being a skill as does knowing how to play a musical instrument or speak a foreign language. These facts by themselves, apart from the many other difficulties to which the non-survivalist hypothesis is exposed, seem sufficient to discredit that hypothesis. For Mrs. Willett almost certainly could not have acquired the skill in question in any normal way; and there is no independent evidence that skills can be acquired by ESP.

As an epilogue to Mrs. Willett's mediumship, we might note that after she died in 1956, extensive communications ostensibly from her began to appear in the scripts of the medium, Geraldine Cummings. They began after W.H. Salter of the SPR asked Miss Cummings to try to get in touch with the deceased mother (viz., Mrs. Willett) of a Major Coombe Tennant. The forty scripts that emerged over a period of two-and-a-half-years provided extensive, detailed information about her life—her early married years, her family, her husband's family, her friends, and her associates in public affairs—all conveyed in a manner reflective of a personality that seemed to the people who knew her to be a strikingly faithful portrayal of her own.[8] Almost all of the great amount of verifiable information provided was corroborated, either by existing records or from the memories of people who remembered her. Several investigators concluded that these scripts constituted the best evidence ever to have come through a single medium for the identity of some particular deceased communicator.

Proxy Sittings

A proxy sitting is one in which the sitter (who is, of course, physically present with the medium) is acting on behalf of a third party, about whom both medium and sitter know nothing or as little as possible, in an effort to establish communication between the third party and some particular deceased person. The third party, who is the real sitter, though not physically present at the sitting, may try to facilitate contact by providing something (but only the bare minimum needed) that might allow the medium to identify the deceased person being sought—perhaps a name, an identifying description, or an object that once belonged to the deceased. The intention motivating the proxy sitting is to greatly reduce the likelihood that the source of the information provided by the medium is telepathy from those present at the sittings.

The British medium, Mrs. Gladys Osborne Leonard (1882–1968), whose mediumship activity rivals in importance that of Mrs. Piper and Mrs. Willett, was especially successful in proxy sittings.[9] In several of the successful ones, much of the information she provided was probably not gained by way of clairvoyance on her part, due to the apparent absence of clairvoyantly accessible sources that might have yielded it. Instead, its source (if not the deceased persons themselves) was likely the same source that was consulted to verify it—namely, the memories of relatives and friends of the deceased persons. Telepathy with one of these persons—someone who possessed all of the information provided—would be a much more plausible explanation. However, it seems that in at least two of these proxy cases, no single living person possessed all the information provided. In these cases, Mrs. Leonard's trance personality (LTP) would have had to identify the different persons who had the needed information, select and acquire from their minds the items needed, and then collate and synthesize them.

When we reflect upon the various ways in which the source or sources of needed information are remote from LTP in the proxy sittings we come to see what an extensive amount of ESP would be needed for success in them. The real (or principal) sitter is not only physically remote—sometimes far from the location of the sitting—but epistemically remote as well, in that the identity, and sometimes even the existence, of the principal is unknown to the sitter. Apparently, LTP must gain access to the mind of the principal to learn the identity of the deceased person whom the principal is seeking. But how is LTP to achieve this other than by accessing telepathically the mind of the sitter—a sitter who typically has at least no normal knowledge of the principal's identity? Even if we put aside this difficulty and suppose that LTP does somehow access the mind of the principal and thereby learns something that might be useful in a search for the deceased person the principal has in mind, this achievement would be only the beginning of a complicated search process. The clues received from the principal might be used to discover other clues that, in successful proxy sittings, eventually result in disclosing the identity of the deceased as well as revealing sources of information about this person—either the minds of living persons or existing records or both. Proper names, dates, addresses and other details that identify a person *uniquely* would have to be acquired. But, as Gauld points out, such items are among the most difficult for mediums to obtain.[10] These difficulties become even more formidable when all the information provided fails to be possessed by one person or contained in a single existing record. Again it seems clear that the non-survivalist ESP explanation requires an appeal to ESP on a grand scale—a super ESP.

"Drop-In" Communicators

Though a defender of the non-survivalist psi theory might argue, however implausibly, that in successful proxy sittings there exists some connection between medium and principal by way of which psychic communication is established, even that defense is apparently blocked in the case of a drop-in communicator. Such a communicator is one who drops in unexpectedly in a sitting set up for the purpose of contacting someone else. No one involved in the séance had any intention of trying to contact the deceased person who the communicator claims to be. Indeed, that person is ostensibly unknown to everyone involved. The intrusion of the communicator is not only uninvited but sometimes annoying to sitters who had other plans for the séance. Given the absence of any grounds for postulating some connection between the medium and the deceased in the typical drop-in case, the appeal to a super-psi exercised by the medium would seem even less plausible here than in the proxy cases. Even if we set aside questions about how and why, without any apparent motive, the medium selects one deceased person to portray as communicating rather than another, the problems involved in identifying someone unknown to her and then acquiring information about that person seem to stretch the super-psi hypothesis to the breaking point.

Of course, the significance of a drop-in case depends upon whether the medium has any normal knowledge of the deceased or of someone who knew that person—a matter that may be very difficult to settle in a particular case. Since the attempt to establish that the medium was never exposed to anything that could connect her to the life of the deceased and thus did not have any such knowledge is an attempt to prove a negative—a notoriously difficult task—we must be content with something less than proof, perhaps extraordinarily good reasons to believe that the negative is true.

While noting that drop-in cases are in general especially problematic for the psi-hypothesis, we shall focus on a couple that apparently provide compelling reasons to reject it in favor of the survival hypothesis. These cases approach what Gauld calls the ideal case: the medium almost certainly lacked any normal knowledge of the deceased, the drop-in communicator had a much stronger and more understandable reason to communicate than the medium or sitters could have had for selecting the deceased person the communicator claims to be, and the information communicated was not all possessed by a single living person or contained in a single record.[11] The first we will examine is the "Stockbridge" case.

A communicator calling himself "Harry Stockbridge" (a pseudonym) provided a number of items of information about himself at several sittings between 1950 and 1952. He spelled out, though in a very abbreviated form, that he had been a Second Lieutenant of the Northumberland Fusiliers and had been transferred to a Tyneside Scottish battalion before his death on July 14, 1916. He said that he was tall, dark and thin, with large brown eyes, and that he hung out in Leicester where he is referred to in a record. When asked about his likes and dislikes he wrote, "Problems any. Pepys reading. Water colouring." In response to a question about whether he knew a "Powis Street," of which two sitters had dreamed, he responded, "I know it well. My association took my memory there." When asked about his mother, he said that she was with him.[12]

The sitters made one attempt to confirm these statements, but were unsuccessful. No further attempt was made until Gauld began his investigation of this case in 1965. Though checking out such claims would be a prodigious task, involving a time-consuming search of old books and records as well as tracking down any surviving relatives, Gauld was able to acquire information that confirmed virtually all of Stockbridge's claims. He established that Stockbridge was born in Leicester and presumably "hung out" there, that there was a Powis Street near the house in which he was born, that he was a Second Lieutenant in a Tyneside Scottish battalion of the Northumberland Fusiliers when he was killed on July 14, 1916 (not July 19 as an HMSO publication erroneously reports), that he had the physical appearance he described, that his name is on a war memorial in his old school in Leicester, and that his enthusiasm for solving problems is indicated by his having won a form prize for physics and mathematics. All that Gauld had to leave unanswered was that he read Pepys, enjoyed water coloring, and, of course, that his deceased mother was with him.

That neither the medium nor the sitters had any normal knowledge of the deceased is effectively ruled out in this case. Gauld established that none had any contacts in Leicester, had ever visited it, or (insofar as such things are determinable) had any line of contact with any member of the Stockbridge family. Cryptomnesia is also virtually ruled out by the fact that most of the details communicated were not made available to the public in a way such that the medium might have accessed them, even subconsciously.

As we turn to the paranormal interpretations, we note that though Stockbridge does not have an especially strong reason for communicating (viz., a wish to help one of the sitters who was a serviceman), it is a stronger reason than any the medium or sitters had for selecting facts about him as targets for ESP. Also reducing the plausibility of the ESP hypothesis is the need to assume super–ESP powers. Since facts about Stockbridge were singled out even though they apparently had no special interest or relevance to the medium or sitters, the indications are that these facts constituted only a tiny fraction of an enormous (perhaps unlimited) number accessible to the medium, any others of which might have been singled out instead. Moreover, in the Stockbridge case these super–ESP powers must be supplemented by an ability to bring together just those facts that are facts about a single person even when a variety of sources must be accessed to find all of them. For in this case, there seems to have been no living person or persons whose minds could have been accessed telepathically to obtain all the needed information. And a clairvoyant apprehension of all of it from existing records would have required locating, and synthesizing the contents of, at least four separate sources. This case might have been an ideal one in Gauld's sense if it had been thoroughly investigated shortly after it occurred. For at that time one might have been able to rule out completely the possibility that some person alive then possessed all of the communicated information. However, Gauld's painstaking investigation did not begin until thirteen years later. Still, this fact might not diminish the evidential value of this case. After contacting surviving relatives and finding that they had only the vaguest recollections of Stockbridge, Gauld said, "My own guess is that the situation would not have been substantially different at the time of the sittings."[13]

Perhaps even more persuasive evidence that a drop-in communicator is who he claims to be is provided by the case of Runolfur Runolfsson ("Runki"). Like the Stockbridge case, this one was very carefully investigated (by Haraldsson and Stevenson),[14] but it is even more problematic for the super–ESP hypothesis. For in this case, the totality of the information provided by the Runki communicator could not have been acquired telepathically from a single source, as no one person alive at the time possessed it. Though in the Stockbridge case the possibility of there having been a single telepathic source cannot be conclusively ruled out, in this case it can be. And in both cases, there was no single document or other existing record that, by itself, contained the totality of communicated information, and thus no single source that might have been accessed clairvoyantly.

The main details of the Runki case, in a very abbreviated form, are as follows. The medium was Hafsteinn Bjornsson and the place was Reykjavik, Iceland. During 1937–38 a highly eccentric drop-in communicator appeared by way of the entranced medium, claiming to be looking for his leg and refusing to give his name. He became very interested in a new sitter, a Ludvik Gudmundsson, who joined the group in January 1939 and who lived in the village of Sandgerdi, about 36 miles from Reykjavik. Eventually he stated that his leg was in Gudmundsson's house in Sandgerdi.

After considerable pressure from the sitters, he finally gave his name as Runolfur Runolfsson and went on to tell about how he came to meet his death and what then happened to his body. He was walking to his home near Sangerdi from a neighboring town late in the day and was drunk. The weather became very bad and he was wet and tired. When less than fifteen minutes from his home, he drank some more from his bottle and fell asleep on the beach. The tide came in and carried him out to sea. Three months later his body was found on the beach after the tide carried it in, but only remnants of it were recovered, as dogs and ravens had torn it to pieces. These remnants were buried in Utskalar graveyard near Sandgerdi. But the thighbone was missing. It was carried out to sea and later washed up again at Sandgerdi. After being passed around it ended up in Ludvik's house.

This remarkable tale was later verified in considerable detail. Though Ludvik Gudmundsson had no knowledge of any thighbone in his house, he learned from some of the older local inhabitants that sometime during the 1920s such a bone, believed to have been washed up from the sea, had been found and was later placed in an interior wall of his house. Though no one knew whose bone it was, nor was there any record of a thigh bone missing from the remnants that were found in 1890, it was a very long bone, indicating that it was a bone of a very tall man. The fact that Runki had been tall was confirmed by his grandson who, however, had not known him. Nor was the grandson aware of a bone or of many other facts provided by the Runki communicator. Nearly all of the other statements made by this communicator were verified by entries distributed over two manuscript sources, both located in Reykjavik. One is the Church Books of Utskalar in the National Archives and the other a work in the National Library.

The investigators considered the possibility that the medium acquired all the communicated information in normal ways, but deemed this extremely unlikely, partly because the latter source, which alone contained some of the details, was little known and unpublished at the time of the sittings. So the plausible alternative explanations are the paranormal ones. But once again the non-survivalist psi hypothesis must include the assumption that ESP exists on a grand scale. As we noted in the Stockbridge case, in addition to the extensive psychic powers needed to acquire the communicated information and the virtually unlimited fund of information from which it is selected, the trance personality of the medium would have had to integrate the information acquired from different records or different persons. But how plausible an explanation does this line of reasoning yield? Haraldsson and Stevenson remind us that, "It may be simplest to explain this integration as due to Runki's survival after his physical death with the retention of many memories and their subsequent communication through the mediumship of Hafsteinn."[15] We should also remind ourselves that Runki's reason for communication, though extraordinary, is more understandable than any the medium or sitters might have had for singling out facts about him to appear as coming from him communicating, especially since they apparently had no normal knowledge that such a person ever existed.

We must keep in mind that (as Haraldsson and Stevenson hasten to add) "sensitives have been known to achieve remarkable feats of deriving and integrating information without the participation of any purported discarnate personality."[16] But when we add to our deliberations *what else* the medium must be able to achieve in the drop-in cases of the kind we have considered, the most we should infer from their point is that drop-in cases fail to provide conclusive support for the survival hypothesis. To reiterate a point we have noted in several contexts, the mere possibility that ESP exists on a grand or even unlimited scale, and thus in much greater quantity than is independently evidenced to exist, does not prevent drop-in cases (along with many other paranormal occurrences of the kinds we have considered) from constituting good evidence for survival, even though it does not attain the level of conclusiveness that one might have hoped it would.

The Cross-Correspondences

Impressive as some of the drop-in cases may be as evidence of survival, their evidential force seems to be exceeded by those mediumistic phenomena that came to be known as the Cross-Correspondences. They are correspondences between the scripts containing the communications provided by several different mediums under conditions such that each medium was ignorant of what the others were producing. What was written or spoken by or through one medium corresponded to what was written or spoken by or through another to an extent that did not admit of normal explanation (e.g., by attributing it to chance coincidence). The principal mediums involved were widely separated, and some of the mediums had never met. Yet their scripts included fragments which, though meaningless when taken alone, seemed to fall into place in a meaningful pattern when pieced together with similar cryptic fragments from the script of another medium. These fragments in most cases pertained to recondite details of the Greek and Latin classics. Not only did they share a subject matter, but they seemed to complement one another in a manner analogous to the way in which the individually meaningless pieces of a jigsaw puzzle form a meaningful whole when fitted together. The meaningful patterns that seemed to emerge upon careful study of the scripts had, in the view of the investigators, every appearance of having been designed by an intelligence with an expert knowledge of the classics.

A detailed examination of the cross-correspondences is not possible in the space available here.[17] The period in which the scripts containing them were produced lasted for over thirty years (from 1901–1932) and the volume of material produced is enormous, consisting of some 3000 scripts. In addition, the significance of the correspondences turns on references to abstruse items in the Greek and Latin classics—references that would not be even recognized without extensive knowledge of these classics. Yet their evidential weight can be appreciated by a general description of the conditions under which they arose and eventually became recognized as connected, their apparently meaningful character, the principal mediums involved, the chief investigators, and the purported identities and purposes of the communicators.

All the principal mediums were ladies of excellent reputation who remained above suspicion throughout, as no indications of fraud were ever found. Mrs. Piper of Boston was the only professional medium among them. Those living in Great Britain were Mrs. Winifred Coombe-Tennant (Mrs. Willett), Mrs. M. de G. Verrall, wife of Professor A. W. Verrall who was a well-known classical scholar, and her daughter, Helen. In addition, there was Mrs. Holland (pseudonym for Mrs. Fleming, sister of Rudyard Kipling) who lived in India during important periods of her script-production.

We have already encountered some of the purported communicators in our examination of the mediumship activity of Mrs. Piper and Mrs. Willett. By 1901 three distinguished Cambridge scholars—F. W. H. Myers, Edmund Gurney, and Henry Sidgwick—were dead. They had been founders of the SPR and deeply concerned with the survival issue. Indeed, they had devoted much of their professional lives to a study of it. They were keenly aware of the extreme difficulty in uncovering any evidence of survival that could not be explained by appeal to the ESP hypothesis. For they knew all too well that the verification of any claim ostensibly from the deceased would require that it be checked against existing records or the memories of living persons, that is, against what might have been accessed by a medium possessing sufficiently extensive ESP powers.

Shortly after the death of Myers in 1901, Mrs. Verrall began to write automatically scripts that were signed "Myers." Though poorly expressed at first, they gradually became better expressed and more coherent. But they remained cryptic, as though their meaning were being concealed. About one year later, allusions to the same subjects began to appear in Mrs. Piper's scripts. They too included the claim that they had come from Myers. Shortly afterwards, Helen Verrall began to write automatically. At that time she had not looked at her mother's scripts. When it was discovered later that her scripts too contained allusions to the same subjects, all the scripts were sent to Miss Alice Johnson, secretary of the SPR.

Soon afterwards, Mrs. Holland, who was in India at the time and who had no normal knowledge that such strange scripts had been produced, began to produce scripts automatically that were signed "Myers." In one she was instructed to send it to "Mrs. Verrall, 5 Selwyn Gardens, Cambridge." Though she had read Myers' book, *Human Personality*, and had come across Mrs. Verrall's name in it, she did not follow these instructions as she was very skeptical about her scripts having any external source. The address given was unknown to her, but was in fact correct. Eventually she sent her scripts to Alice Johnson who dutifully filed them away without suspecting that they were related to those produced by the Verralls and Mrs. Piper.

It was not until 1905 that Alice Johnson realized what had been happening, and by that time the scripts contained the immensely intriguing claim that the deceased Myers, Gurney and Sidgwick had devised this plan of giving out through mediums isolated from one another, fragmentary or allusive communications that if considered separately would be unintelligible, but which would become meaningful when pieced together or when a clue to their meaning was given in the script of yet another medium. In an effort to prove their continued existence in a way that would virtually rule out the non-survivalist ESP hypothesis as an alternative explanation of their communications, they would provide evidence of a design that was not in any living mind or contained in any record. The various mediums were to be kept in total ignorance of their scheme by their sending fragments alluding to abstruse details of the classics to various mediums isolated from one another, and making these fragments appear random and pointless to the medium so that she would gain no clue as to the thought behind them. The script intelligences also suggested that their elaborate scheme would not only reveal their continued existence but also would show that in their discarnate state they are not mere automata or set of memories but have retained the most significant capacities that persons possess and cherish.

What should we make of such suggestions? Are the script intelligences nothing more than a dramatic touch to a monumental hoax perpetrated by the dozen or so mediums involved? Or are they manifestations of a super–ESP unwittingly exercised by one or more of the mediums? Finally, are they just what they claim to be?

The fraud hypothesis seems to be a non-starter in this case. As we noted, the principal mediums involved were women of high repute whose mediumship activity never provided any basis for suspicion of fraud. Beside, the hoax would have had to have been of breathtaking dimensions and sophistication. To accept the fraud hypothesis is to believe that the 30-year series of cross-correspondences was an extremely elaborate hoax perpetrated over a period of time spanning decades by a group of women of high personal character who stood nothing to gain but much to lose—a hoax so expertly executed that it was never detected by the alert and highly critical investigators who were in constant contact with the mediums. Such incredibly coordinated cheating would have been accomplished under extremely difficult conditions, as the mediums were scattered throughout the world and would have had to produce script after script containing allusions to matters unknown to most if not all of them while under the watchful eyes of the investigators. These implications cannot be circumvented by charging that the investigators too were involved in the hoax. For that would be a desperate "last-ditch" response that could be directed indiscriminately against any investigative effort whatsoever.

As usual, the appeal to ESP remains as the only serious alternative to the survival hypothesis, although again the ESP postulated must be of a *super* magnitude. Defenders of the super–ESP hypothesis have argued that Mrs. Verrall might have produced the cross-correspondences by telepathically affecting the minds of the other mediums, perhaps acting (as Podmore suggested)[18] like a telepathic broadcasting station. They have pointed out that she knew Myers and Sidgwick personally, was interested in psychic phenomena, and was a very good classical scholar.

But there are a number of serious difficulties with this hypothesis that together, if not individually, seem fatal to it. First, telepathy of the detail and complexity needed would be staggering and her motive for exercising it difficult to understand. One must suppose that for years Mrs. Verrall's subliminal mind directed the subliminal minds of the other mediums to carry out roles in a hoax perpetrated on their conscious minds as well as on her own. In addition to her telepathy-produced effects on their minds, she would need to have been telepathically scanning their scripts and adjusting her telepathic influence on them as needed. She was supposedly doing all this, even though several of the cross-correspondences did not begin in her scripts, and in some she was not involved at all. Second, the cross-correspondences continued for sixteen years after her death. Thus super-psi powers like those of Mrs. Verrall would have to be attributed to one or more of the other participating mediums as well. Supposedly, the mind-boggling capabilities of Mrs. Verrall were matched by those of others. But this might well strike one as unbridled speculation unrestrained by considerations of evidence. As Gauld soberly reminds us "...we have no evidence for unconsciously hatched, telepathically co-ordinated, plots or conspiracies."[19] Third, some of the literary information communicated apparently was not possessed by any of the participating mediums, including Mrs. Verrall. Clearly, the ESP hypothesis fails to provide a plausible explanation of this case. Indeed, however unlikely the continued existence of deceased persons may seem to be, the truth of the ESP hypothesis when applied here seems even more unlikely.

Conclusion: Assessment of the Case for Post-Mortem Existence

Early on in our study we recognized the high antecedent improbability of any post-mortem existence. The case for post-mortem extinction seemed very powerful. But the impression that post-mortem existence is highly improbable is an initial assessment typically made prior to a careful examination of the numerous considerations that must be taken into account if it is to withstand critical scrutiny. What should our assessment be at this point?

Overview of Our Investigation into the Essence of Persons

If some form of thoroughgoing (i.e., ontological) materialism were true and a person were nothing more than a live human being, the case for extinction would be virtually conclusive. Without the miraculous intervention of a divine being (whose own nature would apparently falsify such a materialism), death could not fail to be extinction. But our rather detailed examination of the mind-brain and person-body relations led us to reject such views. We noted the failure of the attempts to reduce the mental to the physical and the overwhelming strength of the case for concluding that the mental is an immaterial reality—a case much too detailed to rehearse here. We also saw that if the person were identical to the live human organism, then the persistence of the person through time would consist in the continuity of the body: bodily continuity would be both necessary and sufficient for personal identity through time. But we examined various (metaphysically) possible situations in which the person does not go where the body goes—situations in which personal identity over time cannot be constituted by continuity of the body. The apparent (metaphysical) possibility of awakening from sleep to find oneself in a different body would show that the continuity of the body is not *necessary* for personal identity, even though such body-switches do not in fact happen. And the fact that the body continues to exist in those (actual) cases of irreversible unconsciousness due to extensive brain damage—cases

204

providing compelling evidence that the *person* has departed—shows that bodily continuity is not *sufficient* for it either.

We were led by such considerations to conclude that the identity of a person must consist in something other than the body and its continuity over time. We noted that though we are persons who are human beings, and that if a self or person is something (contingently) embodied in humans and some possible non-humans, it is something distinct from these embodiments or perhaps from all of its material embodiments, even if it never actually exists apart from some one or other of them. Thus we were led to psychological theories in our search for the most plausible account of what a person essentially is, i.e., of what is both necessary and sufficient for something to be a person.

We saw that there are two types of theories in which the identity of persons consists in the mental or psychological: (1) those that take a person to be a composite being and (2) those in which a person or self is a single subject of experience. But theories of the first type (viz., the bundle or relational views) have wildly implausible consequences—consequences that clash head-on with what we seem to find ourselves to be in taking the first-person perspective and reflecting upon what it is to have an experience. In maintaining that a person is a composite entity, constituted of an enormous number of individuals—namely, experiences strung out over a lifetime, bearing relations to one another and to the body—it implies that (1) the experience you are having now could have belonged to someone else, (2) only a tiny part of *you* (not merely of your *life*) is present now, (3) it is (metaphysically) possible for some person to be only *partly* you, (4) there (metaphysically) could be several persons existing in the future each of whom is identical to you (i.e., has an equally good claim to be you) and (5) there could be conditions under which you would neither exist nor fail to exist—your existence would be indeterminate! The ambiguity about your existence would be *ontological*, i.e., an apparently impossible state for you or anything else to be in. Since these implications seem, at least upon reflection, to conflict radically with our empirically-grounded concept of what a person is and thus are totally unacceptable, we were led to the single-subject view as the only remaining alternative.

Though many have rejected the single-subject view, arguing either that there is no introspective evidence that such an entity exists or that it cannot be known to last through a lengthy period of time, our extensive investigation of these issues revealed that their arguments are flawed. The fact that the conscious subject or self cannot be found as an object of introspective observation is precisely what we might have expected since, as we saw, self-awareness is entirely nonobservational and, indeed, must already exist for anything disclosed to introspection to be recognized as oneself. As we noted, this fundamental self-awareness consists in a subject's encountering itself in an immediate experience of being itself, and, as such, is unmediated, pre-conceptual, noninferential, not a product of the conceptualizing or interpretive powers of reflective consciousness. We also came to see through our rather detailed examination of the USS (viz., undetected subject-switching) hypothesis that the case for rejecting this hypothesis is virtually conclusive: there is a single subject that endures, rather than a succession of them.

Though our treatment of the subject of conscious states was relatively extensive and complex, its significance to our study is fundamental. For it was central to our case for concluding that a person has a deep, irreducible essence consisting of a unitary, noncomposite, indivisible subject of conscious states that endures through time while its states change. Thus we might say that a (human) person is an embodied subject of conscious states (an embodied "soul"), that is an immaterial individual, distinct from its material embodiment, even if, as a matter of fact, it cannot exist without such embodiment to sustain it. As such, its existence after bodily death is metaphysically possible, even if the natural laws of this world are such that its existence is causally dependent upon the existence and proper functioning of its body. We saw that, given such dependency, we would not in fact survive bodily death, even though we might have survived in some possible world in which the natural laws were different from those in the actual world.

Such considerations led us to focus on the nature of the causal relation in an effort to determine whether there is anything about that relation in general, or in its specific instance in the self-brain relation, that would rule out, or make extremely unlikely, the continuing existence of the self after death has broken the causal connection to its body. But our sustained attempt to determine what the causal relation itself should be understood to be, whether conceived as reducible to noncausal properties and relations or as irreducible, revealed nothing problematic about mind (or self)-brain (i.e., dualistic) causation. Dualistic causation was revealed to be no more dubious or suspect than physical-physical causation. Indeed, our consideration of intentional causation uncovered good grounds for believing that such causation is best explained dualistically and that dualistic causation is in fact occurring. Put somewhat differently, our study revealed good grounds for our fundamental belief that we are agents making things happen in both the mental and physical realms. Though the occurrence of dualistic causation implies that the physical realm is not causally closed, the causal-closure thesis is highly theoretical, conjectural, and all-inclusive in scope, positing much more than current knowledge can verify. Among the many reasons we found to reject this thesis is its implication that the mental is completely powerless to affect the physical—an implication virtually impossible to believe.

Since the intelligibility and factual occurrence of dualistic causation, though of fundamental importance, do not by themselves show that the self can exist in the absence of the causal support provided by its brain, we went on to consider various possible scenarios in which such support is not needed. Though we recognized the deep embodiment of the self and the variety of ways in which its consciousness is causally affected by activities in its brain, these facts fall short of showing that its very existence (along with some of its properties, of course) is brain-dependent. Thus the matter was left open to a consideration of possible ways in which a causal independence of the self's existence might be understood. Accordingly, we considered such possibilities, finding each to be not only intelligible but consistent with the deep embodiment of the self and the respects in which its consciousness is known to be a function of the states of its brain. Perhaps the most intriguing of them is the possibility that although intentional consciousness depends causally upon brain activity for its existence, the self and its non-intentional consciousness do not.

In the end, we found that our rather extensive examination of the causality problem—a problem widely considered to be insuperable for the view that a person is essentially a nonphysical self interacting with a body—revealed that it is no more problematic than physical-physical causation, whatever one understands the causal relation to be. It does not pose a threat to the view that a person is an embodied, nonphysical self that might continue to exist after biological death and to retain its causal powers in its disembodied condition. Of course, its continuing after death to causally interact with other selves and/or the physical realm would be paranormal causation. But this is not problematic, for, as we noted (mainly in our study of psychic phenomena), the evidence for the actual occurrence of paranormal causation, as instanced in cases of apparent ESP and PK, is very strong. Indeed, such causation might be what occurs when an embodied self interacts with its own brain. In any case, our study of the causal connection between our minds (or selves) and our bodies in our present, embodied condition revealed that there is no problem in conceiving of the causal powers we possess now as extended to include psi and for it to have an importance after death that it does not presently have.

Dispositions and the Self

Though we have identified the essential self with the subject of conscious states and have focused on its currently having or being in such states (i.e., its *occurrent* states) we were not implying that its having such states constitutes the entirety of its being. For we have been assuming implicitly that also essential to its existence is a dispositional base—a set of dispositions to have such and such conscious states when suitably stimulated. But this assumption, though unavoidable, might seem inconsistent with its deep unity, especially if one were thinking of the complex organization of one's personality (which consists largely of dispositions to act in certain ways) and were assuming that anything lacking physical characteristics could not be the source of differentiated and recurrent processes needed to carry dispositions. But, as we saw, the subject is properly taken to be a substance—a substance which, though nonphysical and partless, can have a multiplicity of states, characteristics, capacities, aspects, and causal powers and liabilities. The supposition that the self-substance carries the dispositions to have certain kinds of conscious states under such and such conditions—states whose expression leads us to speak of personality characteristics—seems no less intelligible than maintaining that it carries the causal powers needed for intentional action. But, as we saw, the dualistic causation implied by the latter assertion is not only intelligible but apparently is in fact occurring.

Sensory Experience in an Afterworld

One matter that was addressed in an implicit way in our work on the self but which might now be more explicitly and comprehensively addressed is a concern about how we might conceive of the world experienced by a self when existing in the absence of the physical body it once had. When embodied, the self is the subject of a great variety of conscious states: some are cognitive (e.g., thinking, doubting, believing and wondering), some are affective (e.g., emotions, moods, and feelings), some are bodily sensations, and some are perceptual or quasi-perceptual (e.g., the imagery of dreams, hallucinations, memory, and imagination). Since these are already states of the self, as the self is what undergoes or has them, there is no significant problem in *conceiving* of the self continuing to have them (or, in the case of some, states that appear to it to be very much like them) when no longer causally connected to its physical body.

What needs further explication, however, is the question of how one might conceive of the self continuing to have conscious states that appear to it to be like those (viz., bodily sensations and perceptual experiences) in whose production the physical sense organs were causally involved. If the world experienced by a disembodied self lacked the colors, sounds and other sense qualities normally caused to arise in us due to the stimulation of our sense organs, it would be an extremely impoverished world, if possible at all.

But in fact there is no problem lurking here. The "next world," if there is one, could have a qualitative richness and variety comparable to this one. Moreover, the sense qualities could be organized so as to constitute the perceptual (i.e., the phenomenal) objects experienced by a disembodied subject and could have the prominence in that subject's experience as the objects we perceive have in ours. Communication with others about them would be possible but would require ESP. A more detailed conception of a "next world" characterized by a qualitative richness comparable to the world we encounter in our present experience might be described as follows.

Though a disembodied self would no longer be receiving causal stimulation from its physical body, it could have perceptual or perceptual-like experiences of an environment and of its former body due to its memories of perceptual experiences it had while embodied, including those of the body it once had. It could find itself to be in what is in fact a phenomenal world, not unlike the phenomenal world one seems to encounter in dreams. In first-person terms, when I dream I frequently seem to find myself to be embodied in what turns out to be a dream environment. These dreams are often such that they involve the activities of an apparently embodied person whom I take to be myself as long as I am dreaming. In some dreams, my identification with this person becomes explicit and conspicuous, as when I dream that I am looking at my reflection in a mirror. Though the body of this person with whom I identify is only a phenomenal body, it serves as a perfectly good body in the dream experience. I regard it as mine, I seem to act on the dream environment by means of it, and in coherent dreams it forms the persistent center of my perceptual world.

Now, it is surely conceivable that a disembodied self should seem to itself to have a body that, though appearing to be physical, is in fact a phenomenal body. And if, as one might suppose, this body arises due to the influence of the self's memories of its experiences of being physically embodied, its phenomenal body might well resemble rather closely its experiences of its former physical body, perhaps so much so that a disembodied self would fail for some time to realize that it has survived the death of its body. In any case, the self might find itself in what is in fact an environment of phenomenal objects, at the center of which is its phenomenal body. Its environment would be analogous to the phenomenal environment of the dream. Thus it seems that there is no conceptual difficulty in maintaining that the world experienced by a disembodied self could not only exhibit the colors, sounds, and other sense qualities normally caused to arise in us due to the stimulation of our sense organs but to experience them in that integrated, organized form that we experience as the objects of perception in normal sense experience.

If this account should seem highly conjectural and mounted upon the apparent insubstantiality of the dream, we might remind ourselves of how strongly an account along these lines—an account in which colors, tones, tactile impressions, and other sense qualities are attributes of perceptual experience—is supported by what we found to be the most plausible view of our embodied perceptual experience and its relation to the physical world. In that view, which receives powerful support from contemporary physical science, the world of physical objects and events—of matter in motion—provides the stimulation for our sense organs, but not the sense qualities themselves. These qualities appear in, and only in, our sensory experience. They have instances in, and are integrated into, the phenomenal objects that are, in fact, the perceptual objects of ordinary sense experience—the perceptual objects that appear to constitute the world around us and that we assume, uncritically and mistakenly, to be identical to the external physical objects themselves. But these phenomenal objects, along with the sense qualities that have instances in them, have no place in any part of the physical world that causes them to arise in our sensory experience, neither the portion external to our bodies nor the portion that includes our bodies, brains, and nervous systems.

Given that this well-supported view (viz., an indirect realist view of perception) is essentially correct, the difference between the sensory world of a discarnate subject and the sensory world that we now encounter would be a difference in cause, not in sensory content. Both would be sensory worlds constituted of phenomenal objects situated in (phenomenal) space, at the perceptual center of which is a phenomenal body that one takes to be one's own. Thus a discarnate self, though lacking a physical body causally involved in its sensory experience, might well have a phenomenal body that appears to it not unlike the way our physical bodies now appear to us, that is, as phenomenal bodies, though now with physical causes. Whether embodied or not, the sensory realm experienced by the self, and thereby immediately known to it, is phenomenal, whereas an underlying physical world, if present, may be correctly *inferred* to be the cause of the phenomenal, but is *not* immediately known.

Discarnate Communication

A discarnate self might be able to use its phenomenal body to help identify itself to the living or to another discarnate self. Conceivably, it could telepathically project into the visual field of either an embodied or a discarnate self a phenomenal body resembling its own, which, based on its memories of the body it once had (viz., the phenomenal body generated by its physical body), might well be recognizable by others. More generally, any communication with others or any acquisition of information about the physical world would have to depend upon the employment of psi: clairvoyance to acquire information about the physical world, psychokinesis to act upon it, and telepathy to communicate with others.[1]

The Significance of the Ostensible Evidence of Survival

At this point, having completed the extensive and relatively difficult conceptual work necessary to arrive at the most defensible view of the self and its causal relation to its brain, we began our consideration of the ostensible evidence of post-mortem existence, armed with conceptions not only of what it is that might survive but also of how in general communication with the living might occur. In revealing the metaphysical possibility of the post-mortem existence of the self along with its causal powers and its capacity to have a broad range of experiences, our deliberations in effect reduced what might well have seemed to be an enormous initial unlikelihood of such existence. But they fall far short of showing by themselves that survival is quite likely, or even that it is as likely as extinction. For the possibility that we have established, though fundamentally important to our concerns, shows only that the natural laws might be (or might have been) congenial to our continued existence, not that they actually are. And we noted early on the strength of the case for concluding that they are *not* "survival-permitting." In particular, our deep embodiment and the variety of ways in which conscious states are a function of brain activity make the prospects for survival look dim. Still, the empirical evidence of post-mortem existence, largely provided by psychical research, points in the other direction. Is it strong enough to shift the balance of probabilities, to tip the evidence scale, in the direction of survival? Clearly, its evidential weight must be assessed in the light of all the foregoing considerations.

We examined in a relatively detailed, extensive way each of the four major types of phenomena often cited as providing empirical evidence of post-mortem existence: NDEs and NDOBEs, apparitions of the dying and of the dead, cases of apparent possession or reincarnation, and mental mediumship phenomena. Our primary focus was on a few of the strongest cases of each type, recognizing that there are numerous less impressive ones. But this procedure is defensible. The weak cases do not reduce the significance of the strong ones. This point is aptly stated by Paterson when he writes, "a relatively small body of strong evidence for a theory is not in the slightest tainted by an abundance of very weak evidence for the same theory."[2] As we noted, even a single case in which both the naturalistic and the non-survivalist psi explanations are virtually ruled out or extremely implausible would be highly significant, as survivalist explanations would be the only remaining ones. We found several that seem to approach closely, if not to attain, this level of significance. Moreover, they are distributed over the different types of phenomena, giving them a collective evidential force exceeding that which the cases from any single type can provide. They would require a reassessment of the probabilities, certainly increasing the likelihood of survival, perhaps making it more probable than not. But what our final assessment of the probabilities should be is a difficult matter to determine, primarily because the super-psi hypothesis is impossible to rule out.

Super-Psi or Survival?

As we noted, the naturalistic explanations can be effectively eliminated in the strongest cases. Nor is the problem with the psi explanation if the limits of psi are considered to approximate those of the psi capacities that have been independently evidenced to exist. The problem standing in the way of a rather precise or definitive assessment is the problem of determining the significance of the possibility that there exists psi capacities of great or even unlimited magnitude, i.e., that super-psi exists. Since this possibility cannot be ruled out, an appeal to it is always available as the basis of an alternative explanation of phenomena that would otherwise provide convincing evidence of survival. For the verification of what appears to be evidence of survival requires the present existence of records or memories of living persons, all of which could be accessible to someone with super-psi powers. Speaking of super–ESP (rather than using the more general term, super-psi), Gauld provides a clear description of this difficulty:

> If a piece of putative evidence for survival is to be of use, it must be verifiable—we must be able to check by consulting records or surviving friends that the information given by the ostensible communicator was correct. But if the sources for checking it are extant, they might in theory be telepathically or clairvoyantly accessible to the medium or percipient. Since we do not know the limits of ESP we can never say for certain that ESP of the extraordinary extent that would often be necessary—'super–ESP'—is actually impossible.[3]

No matter how persuasive the ostensible evidence for survival may seem to be, our verification of the information communicated, though unavoidable, is what also provides the opportunity for an appeal to super-psi on the part of the living as an alternative explanation. This is, as Gauld points out, the central dilemma involved in the interpretation of such ostensible evidence.

We implicitly encountered this dilemma in our deliberations about the significance of some of the phenomena of each of the major types we considered. In the case of each, we found ostensive evidence of survival that could not be plausibly explained by appeal to either naturalistic theories or ordinary psi. What stood in the way of our interpreting these cases as providing compelling evidence of survival was the possibility that an appeal to super-psi would provide an alternative explanation. But can we find a way out of this dilemma? How plausible should we take such an appeal to be?

We came to grips with this dilemma in our examination of a view espoused by Braude who has argued that, because we must acknowledge the possibility that super-psi is involved in the production of paranormal phenomena, we cannot reject an appeal to psi as a legitimate explanation of such phenomena without unjustifiably assuming in advance what the limits of psi are. His argument, if sound, would block any survivalist interpretation of a paranormal phenomenon because such an interpretation would imply the rejection of the psi explanation and (if the argument is sound) thereby assume unjustifiably in advance a conclusion about the limits of psi. But we rejected his argument. For we saw that we can acknowledge the *possible* existence of super-psi (i.e., Braude's premise) without granting that it is the *actual* cause of some paranormal phenomenon. Acknowledging the possibility of super-psi does not absolve us of the responsibility of searching for positive evidence that this possibility is the one actualized. In fact, the positive evidence provided by some paranormal phenomena might strongly indicate that the possibility actualized is that some deceased person has survived bodily death. Thus we can be justified in judging the survivalist interpretation of some paranormal phenomenon to be the most plausible explanation of it without assuming in advance that psi does not exist on a grand scale. For even if such psi did exist, it might not be the cause of the phenomenon in question. The question of what the actual cause is (or of what possibility is the one actualized) is an empirical one to be answered as best we can by an examination of the positive evidence.

In the final analysis, the evidence for the existence of a psi capacity exercised by the living does not reduce the plausibility of the survival hypothesis. Indeed, the conjunction of a couple of considerations suggests that the overall effect is to increase the likelihood of post-mortem existence. First, there are cases of paranormal phenomena with respect to which the survival hypothesis provides a much better explanation than does an appeal to ordinary psi; and the appeal to the merely possible existence of super-psi, independently of positive evidence that super-psi is in fact being exercised in the case in question, fails to show that the survivalist interpretation of these cases is not the most plausible one. Second, the existence of even the modest amount of psi for which there is independent evidence reduces the antecedent improbability of post-mortem existence, and the existence of super-psi would reduce it further by providing more grounds for rejecting the widespread assumption that the self depends for its existence and all of its activity upon a properly functioning brain.

As we noted earlier, the widespread belief of contemporary intellectuals that death brings extinction is due not to an alternative interpretation of the ostensible evidence for survival but to views of the mind-body relation in which the antecedent probability of post-mortem existence is reduced to virtually zero or, at any rate, so low as to make attention to the ostensible evidence seem unnecessary. As we saw, eliminative and reductive materialism imply that persons are physical organisms and so are destroyed by death. And even those holding views in which the mental is acknowledged to be a reality distinct from the physical would assign a very low antecedent probability to post-mortem existence if they maintained that in fact the mental is, or very likely is, utterly dependent for its existence upon a properly functioning nervous system. But the reality of psi, and especially super-psi, would provide compelling evidence that persons can acquire information about the external world and/or act upon it other than by way of their nervous systems. Such evidence would also be evidence that they are not dependent for their existence and all of their activity upon their brains.

So the relationship between the super-psi and survival hypotheses has crucial importance as we try to bring our study to a conclusion. The logic of our overall argument has led us to see that the survival issue is an issue about which of these hypotheses provides the more plausible explanation of the various cases we have considered and others like them. As we have noted on several occasions, in at least the best cases, all naturalistic explanations and ordinary psi can be effectively eliminated. But super-psi remains as a possibility. Though we have no independent evidence of its actual existence, the existence of ordinary psi makes more plausible the claim that its possible existence must be taken seriously in our attempts to explain psychic phenomena. For a natural world in which ordinary psi is known to exist is thereby revealed to be a world very different from one consisting entirely of matter in motion through space and time, viz., the one to which the ontological materialist is committed, and also different from one in which the self, though distinct from its brain, is utterly brain-dependent for all of its causal transactions. It would be a "super-psi friendly" world in that the issue of whether super-psi exists would be an issue about whether what is known to exist in a limited way also exists on a grand scale.

But, as we noted, such a world would be no less congenial to the survival hypothesis. Since "such a world" apparently is the actual one, we could point out (again) that we have no evidence for super-psi that is known to us independently of the kinds of cases we have considered. But the rejoinder would be that our evidence of survival also arises from and thus depends upon those cases. Belief in the reality of super-psi is, of course, an extraordinary belief—a belief requiring extraordinary evidence. But belief in survival is also extraordinary. At this point we seem to have reached a standoff. Could it be that we can justify nothing more than a weak, disjunctive conclusion: Either at least some persons have survived death or super-psi exists?

The Balance of Probabilities

Fortunately, we can press the matter further. We have, in effect, already done so on several previous occasions when we noted that the survival hypothesis can provide a simpler and more plausible explanation of several features prominent in cases of each of the types we studied. In having the resources to interpret a case as being what it appears to be, it is able to avoid the convoluted, often rather implausible, and sometimes tortuous explanations of some of the features of the case. Though the difficulties standing in the way of accepting a super-psi explanation of cases of each type are too numerous to rehearse here, a reminder of some central ones might be helpful at this juncture.

We saw, for example, that the super-psi hypothesis lacks the resources needed to provide a plausible explanation of the motive for bringing about the paranormal phenomenon in question or of the purpose it is apparently serving. In the case of apparitions of the dead, the motives and purposes displayed are typically those the apparent but not the perceiver or some other living person would be expected to have. It is much more plausible to explain them as being what they appear to be than to invoke the super-psi hypothesis in an attempt to attribute them to the living who lack consciously held purposes of the kind displayed. Cases of apparent reincarnation present a similar problem for any appeal to the super-psi hypothesis in attempting to explain what might motivate a child to identify with a deceased person who is a complete stranger whose very existence was unknown to her and to sustain her strong identification despite considerable negative reinforcement for doing so.

A super-psi explanation of the motivation prompting mediumship phenomena is equally implausible. It seems especially implausible in the case of drop-in communicators when we wonder why the medium, without any apparent motive, selects one deceased person to portray as communicating rather than another from the great number of deceased persons to whose lives her (perhaps) unlimited super-psi powers give her access. Moreover, such explanation conflicts with the fact that some drop-in communicators had a much stronger and more understandable motive to communicate than the medium or sitters could have had for selecting the deceased person the communicator claims to be. In the cross-correspondences especially, if (in accordance with the survival hypothesis) the communicators were who they claimed to be, they would have had *much* greater motivation to communicate than the unconscious minds of the two or more participating mediums gifted with super-psi powers would have had to generate such an incredibly elaborate and sustained conspiracy (lasting over 30 years) to deceive themselves and the other mediums involved, as well as everyone else led to believe that the cross-correspondences are evidence of survival. Any unconsciously wielded motivation to deceive that these mediums could have had seems difficult to understand, let alone the astonishing amount needed to produce the highly sophisticated cross-correspondences initially and then continue to develop them over thousands of scripts for over three decades.

Another general difficulty with the super-psi interpretation comes into view when we see that the person allegedly possessing the super-psi powers typically wields them in a surprisingly narrow way and fails to display any paranormal abilities independent of the paranormal phenomenon in question, in striking contrast to the enormous psychic powers she supposedly has. This difficulty appears most clearly in the reincarnation cases. As we noted, the psychic abilities attributed to the child are exercised narrowly upon the life of a single deceased person, in apparent conflict with the evidence that psychic abilities are *general* abilities. In addition, the children with prior-life memories hardly ever display any psychic abilities independent of those attributed to them to account for these memories. Clearly, the simpler and apparently more plausible explanation is that the child is remembering a prior life.

The paranormal phenomenon that may be the most difficult to explain in either hypothesis is the possession of skills that the subject could not have inherited or acquired. Yet the survivalist account of them seems considerably more plausible. The behavioral component of a skill presents a difficulty for the survivalist, as behavior is activity of the body that, of course, does not reincarnate. But since a skill is a *knowing how* to do something, i.e., a type of *knowing*, it is plausible to suppose that the mental component guides the activity. If so, we might say that the behavioral component is the behavioral *expression* of mental dispositions. But there is no problem in supposing that mental dispositions and capacities are had by substances, in particular, by the nonphysical or mental substance that we have seen compelling reasons to believe the self to be. As such, they would reincarnate with the self whose dispositions they are.

So the survivalist is able to present a plausible account of skills. But they present a formidable, if not insuperable, difficulty for the super-psi theory. For, as we noted, there is no justification for believing that skills can be acquired by ESP, even if it should exist on a grand scale. Yet the possession of paranormal skills seems undeniable. Even if the recognitions of people that children with reincarnation experiences were able to make could be plausibly denied to be manifestations of genuine skills, the cases of recitative and especially responsive xenoglossy could not be similarly dismissed. Nor could sewing skills or skillful playing of musical instruments. Finally, the sophisticated philosophical exchanges between MC, GC, and Balfour are equally resistant to dismissive treatment—the skill of knowing how to philosophize in a sophisticated way.

The conclusion to be drawn from our study seems clear: the survival hypothesis provides the more plausible explanation of at least some of the cases in question. Perhaps this would not be so if we had only the cases provided by *one* of the areas of research we considered. But, as we have seen, the survival hypothesis apparently provides the more plausible explanation of cases in *each* of the areas. Thus each is the source of a line of evidence supporting this hypothesis. And when we view these lines of evidence collectively, as a set of mutually supporting arguments for the same conclusion, we find that they have a cumulative evidential weight sufficient to conclude that the survival hypothesis is probably true, i.e., that survival is more probable than extinction.

How much more probable than extinction? It would be unwise to try to quantity such probability. But the empirical evidence (in conjunction with our conceptual deliberations that cleared the way for its consideration and interpretation) seems sufficient to justify the claim that personal survival is distinctively or significantly more probable than not. It certainly lacks the compelling force needed to eliminate rational grounds for belief in extinction. Such grounds remain. But compelling force or conclusiveness is a level of certitude we should not have expected to reach.

Many of us (and I do mean to include myself) might well find this conclusion surprisingly strong, and perhaps difficult to believe. But we should remind ourselves that we have reached it by following, in a highly circumspect way, the logic of our argument. Though painstaking attention to all the relevant considerations that we find to bear upon our overall conclusion is no guarantee against error, it typically serves us well. Another point to keep in mind is that belief is influenced by numerous psychological factors, some of which have little or no relation to any objective evidence for it. In the case of the survival issue, a powerful influence might well be the prevailing intellectual climate, even if one is fully aware of this influence and has tried to offset it.

On the other hand, many others would likely find our conclusion to be disappointingly weak. A higher level of certitude would have been gratifying, not only to them but also to many of those who have trouble believing that the case for belief in survival is as strong as it apparently is. This is quite understandable, for it seems that few can enthusiastically embrace the possibility of permanent nonexistence after death. It would be the permanent loss not only of departed loved ones but of everything that has been precious to us and thus a loss difficult to regard in a dispassionate way. Indeed, it is easy to see why death looms as the ultimate threat for nearly everyone, even if awareness of it is effectively suppressed much of the time. The threat of reduction to nothingness, of total extinction for all eternity serves as a powerful motivating force leading so many to find the prospects of continued existence immensely appealing. But our conclusion certainly has implications for such concerns—implications that one might find quite uplifting—even if it fails to provide the level of certitude one might have desired.

Though not compelling, our conclusion implies that our prospects for survival are not nearly as dim as they might have seemed early in our study. It implies, of course, that we have rational grounds for belief in survival. But to point that out is actually to understate the strength of the case for such belief. We view its strength more accurately when we realize that our thoughts about death as followed by permanent nonexistence, as the final end to us all and to everything that might have been possible for us to do or to experience are more likely to be *false* than true.

If this is so, we would likely be well served by going beyond our misgivings about what we must leave behind by devoting some attention to what we might expect to take with us. Though this could not be any material possessions, it might well be our minds, in which case our efforts to enhance them would be richly rewarded. Assuming that in the next world (if there is one), in addition to our non-intentional consciousness, we continue to have the variety of intentional conscious states we have now (along with our mental dispositions), that world would likely appear to be physical but in fact would be phenomenal and thus mind-dependent. As such, it might be one in which a well-exercised and informed intelligence, honed to a keener edge by critical and reflective thought, would prove to be of great value in helping us understand what has happened to us and to find our way in unfamiliar terrain. We should be pleased to find that it is whatever wisdom and understanding we have managed to acquire that serves us well not only in this world but especially in a mind-dependent one that might be approaching.

Chapter Notes

Introduction

1. See D. M. Armstrong's *A Materialist Theory of the Mind*, (London: Routledge and Kegan Paul, 1968), and J. J. C. Smart's seminal article "Sensations and Brain Processes," *Philosophical Review* 68 (1959, 141–56).

2. See P. van Inwagen's discussion in *Material Beings* (Ithaca: Cornell University Press, 1990), 145–48.

3. C. McGinn, *The Mysterious Flame: Conscious Minds in a Material World* (New York: Basic Books, 1999), p. 27.

4. A very accessible argument for this conclusion can be found in John Perry's short book, *A Dialogue on Personal Identity and Immortality* (Indianapolis, Indiana: Hackett, 1978).

5. His most cited expression of his private language argument is a number of passages in his book, *Philosophical Investigations*. Translated by G.E.M. Anscombe (New York: Macmillan, 1953). Third edition, New York: Macmillan, 1970.

6. Alvin Plantinga, "Advice to Christian Philosophers," *Faith and Philosophy* 1 (July 1984): 264–65.

7. Metaphysical necessity is a *de re* necessity. It refers to the manner in which a property is possessed by a thing, i.e., necessarily (and thus metaphysical impossibility refers to the manner in which a thing lacks a property). As such, it must be distinguished from logical necessity, which is a *de dicto* necessity referring to the manner in which an entire proposition is true. Both types of necessity are properly characterized as absolute necessity, and are to be contrasted with natural (or physical) necessity, which refers to the fact that, given the (non-necessary or contingent) laws of nature, events must occur in accordance with those laws.

8. As we shall see later, bodily continuity (continuous existence of the body through space and time) is what does this.

9. There is the (metaphysical) possibility that God whisks away the body at death, simultaneously replacing it with a replica body to serve as the corpse that is buried or cremated. Van Inwagen (see earlier reference) has argued that only such a miraculous event renders our survival consistent with our being identical to our bodies and our identity over time being dependent upon the continuity of our bodies.

Minds, Souls and Persons

1. I am, of course, speaking of what we might call *philosophical* materialism, so as to more clearly distinguish it from what people often mean when they say of someone who places excessive value on material things that he is "materialistic."

2. Though one might speak of unconscious mental states, as many philosophers as well as many other academicians do, I shall use the term "mental" synonymously with the term "conscious." In my view, unconsciousness mental states should not be conceived to be conscious states of which one happens to be unconscious, but rather as *dispositions* to have certain conscious states.

3. See David Lewis, "Survival and Identity" and "Postscripts to Survival and Identity" in his *Philosophical Papers*, Vol. 1 (Oxford University Press, 1983).

4. We noted this possibility earlier as one suggested by van Inwagen. We now see that it is, apparently, the only one.

5. Rene Descartes' view of the mental and the mind-body relation proved to be pivotal in the history of philosophy. See his remarkable little book, *The Meditations on First Philosophy*, for an engaging introduction to his thought. It can be found in: *The Philosophical Works of Descartes*, Vol. I, trans. by E. S. Haldane and G. R. T. Ross (London: Cambridge University Press, 1911), reprinted 1969.

6. I have provided a lengthy and detailed analysis of these matters in *The Conscious Self*:

The Immaterial Center of Subjective States (Amherst, New York: Humanity Books, 2005).

7. The possibility that there are matter-points has been suggested by Dean Zimmerman in his article, "Two Cartesian Arguments for the Simplicity of the Soul," *American Philosophical Quarterly* 28, no.3: 217–26. I respond to his suggestion in *The Conscious Self*, p. 307.

8. Although the results of experimentation on commissurotomy patients have been interpreted by some as evidence that one's consciousness has been divided, I argue at length in *The Conscious Self* that this is not the most plausible interpretation. We must acknowledge, of course, that the temporary or permanent *dissociation* of some conscious states is a common phenomenon. One kind of dissociation is a consequence of the passage of time and is revealed by reflecting on the implications of memory. Conscious states that we can remember having have been temporarily dissociated until recalled. Conscious states that we had but cannot remember having had are permanently dissociated. But since conscious states had in the past do not continue to exist as conscious states but rather as dispositions to have or affect present conscious states, they provide no evidence that consciousness is divisible. The other kind of dissociation occurs in the present when, in a non-lucid dream, one continues to have conscious states even though they are temporarily dissociated from one's waking consciousness. But when one awakens and remembers the dream, one remembers it as an episode in the larger, more far-reaching consciousness that one enjoys while awake. We might say that these dream states, though temporarily dissociated from waking consciousness, become integrated into waking consciousness upon awakening. In first-person terms, I then see the dream states to have been states *I* had while asleep—states of the very same undivided consciousness I enjoy while awake. Thus these constitute no evidence of the divisibility of consciousness.

9. I have argued elsewhere that the "use" theory of meaning and the behaviorist analysis of language must fail. See Chapter 3 of *Perception, Mind and Personal Identity: A Critique of Materialism* (Lanham, MD: University Press of America, 1994).

10. There is controversy in physical theory about whether indeterminism reigns on the quantum level and about whether quantum states are indeterminate in themselves. But the issue in highly controversial; and even if the evidence turns out to weigh heavily on the side of (metaphysical, rather than merely epistemic) indeterminacy, any indeterminacy is confined to that level.

11. For more on this see, "The Flight From Mind," by Howard Robinson, in *The Pursuit of Mind*, ed., by Raymond Tallis and Howard Robinson, (Manchester, Great Britain: Carcanet Press, 1991), and *The Conscious Self*. Also see, H. Robinson, *Perception* (London and New York: Routledge, 1994).

12. See, for example, R. Rorty. "In Defense of Eliminative Materialism," *Review of Metaphysics* 24, no 1 (1970): 112–21.

13. For much more discussion of this issue, see my *Perception, Mind, and Personal Identity: A Critique of Materialism*.

14. Of course, others continue to experience other instances of phenomenal color, etc. (instances experienced only by them), and the material objects that ordinarily stimulate our senses continue to exist. But all this is consistent with the claim that every phenomenal quality is experience-dependent.

15. J. Searle is a prominent defender of this view. See J. Searle, *The Rediscovery of the Mind* (Cambridge, MA: MIT Press, 1992), p. 14.

16. Since mental events are mental *particulars*, I am not speaking of those views in which there are no mental particulars but only mental properties that, though nonphysical, are properties of physical particulars. Though these views may be considered forms of property dualism, they offer only a reductionist view of persons.

17. They would follow the lead of the great Scottish philosopher, David Hume, who famously wrote, "For my part, when I enter most intimately into what I call *myself*, I always stumble on some particular perception or other, of heat or cold, light or shade, love or hatred, pain or pleasure. I never can catch *myself* at any time without a perception, and never can observe anything but the perception." D. Hume, *A Treatise of Human Nature*, ed. by L.A. Selby-Bigge (London: Oxford University Press, First edition, 1888. Reprinted, 1968), p. 252.

18. I examine this case at considerable length in "Part I: Self-Consciousness and the Self" of *The Conscious Self*.

19. Galen Strawson, for example, embraces the first alternative when he writes, "I will call my view the Pearl view, because it suggests that many mental selves exist, one at a time and one after another, like pearls on a string, in the case of something like a human being" (1997, p. 424). He is a reductionist about persons but not about subjects. "The Self," *Journal of Consciousness Studies* 4, nos. 5–6, 1997: 405–28.

20. There are, of course, arguments to the contrary. Some have pointed to the commissurotomy cases (involving the severing of the commissural tracts connected the cerebral hemispheres) as empirical evidence that some

persons have been divided (i.e., have undergone fission). Others appeal to thought-experiments in which a person either undergoes fission into two, or merges with another. I argue at length in *The Conscious Self* that all these arguments fail.

21. We might note, in passing, that the difference between PW and the actual world is one that cannot be accommodated in any reductionist view. Though this difference could hardly be greater or more important from your unique viewpoint, no reductionist view can acknowledge its existence.

22. This presentation is, of course, extremely brief. For much more discussion of the difficulty see *The Conscious Self*, especially pp 211–227, along with the references there to other works. We should note here though that, although the actual duplication of a person is extremely unlikely, if the mere conceivability of duplication is ordinarily sufficient to establish its metaphysical possibility (as it seems to be), then reductionist views imply a falsehood. Any view implying a falsehood is itself false.

23. The contention that in this case, conceivability implies metaphysical possibility requires further argument and elaboration. I provide this in Part III, "A Modal Argument for Immateriality," of *The Conscious Self.*

Mental-Physical Relations

1. I show this in *The Conscious Self*, pp. 329–350.

2. I point out some of these difficulties in *Perception, Mind and Personal Identity* and also in *Making Sense of It All*, (Upper Saddle River, NJ: Pearson Education, 1999, 2003) pp. 59–61.

3. This principle owes its name to J. Barnes, who argued that it is false. See his book, *The Presocratics*, vol. 1 (Boston: Routledge and Kegan Paul, 1979), p. 119. See also, J. Hoffmann and G. Rosenkrantz, "Are Souls Intelligible?" in *Philosophical Perspectives*, vol. 5: *Philosophy of Religion*, ed. J.E. Tomberlin (Atascadero. CA: Ridgeview) pp. 183–212.

4. Ernest Sosa, for one, has pointed this out and argued that we have no basis for believing that a non-spatial self and a body can stand in a causal accessibility relation. See his essay, "Mind-Body Interaction and Supervenient Causation" in *Midwest Studies in Philosophy*, vol. 9, ed. P.A. French, T.E. Uehling, and H.K. Wettstein (Minneapolis: University of Minnesota Press, 1984).

5. I do not mean to deny the existence of consciousness in animal life forms lacking a distinct brain but possessing a sufficiently complex nervous system.

6. John Foster, *The Immaterial Self: A Defense of the Cartesian Dualist Conception of the Mind* (London: Routledge, 1991) pp 190–91).

7. R.H. Thouless and B.P. Weisner, "The Psi Processes in Normal and 'Paranormal' Psychology," *Proceedings of the Society for Psychical Research* (London), 48 (1947), 177–196.

8. It is important to see that conceiving of such paranormal causation is not to conceive of a breach of the essential privacy of a mind nor does it imply that such a breach is even conceivable. To affect the mental states of another, even in the direct way in which one affects one's own, is *not to have* those states and therefore not to have the direct epistemic access to them that one has to one's own.

9. W. Hasker, *The Emergent Self* (Ithaca, New York: Cornell University Press, 1999), esp. pp. 188–97.

10. The well-known researcher, K. Lashley, found no evidence for the existence of such traces, despite his thirty-year intensive effort to find them. Though he continues to believe that such traces exist, his own research undermines any empirical basis for such belief. See K.R. Lashley, "The Search for the Engram," primarily pp. 501–3 in F.A. Beach and D.O. Hebb, *The Neurophysiology of Lashley*, cited in H.A. Bursen, *Dismantling the Memory Machine* (Dordrecht: D. Reidel, 1978), pp. 15–16.

General Considerations Supportive of Post-Mortem Existence

1. I. Kant, *Critique of Pure Reason*, trans. by N. K. Smith (London: Macmillan, 1929; reprinted, New York: St. Martin's Press, 1965), pp 372–3.

2. See E. Sosa, "The Essentials of Persons," *Dialectica* 53 nos. 2–4: 1999, 227–41.

3. Roderick Chisholm, *On Metaphysics* (Minneapolis: University of Minnesota, 1989), p. 56.

4. A. Schopenhauer, *The World as Will and Representation*, Vol. II (New York: Dover, 1966), p. 487.

5. Forman, for one, is clear about this. See his *Mysticism, Mind, Consciousness* by Robert K.C. Forman (Albany, New York: State University of New York, 1999), esp. chapters 9 & 10.

6. Forman resists characterizing non-intentional consciousness as personalized, calling such a characterization "a mistake" (p 199). But by this he seems to mean that it is not personalized in the way that we appear to ourselves as objects of our intentional consciousness. He says, "… it would be a mistake to

think that the mystic knows his or her own
consciousness in anything like the same way he
or she knows a desk or a knee twinge....
Rather, one knows it only because one *is* it." (p
171) He speaks of encountering the self in encountering "awareness itself." (p 170). Yet it is
"his or her own consciousness" that the mystic encounters, not, for example, *my* consciousness or *yours*. Neither you nor I have any
memory of the mystic's encounter. Thus it
seems clear that individualization must be involved in some sense, especially in view of the
overall case for believing that we are individuals if we are anything at all.
    7. S. Radhakrishnan, *Indian Philosophy*,
vol. 2 (London: George Allen & Unwin, 1923),
p. 249.

Near-Death Experiences

    1. W. Barrett, *Death-bed Visions* (London:
Methuen, 1926).
    2. *Ibid.*, p. 11
    3. K. Osis, *Deathbed Observations by
Physicians and Nurses* (New York: Parapsy-
chology Foundation, 1961). Parapsychological
Monograph No. 3.
    4. This survey is reported in K. Osis and
E. Haraldsson, *At the Hour of Death* (New
York: Avon 1977).
    5. *Ibid.*, p. 184.
    6. C. Green and C. McCreery, *Apparitions*
(London: Hamish Hamilton, 1975), p. 178.
    7. At *the Hour of Death*, p. 87.
    8. Susan Blackmore, *Beyond the Body*
(London: Paladin, 1983) pp. 140–6.
    9. K. Osis and E. Haraldsson, pp. 193–4.
    10. For an extensive discussion of NDE af-
tereffects, see K. Ring, *Life at Death* (New York:
Coward, McCann & Geoghegan, 1980), chapters 8 and 9.
    11. Robert Kastenbaum, *Between Life and
Death* (New York: Springer, 1979), pp. 16–19.
    12. See Michael Sabom and S. Kreutzinger,
"The Experience of Near Death," *Death Education 1* (1977): 195–203.
    13. See Kenneth Ring, *Life at Death*, pp. 15,
216. He speaks of the core NDE (p. 15) as that
"common set of elements associated with the
onset of death...." On page 216, he lists features of it: "(..., the out-of-the-body state,
paranormal knowledge, the tunnel, the golden
light, the voice or presence, the appearance of
deceased relatives, beautiful vistas, and so
forth)...."
    14. See, for example, the conclusions Rhees
draws from his study. W. Dewi Rhees, "The
Hallucinations of Widows," in *British Medical
Journal 4* (1972): 37–41.

    15. Reported in Grey. See Margot Grey, *Re-
turn from Death* (London and Boston: Arkana,
1985) p. 86.
    16. *Ibid.*, p. 87.
    17. Kenneth Ring, p. 210.
    18. Osis and Haraldsson, p. 187.
    19. Melvin Morse with Paul Perry, *Closer to
the Light* (New York: Random House/Villard
Books, 1990) pp. 191–92. Also see Ring, *Life at
Death*, p. 213. M. B. Sabom, too, speaks of this
in *Recollections of Death: A Medical Investigation* (New York: Harper & Row, 1982).
    20. R.W.K. Paterson, *Philosophy and the
Belief in a Life After Death* (London and New
York: Macmillan and St. Martin's, 1995) p. 144.
    21. Sabom makes this claim about endor-
phins. See pp. 171–72.
    22. R. Siegel, "The Psychology of Life After
Life," *American Psychologist* 35, no 10 (October
1980): p. 923.
    23. Carl B. Becker, *Paranormal Experience
and Survival of Death* (Albany, New York:
SUNY Press, 1993) p. 104.
    24. See, for example, Greyson, 1981. B.
Greyson, "Towards a psychological explanation of near-death experience: A response to
Dr. Grosso's paper," *Anabiosia*, 1, 1981, pp.
88–103.
    25. G.O. Gabbard, & S.W. Twemlow, "Do
"near-death experiences" occur only near
death?—Revisited," *Journal of Near-Death
Studies*, 10, 1991, pp. 41–47.
    26. R. Noyes, Jr., "Near-Death Experi-
ences: Their interpretation and Significance,"
in Robert Kastenbaum, ed., *Between Life and
Death* (New York: Springer, 1979) pp. 83–86.
    27. E.L. Bliss and L.D. Clark, "Visual Hal-
lucinations," in *Hallucinations*, L.J. West, ed.
(New York: Greene and Stratton, 1962), p. 104.
    28. See Sabom, (1982), pp. 160–163.
    29. Bliss and Clark, "Visual Hallucina-
tions," p. 105.
    30. Melvin Morse with Paul Perry, *Closer to
the Light*, pp. 3–9. Also see Sabom and Maurice Rawlings (another cardiologist), *Beyond
Death's Door* (Nashville: Thomas Nelson,
1978).
    31. John Audette, "Denver Cardiologist
Discloses Findings After 18 years of Near Death
Research," *Anabiosis*, vol. 1 (May, 1979), p. 103.
    32. Pim van Lommel, "Near-Death Expe-
rience in Survivors of Cardiac Arrest: A
Prospective Study in the Netherlands," *The
Lancet*, 358 (Dec. 2001), 2039–2045. Also see
the interview-based article, "A New Lease on
Life," in *Ode International Magazine*, Dec.
2005, 24–29.
    33. *Ibid.*, p. 26.
    34. It should seem clear that the attempt
to view the contents of the subject's reports as

predictable by appeal to general probabilities is a non-starter.

35. K. Ring, p. 216.
36. Katie's physician reports the details of her case, among others. See M. Morse with P. Perry, pp. 3–9.
37. Kimberley Clark, "Clinical Interventions with Near-Death Experiences," *The Near-Death Experience: Problems, Prospects, Perspectives*, ed. Bruce Greyson and Charles P. Flynn (Springfield: Charles Thomas Publishers, 1984), pp. 242–55.
38. Elizabeth Kübler-Ross, *On Children and Death* (New York: Macmillan/Collins Books, 1983).
39. Not surprisingly, there are well-known critics who persistently deny that there is reason to believe any theory appealing to paranormal events. Speaking of paranormal perception in NDEs, Blackmore writes, "It is my impression that it probably never does happen. Certainly, I have found no evidence, yet, that convinces me that it does." S. Blackmore, *Dying to Live* (Buffalo, New York: Prometheus Books, 1993), pp. 134–35. Although she acknowledges that the existence of paranormal perception (i.e., ESP) would refute her theory and claims to be on the lookout for corroborated cases of such perception in NDEs, she passes over several reports of such cases in silence. Although she does comment on the case of Maria, she does not take it seriously, dismissing it with the claim that she has been "unable to get any further information," thereby suggesting that what she has is evidentially insignificant. She does not, however, tell us what further information would influence her. She already had the written testimony of an (originally skeptical) health-care professional. For a more extensive critique of Blackmore about this matter see David R. Griffin, *Parapsychology, Philosophy and Spirituality* (Albany, New York: SUNY Press, 1997), pp. 238–60.
40. Hornell Hart, "ESP Projection: Spontaneous Cases and the Experimental Method," *JASPR* 48/4 (Oct. 1954), 121–46.
41. Karlis Osis and Donna McCormick, "Kinetic Effects at the Ostensible Location of an Out-of-the-Body Projection during Perceptual Testing," *JASPR 74* (1980), pp. 319–29.
42. Robert Almeder, *Death & Personal Survival: The Evidence for Life After Death* (Lanham, MD: Littlefield Adams Quality Paperbacks), p. 186.
43. Melvin Morse with Paul Perry, pp. 52–54.
44. E. Kübler-Ross, p. 210.
45. *Ibid.*, p. 208.
46. *Ibid.*, p. 210.

47. S. Blackmore, p. 238.
48. *Ibid.*, p. 259.
49. *Ibid.*, p. 256.
50. Ibid., p. 261.

Apparitions

1. H. Sidgwick, E. M. Sidgwick, and A. Johnson, "Report on the Census of Hallucinations" *(PSPR*, 1894, 10, pp. 25–422).
2. F. W. H. Myers, *Human Personality and Its Survival of Bodily Death* (2 vols. London, Longmans, Green and Co., 1903).
3. Hornell Hart, *The Enigma of Survival* (Springfield, Ill: Charles C. Thomas, 1959), p. 182.
4. C. Green and C. McCreery, *Apparitions* (London: Hamish Hamilton, 1975), p. 188.
5. H. Sidgwick, "Report on the Census of Hallucinations," *PSPR* 10 (1894), 36–44.
6. George N.W. Tyrrell, *Apparitions* (New Hyde Park, New York: University Books, 1961), pp. 116–17.
7. Alan N. Gauld, *Mediumship & Survival: A Century of Investigations* (London: William Heinemann, 1982), pp. 222–3.
8. Hornell Hart, pp. 184–86.
9. Green and McCreery, pp. 189–90.
10. A. Gauld, *Mediumship and Survival*, p. 240.
11. Myers, F.W.H., *Human Personality*, vol. II, pp. 326–329.
12. Robert Almeder, *Death and Personal Survival: The Evidence for Life After Death* (Lanham, MD: Littlefield Adams Quality Paperbacks), p. 100. I am indebted to his work on these kinds of apparitional experiences.
13. This pamphlet is very rare. For a more accessible source of information about this case, see C.J. Ducasse, *The Belief in a Life After Death* (Springfield, Illinois: Charles C. Thomas, 1961) pp. 21–23, 154–55.
14. Robert Almeder, pp. 101–02.
15. John G. Fuller, The *Ghost of Flight 401* (New York: Berkeley Publishing, 1976).
16. *Ibid.*, 165.
17. *Ibid.*, 167.
18. *Ibid.*, 183.
19. *Ibid.*, 184.
20. Fuller, p. 195.
21. This is explicitly acknowledged by Gauld, who speaks of the survivalist as assuming the existence of "the 'weak' form of the super-ESP hypothesis—one that permits telepathy with deceased persons." See A. Gauld, *Mediumship and Survival*, p. 236. However, the survivalist may need to ascribe more psi to deceased persons than what Gauld's comment suggests. As we shall see, the ascrip-

tion of more psi may be unavoidable in a plausible survival hypothesis.

22. See, for example, E.P. Gibson, "An Examination of Motivation as Found in Selective Cases," *JASPR* 38, no 2 (1944): 83–103; and Gertrude Schmeidler, "Investigation of a Haunted House," *JASPR* 60, no. 2 (1966): 139–49.

23. Gauld, p. 238.

24. Stephen Braude, *The Limits of Influence* (London: Routledge and Kegan Paul, 1986), p. 204. See Braude, and also Almeder, pp. 113–17, for discussions of the different forms of the telepathic theory.

25. Myers, 110a, I, p. 268.

26. Myers, 110a, I, p. 266.

27. S. Braude, p. 196.

28. Almeder, pp. 118–121.

Reincarnation

1. Ian Stevenson, *Children Who Remember Previous Lives* (Jefferson, NC and London: McFarland & Co., 2001) p. 30.

2. I. Stevenson, *Twenty Cases Suggestive of Reincarnation*, 2nd ed. (Charlottesville: University Press of Virginia, 1974), p. 349.

3. C.J. Ducasse, *A Critical Examination of the Belief in a Life After Death*, p. 172. This quote is from page 14 of the original document.

4. C.J. Ducasse, *Pacific Forum* (1963) p. 38. Also see Almeder (1992) for a critical discussion of this case.

5. A much more recent example of apparent possession is the Sumitra case, which developed in 1985. The two persons involved in this case came from families living in widely separated towns. For a detailed description and analysis of this case, see Almeder, *Personal Survival*, pp. 143–55. As he points out, many such cases have occurred in nearly all cultures throughout history.

6. This case was reported by Ian Stevenson, who found it to be one of his strongest in this field. He studied it for sixteen years! See his *Xenoglossy* (Charlottesville: University Press of Virginia, 1974). The quoted excerpt was reprinted in *Reincarnation: The Phoenix Fire Mystery* ed. by J. Head and S.L. Cranston. (New York: Warner Books, 1977) p. 439.

7. Stevenson, *Twenty Cases*, 2nd ed. 1974, p. 3.

8. For much more information about this case, see I. Stevenson and S. Pasrichi, "A Preliminary Report on an Unusual Case of the Reincarnation Type with Xenoglossy," *JASPR*, Vol 74, July 1980, pp. 331–348; and I. Stevenson, *Unlearned Language: New Studies in*

Xenoglossy (Charlottesville: University Press of Virginia, 1984).

9. I. Stevenson and S. Pasricha, p. 331.

10. *Ibid.*, pp. 343–44.

11. This case was originally described in L.D. Gupta, N.R. Sharma, and T.C. Mathur. *An Inquiry into the Case of Shanti Devi* (Delhi: International Aryan League, 1936). Also, see, S.C. Bose, *A Case of Reincarnation* (Ligate, Satsang, S.P., 1952).

12. This case and the following case of Swarnlata Mishra are part of the twenty investigated by I. Stevenson in *Twenty Cases*.

13. I. Stevenson, *Twenty Cases*, p. 82.

14. *Ibid.*, p. 81.

15. M. Polanyi, "Tacit Knowing," *Reviews of Modern Physics*, Vol. 34, 1962, 601–616.

16. *Twenty Cases*, p. 88.

17. *Ibid.*, p. 382.

18. M. Polanyi, "Tacit Knowing," p. 603.

19. Stevenson, *Twenty Cases*, pp. 274–320.

20. For more about this, see A. Gauld, *Mediumship & Survival*, p. 182.

21. Stevenson, *Children Who Remember Previous Lives*, p. 159.

22. N. Hintze and J.G. Pratt, *The Psychic Realm: What Can You Believe?* (New York: Random House, 1975) p. 5.

23. Stevenson *Twenty Cases*, p. 385.

24. *Ibid.*, p. 348.

25. Stevenson, *Children*, p. 160, *Twenty Cases*, p. 373.

26. In her case, there can be little doubt that (1) she could speak Bengali responsively and that (2) her knowledge of Bengali does not succumb to normal explanation. With respect to the former claim, Stevenson tells us, "I obtained independent statements about Sharada's ability to speak Bengali responsively from eight Bengali-speaking persons who had conversed with her." One of them, Dr. Roy, testifies, "I conversed exclusively in Bengali with Sharada for approximately two hours. Her answers were sensible and she demonstrated a complete command of the Bengali language." Another, Professor Pal who was born and grew up in an area of Bengal in which Sharada claimed to have lived, writes, "I found her intonation and pronunciation exactly as mine. This was as expected as both of us lived within five miles of each other." (I. Stevenson, *Unlearned Language*, pp. 120–22.) With respect to the latter contention, Stevenson sums up his own conclusions when he writes, "I have found no reason to think that Uttara learned Bengali normally, either inadvertently as a young child or later in fraudulent contrivance." (*Ibid.*, p. 146.) Ian Stevenson, *Unlearned Language: New Studies in Xenoglossy* (Charlottesville: University Press of Virginia, 1984).

27. I. Stevenson, *Twenty Cases*, pp. 203–215.

28. See I. Stevenson, "The Case of Bishen Chand Kapoor," in *Cases of The Reincarnation Type*, vol. l: *Ten Cases in India* (Charlottesville: University Press of Virginia, 1975).

29. Some have argued that the possession hypothesis can never be plausibly excluded. See G.R. Habermas and J.P. Moreland, *Beyond Death: exploring the evidence for immortality* (Wheaton, Illinois: Crossway Books, 1998), pp. 237–53.

30. Stevenson, Twenty Cases, p. 376.

31. I defend in great detail this conception of the subject as the essence of a person in my book, *The Conscious Self: The Immaterial Center of Subjective States.*

32. P. Edwards, *Reincarnation: A Critical Examination* (Amherst, New York: Prometheus Books, 1996), p. 255.

33. *Ibid.*, p. 255.

34. *Ibid.*, p. 255.

35. Edwards, however, does advance several objections to Stevenson's case studies, many of which are summaries of objections made by others as well as some of his own. But all are like those we have already taken in account in our consideration of naturalistic and normal explanations. See his "Reincarnation," *Free Inquiry* (June 1987), pp. 24–48, and *Reincarnation: A Critical Examination.*

Mental Mediumship

1. G. Murphy & R. Ballow, *William James on Psychical Research* (New York: Viking Press, 1960, p. 97.

2. Our earlier deliberations about how an experience or conscious state should be understood and about what essentially constitutes a person justifies our use of the term "person" or "conscious subject" to denote what is manifested in at least the best cases of ostensible communication.

3. R. Hodgson, "Observations of Certain Phenomena of Trance," *PSPR* (London), 13 (1897-8), p. 328.

4. Alan Gauld, a widely respected authority on mediumship and other psychic phenomena, once tried to do this in an attempt to determine whether it is possible. He speaks of how he once devoted a good deal of time to learning all he could about the private lives and habits of Henry Sidgwick and F.W.H. Myers, eventually knowing far more facts about them than it is remotely plausible to suppose that even the greatest of mediums could have acquired by ESP. But it was all to no avail. He could not begin to impersonate them successfully. In his words, "But no amount of such factual knowledge (knowledge *that*) would *per se* have enabled me to imitate them (a skill, knowledge *how*) in a way that their close friends would have found anything other than absurd or pathetic. My performance would have been infinitely less impressive than those of Mrs. Piper or Mrs. Leonard at their best—indeed at their worst!" See his *Mediumship and Survival* (Heinemann: London, 1982), p. 108.

5. R. Heywood, "Death and Psychical Research," *Man's Concern with Death* (New York: McGraw-Hill, 1968), p. 102.

6. *Ibid.*, p. 103.

7. C. D. Broad, *Lectures on Psychical Research* (New York: Humanities Press, 1962).

8. The story of these scripts has been published as *Swan on a Black Sea*, by G. Cummings (London: Routledge and Kegan Paul, 1965).

9. I discuss her mediumship activity at some length in an earlier work, *Death and Consciousness* (Jefferson, NC: Mc Farland & Co., 1985), pp. 128–38. One of the most important series of sittings with her was those with Rev. Drayton Thomas. He described them in two *SPR Proceedings:* "The Modus Operandi of Trance Communications According to Descriptions received through Mrs. Osborne Leonard," 38 (1928), and "A New Hypothesis Concerning Trance Communications," 48 (1949).

10. A. Gauld, *Mediumship and Survival*, p. 56.

11. *Ibid.*, pp. 60–61.

12. *Ibid.*, pp. 68–71. See also, A. Gauld, "A Series of 'Drop In' Communicators," *PSPR*, V. 55, 1971, 273–340, pp. 322–327.

13. A. Gauld, *Mediumship and Survival*, p. 71.

14. E. Haraldsson, and I. Stevenson, "A Communicator of the "Drop in" Type in Iceland: the Case of Runolfur Runolfsson" (*JASPR*, 1975, 69, pp. 33–59).

15. *Ibid.*, p. 57.

16. *Ibid.*, p. 57.

17. For more detail, see Gauld, *Mediumship and Survival*, pp. 77–89; and R. Heywood, *Beyond the Reach of Sense* (New York: E.P. Dutton, 1961).

18. See F. Podmore, *The Newer Spiritualism* (London: Fisher Unwin 1910).

19. *Mediumship and Survival*, p. 89.

Bibliography

Almeder, Robert. *Death & Personal Survival: The Evidence for Life After Death* (Lanham, MD: Littlefield Adams Quality Paperbacks, 1992).

Armstrong, D. M. *A Materialist Theory of the Mind,* (London: Routledge and Kegan Paul, 1968).

Audette, John. "Denver Cardiologist Discloses Findings After 18 years of Near Death Research." *Anabiosis,* vol. 1 (May, 1979).

Barnes, J. *The Presocratics,* vol. 1 (Boston: Routledge and Kegan Paul, 1979).

Barrett, W. *Death-bed Visions* (London: Methuen, 1926).

Becker, Carl B. *Paranormal Experience and Survival of Death* (Albany, NY: SUNY Press, 1993).

Blackmore, Susan. *Beyond the Body* (London: Paladin, 1983).

_____. *Dying to Live* (Buffalo, NY: Prometheus Books, 1993).

Bliss, E. L., and L. D. Clark. "Visual Hallucinations," in *Hallucinations,* L. J.West, ed. (New York: Greene and Stratton, 1962).

Bose, S. C. "A Case of Reincarnation" (Ligate, Satsang, S. P., 1952).

Braude, Stephen. *The Limits of Influence* (London: Routledge and Kegan Paul, 1986).

Broad, C. D. *Lectures on Psychical Research* (New York: Humanities Press, 1962).

Chisholm, Roderick. *On Metaphysics* (Minneapolis: University of Minnesota, 1989).

Clark, Kimberly. "Clinical Interventions with Near-Death Experiences." *The Near-Death Experience: Problems, Prospects, Perspectives,* eds. Bruce Greyson and Charles P. Flynn (Springfield, IL: Charles Thomas Publishers, 1984).

Cummings, G. *Swan on a Black Sea* (London: Routledge and Kegan Paul, 1965).

Descartes, René. *The Meditations on First Philosophy,* in *The Philosophical Works of Descartes,* Vol. I, trans. by E. S. Haldane and G. R. T. Ross (London: Cambridge University Press, 1911), reprinted 1969.

Ducasse, C. J. *A Critical Examination of the Belief in a Life After Death* (Springfield, IL: Charles C. Thomas, 1961).

_____. *Pacific Forum* (1963).

Edwards, P. "Reincarnation." *Free Inquiry* (June 1987), 24–48.

_____. *Reincarnation: A Critical Examination* (Amherst, NY: Prometheus Books, 1996).

Forman, Robert K. C. *Mysticism, Mind, Consciousness* (Albany, NY: State University of New York, 1999).

Foster, John. *The Immaterial Self: A Defense of the Cartesian Dualist Conception of the Mind* (London: Routledge, 1991).

Fuller, John G. *The Ghost of Flight 401* (New York: Berkeley Publishing, 1976).

Gabbard, G. O., & S. W. Twemlow. "Do 'Near Death Experiences' Occur Only Near Death?—Revisited." *Journal of Near-Death Studies,* 10, 1991, 41–47.

Gauld, Alan N. *Mediumship & Survival: A Century of Investigations* (London: William Heinemann, 1982).

_____. "A Series of Drop-in Communicators." *PSPR,* V. 55, 1971, 273–340.

Gibson, E. P. "An Examination of Motivation as Found in Selective Cases." *JASPR* 38, no 2 (1944): 83–103.

Green, C., and C. McCreery. *Apparitions* (London: Hamish Hamilton, 1975).

Grey, Margot. *Return from Death* (London and Boston: Arkana, 1985) p. 86.

Greyson, B. "Towards a Psychological Explanation of Near-Death Experience: A Response to Dr. Grosso's Paper." *Anabiosia,* 1, 1981, pp. 88–103.

Griffin, David R. *Parapsychology, Philosophy and Spirituality* (Albany, NY: SUNY Press, 1997).

Gupta, L. D., N. R. Sharms, and T. C. Mathur. *An Inquiry into the Case of Shanti Devi* (Delhi International Aryan League, 1936).

Habermas, G. R., and J. P. Moreland. *Beyond Death: Exploring the Evidence for Immortality* (Wheaton, IL: Crossway Books, 1998).

Haraldsson, E., and I. Stevenson. "A Commu-
nicator of the 'Drop in' Type in Iceland:
The Case of Runolfur Runolfsson." *JASPR*,
69, 1975, 33–59.
Hart, Hornell. *The Enigma of Survival*
(Springfield, IL: Charles C. Thomas, 1959).
_____. "ESP Projection: Spontaneous Cases
and the Experimental Method." *JASPR* 48/4
(Oct. 1954), 121–46.
Hasker, W. *The Emergent Self* (Ithaca, NY:
Cornell University Press, 1999).
Head, J., and S. L. Cranston, eds. *Reincarna-
tion: The Phoenix Fire Mystery* (New York:
Warner Books, 1977).
Heywood, R. *Beyond the Reach of Sense* (New
York: E.P. Dutton, 1961).
_____. "Death and Psychical Research." *Man's
Concern with Death* (New York: McGraw-
Hill, 1968).
Hintze, N., and J. G. Pratt. *The Psychic Realm:
What Can You Believe?* (New York: Ran-
dom House, 1975).
Hodgson, R. "Observations of Certain Phe-
nomena of Trance." *PSPR* (London), 13
(1897–8).
Hoffman, J., and G. Rosenkrantz. "Are Souls
Intelligible?" in *Philosophical Perspectives,
vol. 5: Philosophy of Religion*, ed. J. E.
Tomberlin (Atascadero, CA: Ridgeview,
1991), 183–212.
Hume, David. *A Treatise of Human Nature*, ed.
by L. A. Selby-Bigge (London: Oxford Uni-
versity Press, 1888. Reprinted, 1968).
Kant, I. *Critique of Pure Reason*, trans. by N. K.
Smith (London: Macmillan, 1929; reprinted,
New York: St. Martin's Press, 1965).
Kastenbaum, Robert. *Between Life and Death*
(New York: Springer, 1979).
Kreutzinger, S. "The Experience of Near
Death." *Death Education 1* (1977): 195–203.
Kübler-Ross, Elizabeth. *On Children and
Death* (New York: Macmillan/Collins
Books, 1983).
Lashley, K. R. "The Search for the Engram,"
pp. 501–3 in F.A. Beach and D.O. Hebb,
The Neurophysiology of Lashley, cited in
H.A. Bursen, *Dismantling the Memory Ma-
chine* (Dordrecht: D. Reidel, 1978).
Lewis, David. "Survival and Identity" and
"Postscripts to Survival and Identity" in his
Philosophical Papers, Vol. 1 (Oxford Uni-
versity Press, 1983).
Lund, D. *The Conscious Self: The Immaterial
Center of Subjective States* (Amherst, NY:
Humanity Books, 2005).
_____. *Death and Consciousness* (Jefferson,
NC: McFarland, 1985).
_____. *Making Sense of It All* (Upper Saddle
River, NJ: Pearson Education, 1999, 2003).
_____. *Perception, Mind and Personal Identity:*

A Critique of Materialism (Lanham, MD:
University Press of America, 1994).
McGinn, C. *The Mysterious Flame: Conscious
Minds in a Material World* (New York:
Basic Books, 1999).
Moody, R. *Reflections on Life After Life* (At-
lanta: Mockingbird Books, 1977).
Morse, Melvin with Paul Perry. *Closer to the
Light* (New York: Random House/Villard
Books, 1990).
Murphy G., and R. Ballow. *William James on
Psychical Research* (New York: Viking Press,
1960).
Myers, F. W. H. *Human Personality and Its
Survival of Bodily Death* (2 vols. London,
Longmans, Green, 1903).
Noyes, R., Jr. "Near-Death Experiences: Their
Interpretation and Significance," in Ro-
bert Kastenbaum, ed., *Between Life and
Death* (New York: Springer, 1979), pp.
83–86.
Osis, Karlis. *Deathbed Observations by Physi-
cians and Nurses* (New York: Parapsychol-
ogy Foundation, 1961). Parapsychological
Monograph No. 3.
_____, and E. Haraldsson. *At the Hour of
Death* (New York: Avon, 1977).
_____, and Donna McCormick. "Kinetic Ef-
fects at the Ostensible Location of an Out-
of-the-Body Projection during Perceptual
Testing." *JASPR* 74 (1980), 319–29.
Paterson, R. W. K. *Philosophy and the Belief in
a Life After Death* (London and New York:
Macmillan and St. Martin's, 1995).
Perry, John. *A Dialogue on Personal Identity
and Immortality* (Indianapolis, IN: Hack-
ett, 1978).
Plantinga, Alvin. "Advice to Christian Philoso-
phers." *Faith and Philosophy* 1 (July 1984):
264–65.
Podmore, F. *The Newer Spiritualism* (London:
Fisher Unwin, 1910).
Polanyi, M. "Tacit Knowing." *Reviews of Mod-
ern Physics*, Vol. 34, 1962, 601–616).
Radhakrishnan, S. *Indian Philosophy*, vol. 2
(London: George Allen & Unwin, 1923).
Rawlings, Maurice. *Beyond Death's Door*
(Nashville: Thomas Nelson, 1978).
Rhees, W. Dewi. "The Hallucinations of Wid-
ows," in *British Medical Journal 4* (1972):
37–41.
Ring, K. *Life at Death* (New York: Coward,
McCann & Geoghegan, 1980).
Robinson, Howard. "The Flight from Mind,"
in *The Pursuit of Mind*, ed., by Raymond
Tallis and Howard Robinson (Manchester,
Great Britain: Carcanet Press, 1991).
_____. *Perception* (London and New York:
Routledge, 1994).
Rorty, R. "In Defense of Eliminative Material-

ism." *Review of Metaphysics* 24, no 1 (1970): 112–21.

Sabom, Michael. *Recollections of Death: A Medical Investigation* (New York: Harper & Row, 1982).

_____, and S. Kreutzinger. "The Experience of Near Death." *Death Education 1* (1977): 195–203.

Schmeidler, Gertrude. "Investigations of a Haunted House." *JASPR* 60, no. 2 (1966): 139–49.

Schopenhauer, A. *The World as Will and Representation*, Vol. II (New York: Dover, 1966).

Searle, J. *The Rediscovery of the Mind* (Cambridge, MA: MIT Press, 1992).

Sidgwick, H., E. M. Sidgwick, and A. Johnson. "Report on the Census of Hallucinations." *PSPR* 10 (1894), 25–422.

Siegel, R. "The Psychology of Life After Life." *American Psychologist* 35, no 10 (October 1980): 923.

Smart, J. J. C. "Sensations and Brain Processes." *Philosophical Review*, 68, 1959, 141–56.

Sosa, E. "The Essentials of Persons." *Dialectica* 53, nos. 2–4: 1999, 227–41.

_____. "Mind-Body Interaction and Supervenient Causation," in *Midwest Studies in Philosophy*, vol. 9, ed. P. A. French, T. E. Uehling, and H. K. Wettstein (Minneapolis: University of Minnesota Press, 1984).

Stevenson, Ian. "The Case of Bishen Chand Kapoor," in *Cases of the Reincarnation Type*, vol. 1: *Ten Cases in India* (Charlottesville: University Press of Virginia, 1975).

_____. *Children Who Remember Previous Lives* (Jefferson, NC: McFarland, 2001).

_____. *Twenty Cases Suggestive of Reincarnation*, 2nd ed. (Charlottesville: University Press of Virginia, 1974).

_____. *Unlearned Language: New Studies in Xenoglossy* (Charlottesville: University Press of Virginia, 1984).

_____. *Xenoglossy* (Charlottesville: University Press of Virginia, 1974).

_____, and S. Pasricha. "A Preliminary Report on an Unusual Case of the Reincarnation Type with Xenoglossy." *JASPR 74*, July 1980, 331–348.

Strawson, Galen. "The Self." *Journal of Consciousness Studies* 4, nos. 5–6, 1997: 405–28.

Thomas, Drayton. "The Modus Operandi of Trance Communications According to Descriptions received through Mrs. Osborne Leonard." *PSPR, 38* (1928).

_____. "A New Hypothesis Concerning Trance Communications." *PSPR, 48* (1949).

Thouless, R. H., and B. P. Weisner. "The Psi Processes in Normal and 'Paranormal' Psychology." *PSPR* (London), 48 (1947), 177–196.

Tyrrell, George. *Apparitions* (New Hyde Park, NY: University Books, 1961).

Van Inwagen, P. *Material Beings* (Ithaca: Cornell University Press, 1990).

Van Lommel, Pim. "Near-Death Experience in Survivors of Cardiac Arrest: A Prospective Study in the Netherlands." *The Lancet*, 358 (Dec. 2001), 2039–2045.

_____. "A New Lease on Life," in *Ode International Magazine*. Dec. 2005, 24–29.

Wittgenstein, L. *Philosophical Investigations*. Translated by G. E. M. Anscombe (New York: Macmillan, 1953). Third edition, New York: Macmillan, 1970.

Zimmerman, Dean. "Two Cartesian Arguments for the Simplicity of the Soul." *American Philosophical Quarterly* 28, no. 3: 217–26.

Index

Almeder, R. 122–123, 137–138, 149, 223–224n
apparitions 129–152; collective 132–133, 136–137, 144–146; collective and iterative 137–142, 144, 150–151; of the dead 136–142; death-related 131; features 129–130; frequency 121; motives exhibited by 143–144, 150–152; and naturalistic interpretation 135, 151; paranormal interpretations 136–152; and perspective problem 144–149; reciprocal 132–135, 147–148, 152; and super-psi hypothesis 142–143, 145–146, 149–151; and survival hypothesis 134, 136, 142–144, 149–152; "third-partied" 144, 152; timing 131, 142, 145–146, 152
Armstrong, D.M. 219n
Audette, J. 222n

Balfour, G.W. 189–193
Ballow, R. 225n
Barnes, J. 221n
Barrett, W. 105–106, 222n
Becker, C. 114–115, 222n
behaviorism, analytical 29–30
Blackmore, S. 108, 127–128, 222–223n
Bliss, E. 222n
Bose, S. 224n
brain: bisection 58–59; and causal closure thesis 74–75; as consciousness dissociator 84–85, 99–100; as consciousness enhancer 85, 99–100; instrument view 25; and non-intentional consciousness 99–100, 102, 207; as source of consciousness 83, 102
Braude, S. 149–150, 177, 213, 224n
Broad, C.D. 193, 225n
Butler Case 137–138

causal closure hypothesis 74–78, 206–207; and epiphenomenalism 75, 206–207; and evolutionary theory 75; and physical science 74–75
causation: and causal accessibility 73; conceived as irreducible 69–74; conceived as reducible 67–69; "deep" 70, 72; direct 80–82; directionality 71; dualistic 206; indirect 80; intentional 71–73, 206; mental-

mental 76–78, 82; mental-physical 63–66, 72–74, 77–78, 80, 88, 206; paranormal 78, 89, 102, 207; physical-physical 65–67, 74; reductive-nomological account 67–69, 71
Chisholm, R. 94, 221n
clairvoyance 78; conceivability 79–80; and direct causation 81
Clark, K. 119–120, 223n
Clark, L. 222n
commissurotomy 220–221n
consciousness: apparent nonspatiality 39; brain-dependence 24–25; concept 10; degrees 94; and generality 41–42; as immediately known 37; intentionality 35, 39, 42; irreducible reality 40; and language 40; necessarily private access to 37; necessary ownership 37–38; and non-actual possibility 40; non-intentional 96–100, 207, 221–222n; and the phenomenal 44–45; "pure" 97; and spatiality 10; subjectivity 37; and truth 41, 45; unity 38–39, 55–56
Cranston, S.L. 224n
cross-correspondences 199–203; allegedly discarnate source 201–202; and the appeal to super ESP 201–203; general description 200–201; normal explanation 200, 202
Cummings, A. 137–138
Cummings, G. 193, 225n

death: indifference toward 4–5; knowledge of 6; philosophical approach to 6–8
death-bed visions 104–108; ESP explanation 105; and mental clarity 108; as non-veridical hallucinations 107; and "other world" apparitions 106–107; and patient expectations 107–108; and the survival hypothesis 105–106
Descartes, R. 36, 219n
disembodied existence 12–16; and causal powers 207; conceivability 12, 15–16, 208; and paranormal causation 207; and sensory experience 15, 208–210
"drop-in" communicators 195–199; anonymity 195; normal explanation 197, 199; "Runki" communicator 197–199;

231

Murphy, G. 225n
Myers, F. 129, 147–148, 151, 183, 189–191, 193, 200–202, 223–224n
mystic 97–98

near-death experiences 104–127; aftereffects 110; apparently requiring paranormal explanation 118–125; apparitions of the dead 123–125; and appeal to super-ESP 123, 125–126; and ESP hypothesis 121–126; and flat EEGs 116–118, 123; frequency 111; general characteristics 109–111; naturalistic explanations 112–118; and OBEs 121–122; suggestive of afterlife 116–118; and survival hypothesis 127
necessity: logical 219n; metaphysical 219n; natural 219n
non-intentional consciousness 96–100; and bodily death 100, 102; and memory 97–98
Noyes, R., Jr. 115, 222n
Nyaya school 98

OBEs 121–122; and NDEs 121; reciprocal 121–122, 125, 134; and super-ESP 123; voluntarily induced 122
Osis, K. 106–107, 113–114, 116, 122, 222–223n

Pasricha, S. 158–159, 224n
Paterson, R. 114, 211, 224n
perception 40, 43–44; indirect realist view 179–180, 210; *see also* sensory experience
Perry, J. 219n
Perry, P. 113, 222–223n
persons: and agency 206; deep embodiment 3–4, 24–25; deep irreducible essence 53, 59–60, 93, 206; as embodied souls 62, 206; as endurers 47; essence 1–3, 15, 90, 97, 178–179, 204–206; and God of theism 16–19; and human beings 23–24, 26; identity 15; as including nonhumans 12–13; materialist view 9, 204, 214; and natural law 20–21, 25; as nonphysical 12, 14, 18, 62–63, 206–207; non-reductionist view 47–62; and partial existence 95, 205; as perdurers 47, 53, 62; psychological theories 45, 205; reductionist views 46–47, 61; as subjects of conscious states 47–62, 206; *see also* self
phenomenal: afterworld 209; body 26, 179; color 44; as consciousness-dependent 44; objects 209–210; realm 179–180; sense qualities 44; *see also* sensory experience
Plantinga, A. 17, 219n
Podmore, F. 189, 202, 225n
Polyani, M. 166, 169, 224n
possibility: and conceivability 20, 221n; metaphysical 18–21; natural 19–20
prakriti 98–99
Pratt, J.G. 172, 224n
properties: intrinsic 31; relational 31

property dualism 65
proxy sittings 194–195; and appeal to super-ESP 195; and Mrs. Leonard's mediumship 194–195
psychokinesis 78, 121–122; and apparitions 148; conceivability 79–80; and direct causation 81–82
purusha 98

Rawlings, M. 222n
Radhakrishnan, S. 222n
recitative xenoglossy 156, 177; Swarnlata's 177
reincarnation: belief in 153; coherence of belief in 178–180; vs. discarnate possession 154, 156–157, 159, 163, 177–178, 224n; evidence of 173–174, 177; of mental dispositions 216; what might constitute 178
reincarnation, apparent cases of: and appeal to super-psi 172–173, 176–177; distribution 153–154; exhibiting unlearned skills 166, 176–177; and experience-memory 172–173, 175; features 159–161; involving paranormal recognitions 166, 169, 176; Jasbir Jat case 162–163, 175; normal explanations 156, 158–159, 162–163, 165, 167–169; paranormal explanations 167, 170–180; and the psi hypothesis 171–177; Shanti Devi case 161–162, 177; and subconscious impersonation 174–176; and survival hypothesis 167, 173, 177–180; Swarnlata Mishra case 163–167, 170–172, 174–177
responsive xenoglossy 156–159; Lydia/Jensen case 156–157, 159, 168–169; Shanti Devi case 161–162; Uttara/Sharada case 157–159, 169, 177
retrocognition 78
Rhees, W. Dewi 222n
Ring, K. 113, 118, 222–223n
Robinson, H. 220n
Rorty, R. 220n
Rosenkrantz, G. 221n

Sabom, M. 113, 222n
Samkhya school 98–99
Schmeidler, G. 224n
Schoonmaker, F. 117, 222n
Schopenhauer, A. 96, 221n
science, natural: influence 9–11; and reduction to nothingness 95; scope of 9–11; and sense qualities 43–44
Searle, J. 220n
The self: as agent 206; annihilation 93–96; brain-dependency 24–25, 83–85, 180, 207, 214; emergence 83, 85; as endurer 50–51, 206; as immaterial individual 62, 206; indivisibility 51–53, 59, 206; and non-intentional consciousness 96–100, 102, 207; and object of self-conception 49–50; peculiar uniqueness 52, 85, 221n; and possible-world twin 52, 221n; self-shining nature